MACROECONOMIC MANAGEMENT

Also edited by Soumitra Sharma

DEVELOPMENT POLICY
ECONOMIC DEVELOPMENT AND WORLD DEBT
(*with H. W. Singer*)
GROWTH AND EXTERNAL DEBT MANAGEMENT
(*with H. W. Singer*)

Macroeconomic Management

Edited by

Soumitra Sharma
Professor of Economics
University of Zagreb, Croatia

First published in Great Britain 1995 by
MACMILLAN PRESS LTD
Houndmills, Basingstoke, Hampshire RG21 6XS
and London
Companies and representatives
throughout the world

A catalogue record for this book is available
from the British Library.

ISBN 0–333–63325–3

First published in the United States of America 1995 by
ST. MARTIN'S PRESS, INC.,
Scholarly and Reference Division,
175 Fifth Avenue,
New York, N.Y. 10010

ISBN 0–312–12608–5

Library of Congress Cataloging-in-Publication Data
Macroeconomic management / edited by Soumitra Sharma.
p. cm.
Includes bibliograpical references and index.
ISBN 0–312–12608–5 cloth
1. Economic policy. I. Sharma, Soumitra.
HD87.M24 1995
339.5—dc20 94–44699
CIP

---

10 9 8 7 6 5 4 3 2 1
04 03 02 01 00 99 98 97 96 95

Printed in Great Britain by
Ipswich Book Co Ltd, Ipswich, Suffolk

Contents

List of Figures

List of Tables

Preface

> He who knows the art of the direct and indirect approach will be victorious. Such is the art of manoeuvre (Sun Tse, the great Chinese military strategist in his work, *The Art of War*).

How to stabilise the macro economy through active domestic and international economic policy is a particularly relevant question in a world that swings between intense economic activity and unemployment. To seek an answer to this question is to invite trouble and confusion. However, to restore equilibrium nations must skilfully manoeuvre a variety of forces through direct and indirect policy measures. I call this art macroeconomic management.

Back in 1925 Keynes wrote, 'In the economic field . . . we must find new policies and new instruments to adapt and control the working of economic forces, so that they do not intolerably interfere with contemporary ideas as to what is fit and proper in the interests of social stability and social justice' ('Am I A Liberal?', *The Nation and Athenaeum*, 8 and 15 August 1925)

On macroeconomic management issues, economists are in constant disagreement. They disagree among themselves but believe that a sharpening of the tools and solid empirical tests will eventually prove them right. Some theorists see macroeconomic management as nothing distinct from the usual economic policy measures used by the government, others see it only as a mechanism to handle economic crises. The international institutions visualise it as nothing more than a system of macroeconomic financial control and regulation.

While Keynesians and neo-Keynesians firmly believe that governments can remedy economic ills, monetarists give due credit to governmental policies in the short run, but deny any such influence in the long run. Similarly the new classical economists tend to rely on *laissez-faire* market economics, while post-Keynesians claim that it is now too late for the government to doctor the economy in any significant way and show little sympathy for conventional economics.

From a long-term perspective macroeconomic management could be seen as method of steering the economy out of an economic muddle. In this sense it could be taken to mean a comprehensive set of policy measures designed by national governments and/or international institutions to attain basic economic goals, for example the best possible utilisation of countries' resources and production potential, encouraging growth, remedying structural imbalances, ensuring an equitable distribution of incomes and wealth, and maintaining a balance in international trade.

From a short- or medium-term macroeconomic policy perspective, economists take it as equivalent to macroeconomic stabilisation or a policy aimed at reducing fluctuations in income, employment and prices and stabilising national income at full employment level.

Since the end of the Second World War the overriding international economic policy question for most nations has been whether they can simultaneously attain the multiple objectives of high levels of employment, price stability, economic growth, trade liberalisation and balance of payments equilibrium. To the extent that these objectives may be incompatible, some policy trade-offs and manoeuvres are necessary.

When confronted by policy conflicts most governments have allowed the objective of full employment to dominate national economic policy. The central challenge to the operation of international macroeconomic management, therefore, is how to allow nations to pursue their domestic economic objectives without having to forgo the gains from trade or suffer balance of payments disequilibrium.

The Bretton Woods conference anticipated these problems. It was believed that establishment of the IMF and a fixed exchange-rate mechanism would allow nations to give primacy to their domestic employment policies over balance of payments adjustment. In the late 1960s and 1970s the major assumptions of the Bretton Woods system in terms of the determination of exchange rates, the disturbance in the balance of payments and the provision of international liquidity were severely tested. In fact, for a successful global macroeconomic management policy, the most important issues involve decisions about the need for remedial action to restore equilibrium. The type of policy adopted by a country depends upon the source of its balance of payment problem and on its other domestic objectives. Naturally the country would like to adopt the least costly mechanism of adjusting its balance of payments without sacrificing domestic economic autonomy, which will in turn depend upon the international monetary system and the code of international conduct it imposes.

Textbook solutions suggest that under any international monetary system the sources and amount of international liquidity differ, as does the degree to which the balance of payments exercises discipline on a country. The more it is desired that an international imbalance should exercise discipline on a country's domestic policies, the less access the country should have to international finance. The less the country's access to finance, the more it must resort to other measures to remove its balance of payments problem. Through a tight monetary policy and budgetary surplus, internal measures entail deflation if the country is in deficit, and to this extent the country loses domestic autonomy over its employment policies. External measures constitute the imposition of restrictions on trade and capital movements or a depreciation of the currency; to this extent the country diminishes its gains from trade or incurs the costs of depreciation. While the internal measures can be seen as expenditure-reducing policies that reduce national income and hence the domestic demand for resources; the external measures can be viewed as expenditure-switching policies because devaluation or depreciation of the currency will raise the price of tradables relative to price of nontradables, thereby causing a switch in the pattern of expenditure and production.

In the monetary approach, money is a stock for which the optimal level is related to current output. If the actual stock is not equal to the desired stock, the disequilibrium will be removed through reserve flows in the balance of payments. Remedial policies must therefore concentrate on the change in domestic credit creation relative to the demand for money.

Since the emergence of the floating exchange rate regime the focus is more broadly on changes in asset portfolios as the proximate cause of exchange rate variations in the short run. The capital flow associated with trade in financial assets can be part of the adjustment process as well as a source of pressure on the exchange rate.

If a country has access to sufficient international funds it may be able to eschew both internal and external measures and simply cover its imbalance by drawing upon its international reserves. There would be no need for expenditure-reducing or expenditure-switching policies. Resort to international funds would be expenditure-sustaining and the balance of payments would exercise no discipline over domestic policies.

The range of policy instruments available to a country that is seeking to adjust its balance of payments is limited to the narrow policy space whose boundaries are determined by the nature of the international monetary system and the state of the domestic economy. Naturally, skilful manoeuvring is required.

This volume presents the various domestic and international policy issues that are involved in macroeconomic management. Two important contributions – 'Domestic Stabilisation and the Balance of Payments' (Chapter 5) and 'Does Fiscal Policy Matter?' (Chapter 4) – were originally written in 1982. They are reprinted in this volume for two reasons: firstly because of the increased relevance of the key issues involved and secondly because these seminal works contain lasting theoretical findings. The authors of these chapters are the two best-known names in economic literature: Nobel Laureates James Meade and James Tobin. The volume also deals with such issues as incomplete markets in foreign exchange and asymmetrical financial integration; internal and external stability; international borrowing strategy and sovereign creditworthiness; stopping inflation; and the scope and sequencing of financial sector-reforms (Chapters 6, 7, 8, 10 and 14) by such experts in international economics and finance as Pan A. Yotopoulos, E. M. Claassen, Ronald Solberg, Karl Socher and Theresia Theurl, and Tomás J. T. Baliño. Globalisation, being the theme of the 1990s, is dealt with at length by Paul Streeten in Chapter 2 and Zoran Jašić in Chapter 3. The impact of Japanese overseas investment is analysed by Kiyoshi Abe in Chapter 15. Macroeconomic issues in Eastern Europe are dealt with in Chapter 13 by Ivo Družić. Chapters 11 and 12, by Tomislav Presečan and Pero Jurković respectively, reflect on foreign trade management problems and fiscal constraints in a transitional economy.

I feel obliged to mention that the contributions included in this volume may not necessarily by themselves be sufficient for a full elaboration of the concept and issues involved in macroeconomic management, nor are they the last word on the subject, but they certainly shed light on relevant issues. To reflect the spirit with which I present this volume to the readers, I quote here a passage from an article by J. M. Keynes ('The General Theory of Employment', 1937):

> I am more attached to the comparatively simple fundamental ideas that underlie my theory than to the particular forms in which I have embodied them, and have no desire that the latter should be crystallised at the present stage of the debate. If the simple basic ideas can become familiar and acceptable, time and experience and the collaboration of a number of minds will discover the best way of expressing them.

Finally, I wish to express my sincere gratitude to all those who have contributed to this volume. My thanks also go to my friends Emeritus Gerald M. Meier (Stanford) and Emeritus Sir Hans W. Singer (Institute for Development Studies, Brighton) and to Mr Keith Povey for their useful suggestions during the preparation of this book.

SOUMITRA SHARMA

Notes on the Contributors

Kiyoshi Abe is Professor of International Economics at the Faculty of Law and Economics, University of Chiba, Japan.

Tomás J. T. Baliño is Chief of the Monetary Operation Division, Monetary and Exchange Affairs Department, IMF, Washington, DC, USA.

Emil-Maria Claassen is Professor of Economics and Finance at the University de Paris-Dauphine, France.

Ivo Družić is Associate Professor of Economics at the Faculty of Economics, University of Zagreb, Croatia.

Zoran Jašić is Minister of Finance of the Government of Croatia and Professor of Public Finance at the Faculty of Economics, University of Zagreb, Croatia.

Pero Jurković is Governor of the National Bank of Croatia and Professor of Public Finance at the Faculty of Economics, University of Zagreb, Croatia.

Rolf Kappel is Professor of Economics at the NADEL-ETH Swiss Institute of Technology, Zurich, Switzerland.

James Meade is Nobel Laureate and an Emeritus Professor of Political Economy at Cambridge University, Cambridge, England.

Tomislav Presečan is Lecturer in International Economics at the Faculty of Economics, University of Zagreb, Croatia.

Soumitra Sharma is Professor of Economics and Chairman of the Department of Macroeconomics and Economic Policy at the Faculty of Economics, University of Zagreb, Croatia.

Karl Socher is Professor of Political Economy at the Instituts für Wirtschaftstheorie und Politik, University of Innsbruck, Austria.

Ronald Solberg is President of International Economic Consultants, Los Angeles, California, USA.

Paul Streeten is a former Director of the World Development Institute of the University of Boston and is currently attached to the UNDP, New York, USA.

Theresia Theurl is Assistant Professor of Finance at the Instituts für Wirtschatstheorie und Politik, University of Innsbruck, Austria.

James Tobin is Nobel Laureate and an Emeritus Professor of Economics at the Cowles Foundation for Economic Research of Yale University, New Haven, Connecticut, USA.

Pan A. Yotopoulos is Professor of Economics at the Food Research Institute of Stanford University, Palo Alto, California, USA.

1 The Evolution of Macroeconomic Management[1]

Soumitra Sharma

THE CONCEPT

As there are a variety of approaches to the concept of macroeconomic management, the task of defining the concept is perhaps as difficult for us as explaining the concept of an 'elephant' was for the seven blind men in the story in the Buddhist literature.[2] While some theorists see macroeconomic management as very similar to macroeconomic policy, the policy makers generally consider it to be a mechanism for handling an economic crisis, and the experts in international institutions visualise it as a system of macroeconomic financial control and regulation.

Economists discussing macroeconomic thought from the point of view of general equilibrium analysis may view macroeconomic management as a mechanism for ensuring equilibrium in the economy, so that even if disturbed the system should return to a position of equilibrium after a certain period of time.[3] Theorists of modern trade cycles are likely to interpret macromanagement as a system that ensures a minimum of volatility in economic activity over time.[4] While Keynesians[5] would consider macroeconomic management as a set of measures aimed at effective demand management, counter revolutionists[6] would insist on the supply side[7] management of economy. Similarly, and with equal enthusiasm, growth theorists are likely to view it in terms of a steady growth path or a balanced growth model.[8]

From the point of view of long-term policy, macroeconomic management could be seen as method of efficiently steering the economy through troubled economic waters. In this sense it could be accepted as a comprehensive set of policy measures designed by a national government and/or international institutions to attain the basic economic goals – for example the best possible utilisation of a country's resources and production potential for a stable and long-term rate of growth, remedying the existing structural imbalances, ensuring an equitable distribution of incomes and wealth, and maintaining balance in the external payment position of the country.

From a short- or medium-term perspective macroeconomic management is seen as synonymous with macroeconomic stabilisation, or simply as an attempt to reduce fluctuations (in income, employment, price levels) and to stabilise national income at full employment level. The policy is normally persued by using techniques of demand management. In the vocabulary used by the IMF and the World Bank, macroeconomic management is seen as economic stabilisation and is taken to mean financial programming.[9] The model is aimed at shortening the duration and lessening the degree of disequilibrium in the international balance of payments of the country. For these institutions macroeconomic management has in fact meant debt settlement, adherence to cross conditionalities, stabilisation, structural adjustment and change, and liberalisation of trade policy.

Macroeconomic management should, in fact, be seen as an integrated system of several kinds of policies aimed at overall balance and could include:

1. Macroeconomic stabilisation – the use of fiscal, monetary and other policies affecting national output, employment and prices, and other variables.
2. Resources allocation: national priority among various probable choices in various public and private goods.
3. Regulation of economic activity and markets.
4. The use of public resources to redistribute income and wealth so as to ensure economic equity.

Accordingly, this sort of management strategy could be termed a cocktail or a policy-mix approach.

EVOLUTION AND BACKGROUND

Since the time of Confucius and Kautilya,[10] some form of management of a nation's economy has been used. The Greek philosophers,[11] while laying down the principles of *Oeconomicus*, paid due attention to the efficient economic management of the Hellenic city state, or *polis*. During the eighteenth century and even before, from the time of the Mercantilists to Adam Smith and other Classicists, the major concern was internal and external macroeconomic balance.[12] Marx elaborated a complex two-sector equilibrium model of national economics. His theory of reproduction, along with that of Leon Walras, can safely be considered as parent of the modern dynamic theory of general equilibrium.[13] Until the early years of this century macroeconomic management could be traced back to the anti-cyclical policies suggested by popular trade cycle theorists.[14]

Until the 1930s it was the privilege of individual scholars to write and talk philosophically of the need to macromanage national economies. Perhaps for the first time in economic history, during the Great Depression nations and their governments were forced by circumstances to rescue their sagging economies and adopt available measures in order to improve the management of macroeconomies.

The beggar-my-neighbour policies that existed before the First World War and the depression of 1929–33 brought an end to the ancient stability of the gold standard and ushered in a period of experimentation in exchange regimes, which coincided with the Depression. Because of mass unemployment, governments had to cast around for any measure, no matter how extreme, that might alleviate the problem. One superficially plausible way of doing this was to cut back on imports and produce those goods domestically. If one country could manage to reduce its imports, then its unemployment might be reduced because people would be put to work producing replacement goods at home. Other countries would, however, find their exports falling and unemployment rising as a consequence. This was considered to be a method of attaining internal and international equilibrium at the same time. If the policy worked, it was an example of successful macroeconomic management and an argument in its favour. But, in fact, the policy worked only so long as other countries did not protect themselves by taking similar measures. The net effect of such policies was a reduction in the volume of trade, thereby sacrificing the gains from trade without increasing worldwide employment.

The beggar-my-neighbour policies of the 1930s used methods such as import duties, export subsidies, quotas, prohibitions and exchange-rate depreciations. If a country with a large portion of its labour force unemployed devalued its exchange rate, two effects could be expected: exports would rise and consumers would buy fewer imports and more domestic goods. Both these changes would have the effect of lowering the country's unemployment level. But such policies definitely led to competitive countermeasures being adopted by other countries, causing the collapse of global and national economic management.

The publication in 1936 of Keynes' *The General Theory of Employment,*

Interest and Money marked the beginning of a new era of thought that sharply departed from classical, liberal economic philosophy. Keynesian theory and the pragmatic policy of President Roosevelt in the US – the New Deal – gave a new significance to the concept of macroeconomic management and what is sometimes known as state interventionism. It must, however, be noted that the positive role of the state in economic management is not to be confused with state ownership of the public sector.

In modern macroeconomics it is definitely Keynes who should be credited with devising an elaborate and consistent theory of equilibrium of output, income and employment that also incorporates money and prices. From the point of view of practical policy the guiding principle of his vision for a new postwar international order was 'never again' – the unemployment, the beggar-my-neighbour policies, the collapse of commodity prices, the deflationary policies, the protectionism and so forth of the 1930s. Accordingly Keynes became one of the key architects of the postwar Bretton Woods System.

In the post Second World War period the creation of the Bretton Woods System, which respected most of Keynes's original ideas[15] and resulted in the creation of the International Monetary Fund (IMF) and the International Bank for Reconstruction and Development (now the World Bank), laid down the foundations for solid global macroeconomic management. It was the failure of the international community (non-ratification of the treaty) that ITO – the third pillar of Keynes's system – was not created (the UN being the fourth), leaving the system crippled for ever. While the IMF was entrusted with the task of maintaining stable exchange rates – through the dollar standard (which could be converted into gold), thereby ensuring relatively stable exchange rates and commodity prices in the international market – the World Bank was supposed to provide soft loans for reconstruction and development.

The golden years of Bretton Woods (1948–71) saw an immense improvement over the situation of the 1930s. The 1950s and 1960s marked a period of global expansion of production and trade, full employment, and low inflation in developed countries – a favourable environment for the developing countries. There was often an excessive emphasis on physical capital accumulation; but the initial equation, that is, development with capital accumulation supplemented by foreign aid, later led countries into increased problems as the golden years went by. The emphasis on physical capital formation was also linked to optimism regarding the capacity to utilise surplus labour and to disguise unemployment. Domestic savings did increase, not because of the mobilisation of domestic manpower, but rather as a result of squeezing the agricultural sector; and an inegalitarian pattern of development emerged. Thus, although the golden years did show rapid economic growth, they were certainly not solid gold years.

The 1970s saw the breakdown and disintegration of the Bretton Woods system. The engine of growth that had supported the developing countries during the golden years began to stutter and then violently change gear. The opportunity to assert oil and commodity power appeared briefly but was not fully utilized. Even in the face of reduced growth and serious recession in the industrial countries the developing countries continued to grow and made vigorous progress in their competitive position in world trade and manufacture. Although aid and official development assistance stagnated and dwindled well below the targets set by the UN Development Decades, the flow of private capital into the developing countries flourished. The continuation of growth was debt-led, and to that extent it was an illusion.[16]

As the 1980s drew to a close, turbulence and uncertainty persisted, and growth slowed substantially. Some African and highly indebted, middle-income countries suffered a significant decline in per capita income. Their investment sagged to levels where even minimal replacement could no longer occur in important sectors of their economies. Their debts grew and their debt-service obligations were exceeded, leading to negative net resource transfers. In some countries the severity of this prolonged economic slump surpassed that of the Great Depression.

Compared with the golden years, the 1980s were years of poor development. In the period that followed the illusory debt-led growth, national governments and international institutions shifted their attention from growth to debt settlement, stabilisation, structural adjustment, structural change and liberalisation. This was not just a lost decade but was a time of major reversal of development with an alarming run-down of human capital. The adjustment policies in many countries failed miserably in laying down the foundations for subsequent sustainable growth.[17]

In the 1990s the global economy remains fragile – primarily due to the poor performance of macroeconomic policies in the industrialised countries, on the one hand, and unsuccessful adjustment policies in the developing countries on the other.

THE FINANCIAL PROGRAMMING MODEL

The International Monetary Fund has for a long time advocated macroeconomic management through structural adjustment programmes consisting of a comprehensive set of economic measures designed to achieve broad macroeconomic goals. Fund members are free to seek advice and financial support for such programmes. A fundamental objective of IMF-supported programmes is to provide an orderly adjustment of both macroeconomic and structural imbalances so as to foster economic growth, while bringing about a balance of payments position that is sustainable in the medium term.

The programmes are usually formulated by the member countries with the assistance of IMF staff. Understanding the role and use of monetary and fiscal policy to influence macroeconomic performance typically plays a major part. The use of these primary demand management instruments is supplemented by a variety of other measures such as exchange-rate policy, structural policies – for example prices, income, trade policies and specific aspects of taxation or public spending policies.

The IMF's approach to macroeconomic management (what it generally prefers to call economic stabilisation) is known as financial programming and is based largely on oral tradition. Surprisingly, there is little readily available material on its theoretical underpinnings. In the 1950s and 1960s IMF programmes were articulated and formalised by IMF staff, and their papers remain the theoretical mainstay of the programmes.[18]

Since the 1970s the concept and structure of the adjustment programme has evolved, but its methods – such as floating exchange rates among major currencies, large fluctuations in real interest rates in international credit markets, extended periods of recession in industrialised countries – have aggravated the adjustment problems of developing countries and seriously complicated the task of macroeconomic management.[19] Finally, as the matter stands today, the IMF-supported adjustment programmes have gradually absorbed many of the developments that have taken place in the past.

Programme Design

When negotiating an IMF-supported programme with a member country, technical analysis and political processes are intimately linked. An integrated system of accounting, covering national income and expenditure as well as financial flows and associated stocks, lies at the heart of macroeconomic appraisal and analysis of the performance of any economy. For the purpose of financial programming it is useful to divide the economy into sectors and record the transactions taking place among them. The four sectors usually distinguished are the private non-financial sector, the government sector, the banking sector, and the foreign sector. For each sector the transactions between its members and those of other sectors can be divided into two: transactions arising during the course of production, and financial transactions. The balance of all transactions for each sector is necessarily equal to zero, and the balance of income-expenditure transactions is equal and of an opposite sign to the balance of financial transactions. Indeed the complete framework of income and flow-of-funds accounts shows numerous identities among the recorded surpluses in the accounts. These and other identities can be useful in gauging tendencies in an economy and in assessing the effects of policy changes. These identities are complemented by behaviourial relationships, and a model is created.

Economic models can provide a quantitative framework for forecasting and policy analysis. They can be used in either of the following ways: by assessing the consequences of foreseen or assumed changes in exogenous variables, which are determined independently of the processes illustrated in the model; for the magnitude of endogenous variables, which are determined within the model; or by determining the changes in policy instruments needed to achieve the changes in some of the endogenous variables considered to be the objectives of economic policy. Financial programming involves the models in the latter mode.

In considering the framework used by the IMF to analyse adjustment programmes, it may be useful to distinguish between a balance-of-payment disequilibrium that is reversible within a period of two to three years and a disequilibrium involving serious structural impediments to growth or such a large accumulated external debt that the strategy of returning to equilibrium can only be considered for a longer period. The two cases differ primarily in respect to the emphasis placed on measures aimed at growth or utilisation of productive capacity.

In the short term the formulation of the model assumes productive capacity to be fixed and not necessarily fully utilised. Output (income) could, therefore, change within the limits set by the existing productive potential. Residents' expenditure on domestic and foreign goods (commonly called absorption) could either fall short or exceed domestic income. The difference between the value of domestic production (Y) and absorption (A) is the balance of trade in goods and services, which is sometimes loosely referred to as the current account balance (CA):[20]

$$CA = Y - A \tag{1.1}$$

The current account shows either a surplus or a deficit. This demonstrates an important principle, that a current account deficit can be reduced by a decline in absorption (relative to income) or by an increase in income (relative to absorption). The desired current account balance is of course not likely to be zero. Foreign residents may make investments in and transfers to the economy, and domestic residents may in turn do the same abroad. The net balance of transfers and capital transactions is itself affected by changes in domestic economy and in the rest of the world.

Adjustment programmes for which IMF support is generally requested typically involve the problem of reducing a current account deficit to fit a sustainable net inflow of capital; and they may also be aimed at restoring a sustainable net capital inflow. In directing economic policy to this objective, the authorities are faced not so much with target outcome but with a binding constraint that it may not be easy to change for long periods and by large margins.

The way in which the balance of payments acts as a constraint on the use of resources in the economy can be illustrated by an extension of equation 1.1:

$$\Delta R = CA + \Delta FI \tag{1.2}$$

where ΔR is the change in net foreign assets of the banking system, including net international reserves of the Central Bank and ΔFI is the change in net foreign indebtedness of non-bank residents. By combining the two equations one gets:

$$\Delta R = Y - A + \Delta FI \tag{1.3}$$

which shows that an excess of absorption over income not financed by foreign borrowing leads to a run-down of net foreign assets.

It follows from the definition of the current account balance that a desired reduction in a current account deficit can be achieved through some combination of increased output and reduced absorption. It is generally easier to reduce absorption than to increase production. For this reason, policies affecting absorption are often put in place first when a rapid decline in the current account deficit is mandatory.

Demand management policies directly affect absorption and thereby internal balance, which refers to the conformity between aggregate expenditure (equal to absorption plus exports minus imports) and potential output at stable prices. Since output of domestic goods and services is by definition equal to aggregate expenditure by domestic and foreign residents on these goods and services, a change in the latter necessarily produces a corresponding change in the former. If aggregate expenditure exceeds the productive capacity of an economy at the existing price level, the result would be a rise in prices that would continue until the excess demand was eliminated. If aggregate expenditure fell short of productive capacity, prices could fall – the more likely immediate outcome would, however, be a fall in employment without much reduction in prices.

In general, external and internal balance can not be simultaneously achieved without employing at least two separate instruments, one acting to reduce domestic expenditure and other to change the composition of foreign and domestic expenditure between foreign and domestic goods.[21] If absorption exceeds output while aggregate expenditure on domestic goods and services exceeds potential output at existing prices, policies restraining aggregate demand could alleviate both external deficit and the inflationary pressure resulting from the internal disequilibrium. But the demand restraint will only by coincidence lead to simultaneous external and internal balance. What is needed in such a situation is a policy that can increase the global demand for domestic goods without at the same time increasing domestic absorption of all (domestic and foreign) goods and services. This can be achieved by expenditure-switching policies, which, in conjunction with expenditure reducing policies, can reduce a current account deficit.

It must be noted that in order to sustain an improvement in a country's external position, growth in expenditure can not be allowed to exceed the growth in output. It is often suggested that in debt-ridden countries where growth has been slow because of contraction in domestic expenditure and unfavourable external conditions, or because of severe structural problems, economic recovery could be achieved by government expenditure. But if the rate of growth of output is not adequate and sufficiently outward oriented, it will in the long run not be possible to service the external debt without reducing absorption and, inevitably, the economic well-being of the people. Economic growth and external equilibrium are therefore complementary and mutually supporting objectives of economic policy.

The supply-side policies have two distinct effects: One is to increase output from existing productive capacity; and the second is to increase the rate of growth of productive capacity itself.

Basic Financial Programming Model

While the adjustment programmes for each country differ considerably in their details, there is nevertheless a common feature – namely, the need to restore balance of payments equilibrium while maintaining and strengthening the conditions for noninflationary, long-term growth of output. Accordingly, a necessary condition for achieving this outcome is that the basic structure of all programmes is built on a financial analysis that ensures consistency between the impact of proposed policy measures and the desired balance of payments outcome.

Balance of payments has long been viewed as a monetary phenomenon in economics.[22] The absorption approach has played a key role in the design of IMF-supported programmes and has changed the thinking on balance of payments issues by posing the problems of adjustment in a way that has highlighted the policy aspects. The basic proposition of the policy model of the IMF programme is that an open economy works under the rule of a fixed exchange rate, the money supply is considered as an endogenous variable influenced by surpluses and deficits in the balance of payments, and it is not just an exogenous policy instrument.[23]

The model is based on three fundamental equations. The core of every programme starts with the financial identity expressing the change in the money stock as the sum of the changes in international and domestic components:

$$\Delta M = \Delta R + \Delta D \tag{1.4}$$

where M is the stock of money, R the domestic currency value of net foreign assets and D the net domestic asset of the banking system.

The second founding block of the model is the demand for money. In its restrictive mode it is the change in nominal money (ΔM^d) in relation to changes in nominal income ($k\Delta Y$)

$$\Delta M^d = k\Delta Y \tag{1.5}$$

The third building block is a condition defining flow equilibrium in the money market, that is:

$$\Delta M^d = \Delta M \tag{1.6}$$

By combining the three components, we get:

$$\Delta R = \Delta M - \Delta D = \Delta M^d - \Delta D \tag{1.7}$$

The model defined in equation 1.7 can also be put in a more general framework by considering income and expenditure relationships and the role of private capital movements in an open economy. Recalling equation 1.1, the current account must be matched by changes in the net foreign assets of the banking system (ΔR) and the net foreign indebtedness of all non-bank residents (ΔFI), that is:

$$CA = \Delta R - \Delta FI \tag{1.8}$$

By combining 1.7 and 1.8 we get:

$$CA + \Delta FI = \Delta M - \Delta D \tag{1.9}$$

and in terms of national income and absorption the equation can be rewritten as:

$$Y - A + \Delta FI = \Delta M - \Delta D \tag{1.10}$$

In other words, residents' use of resources (absorption) will exceed the sum of the supply of domestic resources (income) and foreign savings (changes in net foreign indebtedness) when the changes in domestic credit exceed the change in net domestic assets.

If it is assumed that M^d is a function of a few variables that are independent of ΔD, then the conclusion remains that a ceiling for ΔD will determine ΔR.

With the overall outline of financial programming in mind, it is easy to show how the basic relationship between change in net foreign assets and changes in domestic credits can be used for the design of a financial adjustment programme. In a simplest case, only three steps are required:

1. To set a target for changes in net foreign assets over a specified time period.
2. To make an estimate of the probable course of the demand for money over the same period, involving setting targets for principal determinants of money demand such as real income and prices.

3. To forecast the demand for money and overall targets for the balance of payments, deducting the change in net domestic assets of the banking system from the balance sheet identity of assets and liabilities.

It is obvious that in the financial programming approach there is no conceptual difficulty in deriving a domestic credit ceiling consistent with a desired change in net foreign assets. The whole exercise involves manipulating only the balance sheet relationships.

MACROECONOMIC MANAGEMENT: AN ALL-SIDED APPROACH

During the past twenty years or so, particularly since the international debt crisis of the late 1970s, frantic attempts have been made to macromanage the debt-ridden economies. Unfortunately, under the pressure of the IMF these countries had to adopt so-called structural adjustment programmes with strict financial programming strategies. The results were as follows: in Africa, near failure; in Latin America, some success; in the rest of the world, a moderately good record. But everywhere there were social tensions and unrest, retardation of the growth process and a severe running down of human capital.

There are a variety of reasons for these results: inappropriate analysis of a country's real economic health when designing the programme; a lack of understanding of the local socio-political economic conditions in the country concerned; a lack of determination on the part of the governments of countries to implement the programme; and the absence of social safety nets in the adjustment programmes for these countries. However pious the intention to help a country and support its adjustment programme, the fact remains that managing the macroeconomy of a country is not just an exercise in financial programming and balancing its books. Macroeconomic management is an all-sided approach.

Countries suffer from a broad range of economic problems, the most common being external imbalances as, reflected in current account deficits, capital flight and high levels of indebtedness; accelerating inflation, frequently accompanied by falling private investments and stagnant growth; growing administrative regulation of credit, imports, prices, wages and so on, thereby reducing capacity utilisation and increasing structural maladjustments; and above all, an increase in unemployment. In order to restore growth, create employment and achieve internal and external equilibrium, what is needed is an appropriate, all-sided, coordinated use of a variety of policy measures that include demand management policies (monetary and fiscal measures), exchange rate policies, external debt policies, policies affecting capacity utilisation and production potential, and trade and social policies.

The effectiveness of fiscal policy is a major factor in determining a country's macroeconomic performance. This follows from the fact that the public sector alone in most developing countries constitutes roughly one quarter of GDP. Furthermore the governments in these countries have exercised taxing, borrowing and spending powers both to maintain a certain level of economic growth and manipulate the allocation of resources to achieve growth with redistribution.[24] It must be noted that while fiscal policy is a major tool for achieving growth-oriented adjustment, it may also become a possible source of disequilibrium.[25] For countries with unsustainable fiscal deficits, macroeconomic management should be a top priority, involving a review and reform of the tax structure and control over government spending. In the context of fiscal policy, three major issues need consideration: the size of the budget deficit; the budget and external balance; and financing the budget deficit.

The task of monetary policy is to ensure that expansion in domestic liquidity is consistent with the objectives of growth, inflation, and the balance of payments position. In this context money control policies play a central role. From the stabilisation policy point of view, these policies usually involve the prevention of expansion or reduction of overall spending. Balancing the demand and supply of money requires direct action (imposing a credit ceiling on bank loans, control of interest rates and so on) or indirect action (purchase and sale of securities) on the one hand, and control of the money supply on the other.

Exchange rate policy involves choosing an exchange rate system and determining the particular rate at which foreign exchange transactions will take place. A country's exchange rate policy affects both its relative price structure in domestic currency terms between goods that are traded internationally and those produced for the domestic market as well as the level of its domestic prices. Thus the particular exchange rate system (pegged to a single or a basket of currencies, or independently floating) and its level, in terms of price incentives, will have a widespread impact on the entire economy. A country's economic structure and the institutional characteristics are important considerations in determining its exchange rate policy.[26]

Trade policy also has an immense impact on the macroeconomic health of a nation. Even the IMF places increased attention on trade policy and supports it through EFF (Extended Fund Facility), SAF (Structural Adjustment Facility) and ESAF (Enhanced Structural Adjustment Facility) as well as through standby arrangements. The main issue in trade policy, however, remains protectionism versus free trade. The latter promotes competition in domestic markets, stimulates innovations, provides consumers with a wider choice of goods, and allows firms to take advantage of competition and economies of scale. It also unleashes dynamic forces to raise the growth rate in the economy. Despite these advantages, protectionism has a strong hold not only in countries left behind in the process of development and structural change, but also among the highly industrialised countries.

In recent years external debt policy has become one of the corner stones of macroeconomic management. The debt crisis of the late 1970s had a major impact on the issue. Clearly defined policies on the part of the borrowing country and the extent of its external indebtedness play a crucial part in determining its macroeconomic management strategy. While the appropriateness of borrowing depends on the use of resources, the effectiveness of debt management depends on the appropriateness of other policies. Growth and stabilisation are the central objectives of debt management policy, its two basic aspects being the capacity to borrow and the ability to service the debt.

In addition there are two supply-side options to consider. The first is designed to increase current output by improving the efficiency of the ways in which capital, labour and land are utilised and allocated. This option involves measures that reduce the distortions arising from price controls, imperfect competition, taxes, subsidies, trade restrictions and so on, and drive a wedge between prices and marginal costs. The second option involves measures designed to raise the long-term rate of growth of capacity output by providing incentives to stimulate domestic savings and investments as well as educational and technological innovation. Policies that increase the inflow of foreign savings are also important.

The social dimension of macroeconomic management is the most vital part of the concept and includes employment, education, health and sanitation, housing and so on. Policies that develop the basic infrastructure (allowing for services such as the media, the press, information and communication systems and so on) and maintain ecological balance also have a special place in macroeconomic management, as do policies aimed at the reduction of inequalities of income and wealth – especially in view of the adjustment programmes supported by the IMF that brought to the surface many deeper social problems in adjusting countries. Development with a human face need not only be proclaimed but must also be pursued.

Objectives and Policy Instruments

Although it is a fact that a diversity of social, political and institutional characteristics determine the macroeconomic goals of management strategy, it is still possible to discern a set of fundamental objectives, external and internal balance and speedy growth being the most important. The question arises as to how these objectives relate to each other and to other policy objectives. Although governments peruse a wide variety of policy objectives that may conflict, the functions of government are classified as stabilisation, allocation and distribution.[27]

In the theory of economic policy, the process of using the various instruments of policy to achieve simultaneously the desired levels of the target variables is approached two ways. Jan Tinbergen's fixed targets approach to economic policy is concerned with the basic requirement of simultaneously achieving the desired levels of the target variables. His approach views economic policy in terms of the dichotomy between targets and instruments. Fixed values are chosen for the target variables, and the instruments are varied in order to attain the predetermined targets. Another approach to policy is that of Henri Theil, which is concerned with the situation where all the desired levels of the target variables can not be achieved simultaneously and where choices therefore have to be made.

In balancing the competing objectives, a government may be faced with various conflicts. The problem of conflicting interests is not entirely caused by noneconomic and distributional aims.[28] For instance it is not always clear whether price stability or a law rate of inflation is implied by, or is a necessary condition for, the achievement of external balance and economic growth. First, price stability could appear to be implied in a financial programme for bringing aggregate expenditure into line with aggregate output. Second, there are reasons to believe that a chronic environment of high inflation eventually discourages saving and investment. Third, a sharp improvement in the current account deficit may lead to inflationary pressures that are difficult to correct with other policies, in part because of wage rigidities in lagging sectors. Finally, achieving policy objectives may have an initial inflationary impact.

Targets set for some objectives may be open ended, that is they are regarded as ceilings and floors rather than point targets. Over- and underperformance may lead to a redesign of management strategy. Derivation of intermediate targets from ultimate objectives may pose another problem and may be difficult to relate directly to available policy instruments.

A further factor influencing the availability of different policy instruments is the role of central government planning and direct control over facets of economic activity. The institutional setting in these respects may reflect political ideology, making it difficult to implement the programmes.

The choice of policy instruments is heavily influenced by the stage of development of economic institutions such as markets, banks and so on. In a country with relatively undeveloped and segmented financial markets, the economy is likely to respond much less flexibly to changes in monetary policy. Moreover, where there are severe policy-related distortions arising from price controls, exchange and trade restrictions, overvalued exchange rates and so on, the efficacy of demand management policies is sharply reduced.

Economic theory provides a guide to basic equilibrium relationships only and not to the length of time it takes for changes in exogenous variables (including policy instruments) to have an impact on endogenous variables. In practice, however, policies operate with time lags that can be substantial. Another problem is of proper timing in the case of supply-side policies, as the results of these policies may not become evident for several years.

The interaction between supply-side policies and demand management policies pose further problems in designing the strategy of macroeconomic management. Specifically, the liberalisation of import restrictions, of domestic financial markets, and of foreign exchange markets alters the way in which the economy reacts to fiscal, monetary, exchange rate and other policies.

CONCLUSIONS

Macroeconomic management is a requirement of our times. Nineteenth century liberal economic philosophy that ignored the role of state intervention in macroeconomic matters is a thing of the past. Today no country, whether rich or poor, developed or developing, large or small, can afford to leave management of its economy unattended. Although the problems and priorities of every country are different, the basic goals are the same: growth of employment with equitable distribution of incomes and wealth. While equilibrium, both on the domestic and external fronts, remains the focus of attention of every government, the mainstay is a stabilised economy with low inflation. The adopted instruments of each policy will differ according to the degree and intensity of the problems of macroeconomies, and thus the results will vary. IMF supported adjustment programmes are highly desirable as they emphasise financial discipline, but there is no substitute for a proper macroeconomic management strategy.

Notes

1. This chapter draws on some of the research material of the IMF, Washington DC. The contributor greatefully acknowledges the permission to use the same. – Editor.
2. The *Jataka Kathayen*, or the *Jatakas* (the story books) as they are popularly known, narrates the story.
3. Perhaps the greatest support for general equilibrium analysis could be traced back to the works of J. von Neumann, P. A. Samuelson, K. J. Arrow, J. R. Hicks, G. Debreu and many others.
4. For modern business cycle theories one could cite the works of J. R. Hicks, R. M. Goodwin, M. Friedman and A. J. Schwartz, P. A. Samuelson, L. A. Metzler, E. J. Shapiro and P. Cagan.
5. Today James Tobin is definitely one of the greatest supporters of J. M. Keynes and his policies. He stands for a modified version of Keynes' liquidity preference theory and improvements in Keynesian 'market failures'.
6. The rational expectation counterrevolution was started by R. E. Lucas and others. This is the basis of the new classical macroeconomics. The panglossian conclusion of the theory is that macroeconomic performance is always as good as it can be under the circumstances and certainly can not be improved by the usual Keynesian monetary and fiscal policy.
7. In the 1970s the term supply side (coined by Herbert Stein) became the vogue, making Arthur Laffer with his cocktail-napkin curve (drawn for the instruction of Congressman Jack Kemp) the star economist. While R. Mundell, D. Stockman and A. Laffer were the ideologists, Jack Kemp and President Ronald Reagan were the political protagonists of the idea that tax cuts and reduced public spending would stimulate work, savings and investment, thereby augmenting productivity and raising the economy's capacity to produce from a given employed labour force. But the essential message of supply-siders and its sure result, at least in the US, was the redistribution of wealth in favour of the richer sections of the population (see Tobin, 1987).
8. See the work of growth theorists such as N. Kaldor and J. Mirrleet (1962), T. W. Swan (1963), Robert Solow (1969), L. Pasinetti (1962) and many others. Among the balanced (steady-state) growth protagonists the following names are worth mentioning: R. Nurkse, P. N. Rosenstein-Rodan, W. A.

Lewis and T. Scitovski. Their doctrine stresses that the percentage rate of change of the constituent variables of the economy are the same.

9. See IMF Research Department Paper (1987).

10. In the writings of the famous Chinese politician–philosopher Kung Fu Tse (Confucius) (551–478 BC), we find a highly developed public administration that dealt with current agrarian, commercial and financial problems. Similarly, from the writings of Meng Tzu (Menicius) (372–288 BC), it is possible to compile a comprehensive system of economic policy, especially of monetary management and exchange control.

    The Indian teacher, philosopher and politician Vishnugupta (Chanakya or Kautilya, as he is popularly known in literature of 320 BC) could be considered among the first whose work on the management of state affairs, the *Arthashastra*, is today considered as an important contribution to the principles of political economy. It was first translated in English from Sanskrit in 1909.

11. Fragments of Greek economic thought that are accessible to us may be gleaned from the works of Plato (427–347 BC) and Aristotle (384–322 BC).

12. In *An Inquiry into the Nature and Causes of the Wealth of Nations*, Adam Smith argued that in a freely competitive economy the self-interest of individuals will lead automatically to an efficient distribution of society's resources, as if they have been guided by an invisible hand. This natural order in a freely competitive economic system would be upset by government intervention, and Smith consequently disapproved of any restrictions on the free working of the economy. In his view, the role of the government should be confined to safeguarding property rights, the maintaining particular public works, and national defence. He stressed that the free-market system would only produce harmonious results within a definite legal and institutional structure and that self-interest in other circumstances can easily thwart rather than promote public welfare.

    David Ricardo's theory of international trade, based on the law of comparative costs, and T. R. Malthus' law of population are examples of concern for domestic and external equilibrium of the economy.

13. For an elaborate explanation of the theory, see M. Morishima (1973).

14. See, for example, theorists such as R. G. Hawtrey, F. A. von Hayek and J. A. Schumpeter.

15. The World Economic Conference of 1933 was the first attempt to create an international economic order. Although this attempt ended in failure, the ideas then brought forward continued to reverberate in Keynes's mind. In 1942 he and his associates prepared the three famous memoranda on the International Clearing Union, on Commodity Buffer Stocks and on Plans for Relief and Reconstruction. The structure envisaged by Keynes, arising from his belief in the possibility and sustainability of full employment through active government policy – later expanded by Harrod to full employment growth – was embodied in the 1942 memoranda, the central point being global, macroeconomic, monetary and financial management; an investment fund for relief and reconstruction; the stabilisation of primary commodity prices; and the use of soft aid programmes. These ideas were put forward again by Keynes at the Bretton Woods meeting as the British proposal.

16. For an interesting analysis of post World War development, see H. W. Singer (1992).
17. See Sharma and Singer (1988).
18. See S. J. Polak (1977).
19. According to the World Bank Policy Research Bulletin of March–April 1994 twenty nine African countries drew up programmes in the 1980s – programmes intended to improve the poor policies that were the primary cause of the 15 per cent fall in Africa's GDP between 1977 and 1985. On the macroeconomic front, six of the adjusting countries experienced a large improvement in their policies; nine, a small improvement; and eleven a deterioration. There has been much talk about the costs of adjustment but less about the substantial benefits. Most countries that improved their policies have returned to positive growth rates of per capita GDP.
20. This approach was first developed by S. S. Alexander (1952).
21. This of course is an example of J. Tinbergen's (1952) rule that in general a specified number of policy objectives cannot be attained without using at least the same number of policy instruments.
22. See J. Frankel and H. G. Johnson (1976); R. R. Rhomberg and H. R. Heller (1977).
23. The papers written by S. J. Polak (1977) and E. W. Robichek (1967) influenced greatly the subjects within the IMF, particularly the issue of stabilisation policy and the theoretical aspects of the present-day philosophy of adjustment programmes.
24. See Hollis Chenery *et al.* (1974).
25. Unfortunately, despite impressive objectives, the results of fiscal policy intervention in developing countries have often been far from favourable. Indeed substantial evidence exists that in many cases poor fiscal management has been a major factor underlying problems of internal and external balance and low growth rates.
26. In this context a number of characteristics can be noted common to many developing countries: reliance on primary commodity production and exports; the limited substitutability of domestically produced goods for imports; dependence on the external sector for essential imports, particularly capital equipment and intermediate goods; the importance of capital flows, including direct foreign investments and private and official lending; the presence of underdeveloped financial markets, and so on.
27. This classification was first proposed by R. Musgrave (1959) and has been reasserted by V. Tanzi (1986).
28. See M. I. Blejer (1983) and O. E. G. Johnson (1984).

References

Alexander, S. S. (1952) 'Effects of a Devaluation on a Trade Balance', *IMF Staff Papers*, vol. 2.

Blejer, M. I. (1983) 'On the Anatomy of Inflation: The Variability of Relative Commodity Prices in Argentina', *Journal of Money, Credit and Banking*, vol. 15.

Black, S. W. (1982) *Politics versus Markets* (Washington: American Enterprise Institute for Public Policy Research).

Chenery, H. B. *et al.* (1974) *Redistribution with Growth* (London: The World Bank and Oxford University Press).

Davis, J. M. (ed.) (1992) *Macroeconomic Adjustment: Policy Instruments and Issues* (Washington: IMF Institute).

Frankel, J. and H. G. Johnson (1976) (eds) *The Monetary Approach to the Balance of Payments* (London: Allen & Unwin).

Johnson, O. E. G. (1984) 'On Growth and Inflation in Developing Countries', *IMF Staff Papers*, vol. 31.

Hardy, D. C. (1992) 'Soft Budget Constraints, Firm Commitments and the Social Safety Net', *IMF Staff Papers*, vol. 39, no. 2.

Kaldor, N. A. and J. Mirrlees (1962) 'A New Model of Economic Growth', *Review of Economic Studies*, vol. XXIX.

McKinnon, R. I. (1991) *The Order of Economic Liberalization: Financial Control in the Transition to a Market Economy* (Baltimore: The Johns Hopkins University Press).

Meade, J. E. and M. Weale (1991) 'On the Stability of Monetary and Fiscal Policy', *DAE Working Paper*, no. 9177 (Cambridge: University of Cambridge).

Morishima, M. (1973) *Marx's Economics: A Dual Theory of Value and Growth* (Cambridge: Cambridge University Press).

Musgrave, R. A. (1959) *The Theory of Public Finance: A Study in Public Economy* (New York: McGraw Hill).

Pasinetti, L. L. (1962) 'Rate of Profit and Income Distribution in Relation to Economic Growth', *Review of Economic Studies* vol. XXIX.

Person, T. and G. Tabellini (1990) *Macroeconomic Policy, Credibility and Politics* (New York: Harwood Academic Publishers).

Polak, S. J. (1977) 'Monetary Analysis of Income Formation and Payments Problem', *IMF Staff Papers*, vol. 5.

Polak, S. J. (1987) *Theoretical Aspects of the Design of Fund-Supported Adjustment Programs* (Washington: International Monetary Fund).

Rhomberg, R. R. and H. R. Heller (1977) 'Introductory Survey', in *The Monetary Approach to the Balance of Payments* (Washington: International Monetary Fund).

Robichek, E. W. (1967) 'Financial Programming Exercises of the International Monetary Fund in Latin America', *Address to Brazilian Professors of Economics*, Rio de Janeiro.

Sharma, S. and H. W. Singer (1988) 'Preface' in *Growth and External Debt Management* (London: Macmillan).

Singer, H. W. (1992) 'Lessons of Post War Development Experience', in Soumitra Sharma (ed.), *Development Policy* (London: Macmillan).

Solow, R. M. (1969) *Growth Theory: An Exposition* (New York: Oxford University Press).

Swan, T. W. (1963) 'Growth Models of Golden Ages and Production Functions', in K. E. Berrill (ed.), *Economic Development with Special Reference to East Asia* (London: Macmillan).

Tanzi, V. (1986) 'The Growth of Public Expenditure in Industrial Countries: An International Historical Perspective', Unpublished Monograph (Washington: IMF).

Tanzi, V. (1992) 'Financial Markets and Public Finance in the Transformation Process, paper presented at the CEPR Conference on The Economic Consequences of the East, held at the Deutsche Bank, Frankfurt/Main.
Theil, H. (1956) 'On the Theory of Economic Policy', *American Economic Review, Papers and Proceedings*, vol. 45.
Tinbergen, Jan (1952) *On the Theory of Economic Policy* (Amsterdam: North Holland).
Tobin, J. (1983) 'Keynes' Policies in Theory and Practice', *Challenge*, vol. 26, no. 5.
Tobin, J. (1987) *Policies for Prosperity: Essays in a Keynesian Mode* (edited by P. M. Jackson) (Cambridge, Mass.: The MIT Press).
World Bank Policy Research Bulletin, March–April 1994.
Whitehead, L. (1990) 'Political Explanations of Macroeconomic Management: A Survey', *World Development*, vol. 18, no. 8.

2 Global Prospects in an Interdependent World

Paul Streeten

DOMINANCE – A CONDITION FOR GLOBAL ORDER

What are the characteristics of a working international order that is concerned with the evolution of underdeveloped regions in a growing world economy with an equitable distribution of the gains from growth?

There are at least four. First, for the benefit of the developing regions there should be a centre to generate a balance of payments surplus and an excess of exports over imports.

Second, there should be financial institutions such as banks, corporations and aid agencies to convert surpluses into long-term loans or equity investments on acceptable terms. In addition to this there should be supportive financial functions for foreign lending to be countercyclical, so that when the centre contracts, the periphery can expand and contribute to the stabilisation of the system. It would also be helpful if the centre could act as lender of last resort and as provider of the means of payment for international transactions.

Third, there must be the industrial capacity and technological leadership to produce the capital goods or intermediate products and the technology required for industrialisation, which will contribute to the trade surplus. This capacity will be mainly in the centre that originates the surpluses and the loans, at least in the early stages of the development of the periphery. The fourth is the controversial characteristic of supporting the three other characteristics with a strong military power to enforce contracts and keep the peace.

Between the Napoleonic wars and 1914 Great Britain – under the Pax Britannica – embodied these characteristics. The surpluses were generated by Britain; the financial institutions were established in the City of London; the 'dark satanic mills' of the north of England manufactured the industrial products, and the British navy ruled the waves. The management of the gold standard after 1910 placed the burden of deflationary adjustment on other countries. However, although this order was dominated by Britain and run in its interests, it contributed to the development of large areas in North and South America, South Africa, Australia and New Zealand.

There was not much of an order between the two world wars. Britain had become unable, and the US was still unwilling, to assume the leadership functions. When agricultural prices fell, the US imposed the Smoot–Hawley tariff in 1930. The US did not function as lender of last resort and did not keep markets open in periods of glut for the purchase of distress goods. There was no countercyclical lending; on the contrary, a boom at home caused an increase in foreign lending and imports. The result of the lack of coordination of the four functions was the Great Depression and the Second World War.

For twenty-five years after the war, and largely as a result of it, the US assumed these functions under the Pax Americana. Large balance of payments surpluses were generated by the US, which led for a time to fear of a chronic dollar shortage. But the US opened its market, and the Marshall Plan, reconstruction aid and long-term direct investment by multinationals soon converted the dollar shortage into a dollar glut and proved correct Keynes' prediction of the US becoming a high-cost, high-living economy. US trade surpluses fell from 4.5 per cent of GNP in 1947 to 0.5 per cent in 1950. In 1968 J.-J. Servan Schreiber predicted in his book, *The American Challenge*, that the power of the US multinational corporations constituted a long-term threat to Europe.

The mighty dollar replaced the pound sterling and New York became an important financial centre, with its institutions soon matching and overtaking those of the City of London. The US became, for a while, the industrial workshop of the world. The nation held a nuclear umbrella over Europe and Japan and used military power to enforce peace. As in the case of Britain half a century earlier, in the 1960s benign dominance turned into predatory dominance. The US began to exploit foreign acceptance of its reserve currency to extract goods and services from abroad. During the inflationary period of the Vietnam War the US offered, in return for large purchases of goods from the rest of the world, depreciating short-term assets in the form of dollar balances in US banks.

After 1970 the power of the US declined, and this process was witnessed as J. Bhagwati's diminished giant syndrome. The country's share of the world's GNP fell from 40–45 per cent in the 1940s to 16–17 per cent in 1988. US competitiveness in both old and new industries and its economic growth rate declined, and the large twin deficits of the budget and balance of payments were symptoms of this decline. In 1970 imports comprised 4.1 per cent of US GNP; in 1980, 9.1 per cent; and in 1989, 18.1 per cent. Other symptoms were the decline in research and development, the failure of primary and secondary education, the falling number of scientists and engineers, and low savings and investment ratios.

There are some who dispute the thesis of the decline of US power in the world economy. Sam Huntington has written of renewal, of a return to a more long-term, prewar trend. Similarly Seizaburo Sato has written that the twentieth century has been the American century and that the twenty-first century will also be an American century. But the evidence is too strong about the reduction of US power and its role as a leader. The US is losing confidence just when others are seeking to imitate it and accept it as leader.

Since 1970 there has been a lack of coordination of the four functions mentioned above. The world has become fragmented and schizophrenic. The US went off gold and abolished dollar convertibility in 1971, just as Britain had in 1931. The current account surpluses were generated first by capital-surplus, oil-exporting desert sheikhdoms, and in the 1980s by Japan and Germany. Financial institutions proliferated, not just in Europe, Japan, Hong Kong, Singapore, Taiwan and Bahrain, but also in the Cayman Islands, the Bahamas, Luxembourg, the Channel Islands, Ireland and other tax havens.[1] Industrial capacity shifted from the US and Britain to Germany, Japan and the newly industrialised countries.[2] Increased military expenditure in the US and the former USSR not only resulted in the loss of their economic power, but also in their decreased ability to maintain peace. Of course many factors other than defence spending contributed to their economic decline, such as growing rigidities, distributional coalitions, over-consumption and so on.[3]

GLOBAL SOLUTION

What future scenarios are likely? Three possible developments of the world economy can be considered, but before doing so one should rule out certain possibilities. In the 1970s there was some talk about a Pax Arabica, with Arab OPEC countries taking over the functions of the dominant economy. Even if the price of oil were to rise again, this scenario has never been a likely one. More plausible is a future Pax Japonica or Nipponica. Some observers have compared the present situation of Japan and the US with that of the US and the UK between the two world wars: as Britain then, so the US is now unable, and as the

US then, so Japan is now unwilling to assume the leadership role. It is not inconceivable that the Japanese, with their immense adaptive power, could eventually become a dominant economic power. But at present Japan lacks a large domestic market for manufactured goods; its imports are not labour-intensive raw materials; it has no military power at present; there is no global appeal or prestige in the Japanese ideology, message or lifestyle; and it does not belong to Judaeo–Graeco–Roman culture.

The fragmentation of the four functions of an international order has contributed to the current confusion, but it has also presented the opportunity for a much better solution. Our present interdependent, pluralistic, multipolar world is less stable and more in need of peace, prosperity and global leadership than past orders, but no single power is both able and willing to assume these functions. This presents us for the first time in history with the opportunity to create a world order based not on dominance and dependence, but on equality, pluralism and cooperation. But this would require creative institutional imagination and the sacrifice of national sovereignty.

Today, institutions lag behind technology. The revolutions in the technologies of transport, travel, communications and information have unified and shrunk the globe, but our organisation into nation states dates back to the Peace of Westphalia in 1648, and to the nineteenth-century unification of Italy and Germany. When the nation states were founded, the city states and feudalism that preceded them had become too small for the scale of operations required by the industrial revolution. The political institutions were therefore adapted to the new industrial technology, to the roads, railways and canals. The nation state was then a progressive institution. The adaptation of institutions to technology is not an inevitable process. In the Middle Ages, for instance, the Roman technology that went into building roads, baths, aqueducts and amphitheatres was lost and they were allowed to fall into disrepair.

But today the nation state, with its insistence on full sovereignty, has become an obstacle to further progress. It has landed us in several prisoners' dilemmas: each nation acts in its own rational self-interest, and as a result every country is worse off. It pays each nation to pursue this mutually destructive course, whether others do likewise or not. If a world government were ever to come about it would probably be the result of a trend where the nation states find it difficult to resolve various issues for themselves (such as the conflict of interests between European farmers, industrialists and the public that has to pay for the common agricultural policy, and the textiles manufacturers of advanced countries aligned in the Multifibre Agreement against Third World textile exporters, and so on).

Clearly, prisoners' dilemma outcomes move the world economy away from a more or less efficient allocation of resources. There are, therefore, potential gains to be had from moving back to more efficient allocations. According to Coase's theorem, which states that in the absence of transaction costs and with full information, a legal framework and well-defined property rights, it pays each state to reach agreements with other states to avoid, by compensation payments, this damage and make all better off than they would have been in the outcome of the prisoners' dilemma.[4] But as we know to our regret, we are far from the outcome of Coase's theorem, but we are not always at the other end of the spectrum – the prisoners' dilemma. Coase's theorem remains useful, in spite of its unrealistic assumptions, in drawing our attention to the fact that there are unexploited mutual profit opportunities to be had from restraint.

Added to the prisoners' dilemma is the free-rider problem, which states that each country relies on others to bear the costs of arrangements that benefit everybody. As a result public goods (such as peace, an open trading system, freedom of the seas, well-defined property rights, international stability, a sound monetary system, conservation of the global environment and so on) are in short supply, while public 'bads' (such as war, pollution and poverty) are oversupplied. The situation is frequently defined in professional literature as the 'social trap', the 'isolation paradox' and so on.

The ranking of preferences by each country is often either/or:

1. A country does not contribute while others do (a case of the free-rider problem).
2. A country contributes together with others (a case of mutual cooperation).
3. No country contributes (a case of the prisoners' dilemma).
4. A country contributes while no other country does (a case of a country being a sucker).

Behaviour by each according to (1) or the fear of (4) leads to outcome (3). Although (2) is preferred to (3), we end up with (3) unless either rewards and penalties, or autonomous cooperative motivations lead to (2). Incentives and expectations should be such that they rule out outcomes (4) and (1), so that nobody ends up as sucker. In the absence of such motivation the public good will be undersupplied.

It has been shown by game theory that iterative games of the prisoners' dilemma type lead to nondestructive outcomes. The partners team up and adopt mutually beneficial strategies.[5] However it is generally more difficult to reach cooperative agreements in international transactions than it is when mutual trust and a sense of duty play a stronger part. There are now many states, and their large number makes it difficult to come to an agreement. The absence of a world government makes it impossible to enforce any such agreement. Changes in the world being rapid, the stability upon which the agreements are based is deeply undermined.

Examples of prisoners' dilemma on the global scale are ubiquitous. Competitive protectionism, through which each country casts its employment problem onto others; competitive exchange rates, whereby inflation or unemployment is exported; research and development; investment; competitive increases in interest rates; environmental pollution; debt crisis – these are only some of the areas in which battles have been fought.

Avoiding these traps requires the coordination and enforcement of policies. But coordination means that each country has to do things it does not want to do.[6] Coordination of policies may mean several types of action: there may be literal harmonisation, such as in the metric system or GMT; it may mean joint expenditure, as in air traffic control under the Civil Aviation Organisation; there could be agreed rules under which autonomous decisions are made; or there could be a continuous exchange of information, such as in public health and macroeconomic policies. Perhaps the most difficult form would be joint decision making.

By realigning modern technology and political institutions, and thus avoiding the negative sum games to which the prisoners' dilemma situation gives rise, institutional innovations at the global or transnational level could be advantageous to all. We could suggest the creation of a set of the following institutions.

International Investment Trust

There is a dire need for the creation of a new institution that would recycle the current account surpluses of countries such as Japan, Germany and others to developing countries in need of capital. The current conventional wisdom is to exhort the Japanese to consume and invest more at home. The slogan 'Japan should eat more, not sell more' seems quite wrongheaded. In a capital-starved world, everybody should be thankful to countries that are prepared to generate excess savings for the rest of the world.

Since the Japanese are inclined to invest the bulk of their excess savings in the most capital-rich countries (the US and Europe), an intermediary institution is required. An International Investment Trust could issue bonds (and perhaps other assets) that are multilaterally guaranteed against devaluation and perhaps indexed against inflation. It is generally agreed that the US will have to reduce its large current account deficit. Unless this reduction is accompanied by an increased loan demand elsewhere (or by domestic expansion in surplus countries), the world economy will be threatened with growing deflation and unprecedented unemployment. Recycling to creditworthy developing countries through the proposed International Investment Trust is a sensible alternative. The rate of return on assets acquired from the Trust might be lower than that on US Treasury Bonds, but it would be a safer investment and thus could attract lenders. The loans could be granted on commercial terms to the newly industrialised countries and on subsidised rates to poor countries.

The point could be raised as to whether existing institutions, such as the World Bank or the regional development banks, could not undertake this task. In principle, they could and this would be better than deflation. But competition in lending procedure, experimentation in alternative lending styles, and some limits to the size and monopoly power of the existing lending institutions are desirable.

It could also be asked whether these surpluses will last. Some have argued that the surpluses are the temporary result of over-adjustment to oil price rises; others claim that they arise from adverse trade policies, or from demographic factors. A few seem to reason a very high degree of disparity between savings and consumption rates. While G. Myrdal, in a much quoted passage in his *An American Dilemma*, said 'separate means unequal', the Japanese say 'for Japan to be equal requires Japan to be separate. If not, it could only be inferior, a colony of the West'. But even if the Japanese surpluses were to come to an end, if some countries have deficits and others have surpluses, it is in itself a sufficient argument for the creation of the IIT.

The purpose of the proposal is to bring together, for the mutual benefit of all and in service of a growing world economy, three now grossly underutilised pools of resources: the current account surpluses of Japan, Germany and other countries; the industrial capacity of the OECD countries; and the vast unskilled labour of the Third World.

World Central Bank

Bankers are not the most popular members of our species, and it is not obvious that we should hand over our fate to a new group of global central bankers. In 1961 J. K. Galbraith wrote, 'The sense of responsibility in the financial community as a whole is not small. It is nearly nil'.[7] Way back in 1931 Keynes wrote, 'Banks and bankers are by nature blind. They have not seen what was coming. . . . Lifelong practices . . . make them the most romantic and least realistic of men . . . if [the bankers] are saved, it will be, I expect, in their own despite'.[8]

In spite of such an image, bankers fulfil an important function. Long-term, capital-intensive investments are needed for economic growth and development. Fluctuating exchange rates discourage this form of investment. In the past the stability of the currency of the dominant economy has played the role of international standard and store of value. After the Second World War Keynes, with this very aim in mind, suggested the creation of Bancor (a name for the proposed world currency), but this did not come about. Later an attempt was made to create special drawing rights, but this was not very successful either. However, if we wish to move in the direction of a pluralistic, democratic world order, sooner or later a world currency will have to be devised.

The International Monetary Fund, as it is not a global Central Bank, could at least be temporarily assigned the power to conduct open market operations so as to regulate the world currency for transactional purposes, to prevent panic runs on deposits and to maintain the stability of international financial system.

In most OECD countries, joint policies for the reduction of interest rates will have to be adopted to increase investment and productivity growth.

International Debt Facility

The proposal of an international debt relief facility combined with government guarantees of the reduced debt is perhaps different from other proposals because it applies to the present situation. It is hoped that from the present situation some good lessons will be learned for the future, as the possibility of another debt crisis can not be excluded. Therefore a global equivalent of a bankruptcy facility might well constitute a permanent feature of the global landscape.

On the assumption that some part of the outstanding debt will have to be written off and relief will have to be provided to the borrowers, two questions arise that call for global solutions. First is the free-rider problem. There is a Laffer Curve at work: debt reduction would lead to increased domestic investment in the debtor countries; higher investment would lead to higher growth, and this would in turn lead to higher debt service payment. Although all banks would benefit from such a general debt relief, because growth and exports could be resumed by debtor countries, each bank would have an incentive to let other banks make the concessions and thus frustrate the purpose of the exercise. At present banks sell their claims at discounted values to other institutions, including the debtor countries, but this helps the debtors only when the debt reduction is passed on to the debtor country. Since it involves a large current liability, the buying back of the debt by the debtor country at a lower value tends to be inflationary. Because of the logic of collective action the free market does not solve the problem of this transfer of debt relief to the debtor. Concerted action to forgo part of the claim is a necessary condition for the relief. Second, after part of the debt has been cancelled, multilateral guarantees are needed for the remaining debt. Here again a concerted effort is required as neither the market nor sporadic efforts can bring about a solution to the debt problem.

Commodity Price Stabilisation Scheme

The failure on the part of developing countries and UNCTAD to reach an agreement on a working scheme of commodity price stabilisation is due partly to the absence of political agreement and partly to the weak analytical basis up on which it was presented. The case was based largely on microeconomic arguments about stabilising or raising producers' or consumers' incomes, or improving incentives. But a stronger case can be made on macroeconomic grounds. Lord Kaldor, R. Kanbur and others have shown that different pricing methods for primary and manufactured goods, combined with the fact that primary products are imported inputs into manufactured goods, lead to inflation and unemployment, with fluctuating and depressed incomes in the exporting countries. Commodity price stabilisation schemes can contribute to reduced inflation and unemployment in advanced importing countries, and to income stabilisation and progress in developing exporting countries. This nexus depends upon a continued link between raw materials and manufactures.[9] The proposal is in line with Keynes' post-Second World War proposal to establish an ITO (international trade organisation) with a mandate to stabilise the prices of primary products.

Global Energy Policy

In the global energy field nobody, neither from the exporters' nor the importers' point of view, could call the events since 1973 satisfactory. The world has suffered from the wild zig-zag movements of oil prices, leading to periods of conservation, high-cost exploitation and exploration of alternatives, followed by periods of waste, the closure of high-cost wells and the cessation of conservation. High oil prices lead to inflation, which, if countered by monetary contraction, is followed by deflation, unemployment and underutilised capacity, depriving industry of incentives, the funds to spend on conservation and the chance to explore new sources and alternatives.

A more sensible course would be for selling and buying countries to agree upon the long-term future price of oil, to increase by, say, 2 per cent per annum. Accordingly investment based on reliable prediction would be stabilised. Inflationary and deflationary impulses and unemployment would be reduced, the exploration of alternatives would be encouraged and resources would readily be made available.

Industrial Investment Board

At present the world economy lurches in between excess capacity and scarcity in products produced by plants that take a long time to be constructed. The problem arises when, in the absence of proper coordination, investment depending on mutual activity (the investment of A depends upon the investment of B and vice versa) leads to an indeterminate outcome. It is not that the market fails, but that there are no relevant market signals or incentives to communicate.

At the minimum, an exchange of intentions about investment plans, say on the pattern of the British National Economic Development Office, would help to introduce greater stability. A further step would be to coordinate the planning of investment decisions. An institution such as a board for fixed investments in durable plants with long gestation periods could provide a forum to discuss such matters.

Global Progressive Tax

In the current climate of retreat from global commitments, such a tax proposal would appear even more utopian. Nevertheless it is worth exploring how such a scheme might work. The basic principle would be to move towards a system of automatic collection, but not of automatic disbursement. This would, however, remain conditional not only on factors such as size of population and level of poverty, but also on performance in macroeconomic policy, human rights record and so on.

Global Competition Policy

In the US the Webb Pomerane Act encourages firms to band together in monopolistic actions against foreigners, while the Sherman Anti-Trust Act forbids similar action in the domestic market. It is true that not many companies are registered under the latter, but the asymmetry between the treatment of monopolistic exploitation of citizens and that of foreigners is glaring. A global order based on fairness, equality and human solidarity would apply the same principles to international transactions as are applied to domestic ones. A global monopolies commission may be required to allow fair competition in the international market.

Global Environmental Protection Agency

Just as in an uncoordinated world each country has an incentive to pour its unemployment problem into the back yard of another country, so does it literally cast its much into neighbouring gardens or into the oceans, atmosphere and land that are common to all. Acid rain that kills forests, the emission of chlorofluorocarbons that destroy the ozone layer, the global warming that results from the burning of fossil fuels, and overfishing in common waters are just some of the examples of global abuse that can be checked by global agreements.

The domestic environmental problems of rich countries are often in conflict with the objective of poverty reduction in developing countries, while the domestic environmental problems of poor countries arise from and contribute to poverty. The poor are both cause and victims of ecological degradation. Global environmental problems are the legacy of the whole of humanity and thus call for global solutions. The creation of a global protection agency would be a step forward in this direction.

Buffer Aid Institution

The aid dialogue, with its conditionality clauses, has given rise to acrimony. Respect for national sovereignty is hard to combine with accountability for taxpayers' money. A mutually trusted buffer institution could resolve these frictions. Either the principle of the Marshall Plan should be revived; or a council for the supervision and use of funds – trusted by both sides – should be created; or there should be a secretariat of aid donors with genuine global loyalities, sensitivity to local socio-political conditions and high professional and technical competence.

International Technological Agency

Its task would be to reduce the chance of nightmares such as electronic invasion of privacy, misuse of bioengineering, a technical elite ruling the masses, and so on. It should also guide overall research and development expenditure and its composition in order to reduce the danger of R&D wars.

Global Health Agency

Health has become a global concern. The spread of AIDS, the impact on human health of environmental decay, deteriorating water and air quality, deforestation, desertification, soil erosion, global warming, ozone depletion and toxic and radioactive waste disposal are some such concerns. An international agency to monitor global health is a dire necessity of the new global order. The World Health Organisation could assume some of the responsibilities.

Global Migration Agency

International migration, now mainly from the poor South, is a subject of growing importance. The growth of political, environmental and economic refugees is producing a self-interested incentive to international governmental cooperation. The currently fashionable free-market ideology has not moved far from *laissez-faire* to *laissez-passer*. Reducing trade barriers, foreign direct investment and aid may be substitutes for reducing barriers to migration. Or alternatively, while perhaps reducing the incentive to migrate by reducing income differentials, they may simply provide migrants with more means to migrate. A coordinated action is required.

A Utopia? Or Desirable and Feasible?

Two types of objection can be raised to these proposals: one on grounds of desirability and the other on grounds of feasibility. First, it may be said that creative institutions are not designed on drawing boards, but are a spontaneous response to challenging situations. Designed institutions, such as the League of Nations, The World Economic Conference of 1933, The International Trade Charter, the special drawing rights, all failed; while the multinational corporations, the Eurocurrency market, the global round-the-clock capital market and the swap arrangements between the Central Banks, none of which are the result of grand designs, are great successes. The Bretton Woods institutions are the exception but they were created after a world war, when international order was in completely disarray. The answer would be for such spontaneous institutions to be regulated by a designed institution. For instance the debt crisis is a direct result of the unregulated recycling of OPEC surpluses by greedy lenders to profligate borrowers. Had something like the proposed International Investment Trust been in existence, the world would have been spared many of the pains.

A different criticism levied is that, though desirable, these proposed institutions are not feasible. They are utterly unrealistic and utopian. There are five replies to such criticism. First, utopian thinking can be useful as a framework of thinking. Second, the utopian vision gives a sense of direction, which can get lost in approaches that are preoccupied with the feasible. In a world that is regarded as the best of feasible worlds, everything becomes a necessary constraint and all vision is lost. Third, excessive concern with the feasible tends to reenforce the status quo. In negotiations it strengthens the hands of the opponents of reform. Fourth, it is sometimes the case that the conjunction of circumstances changes quite suddenly and dramatically, and that the constellation of forces unexpectedly turns out to be favourable to even radical innovation.[10] Unless we are prepared by having a carefully worked out, detailed plan that yesterday may have appeared utterly utopian, reforms will lose out by default. Fifth, the utopians themselves might constitute a pressure group that counterbalances the self-interested pressure of obstructionists.

Note that ideas thought to be utopian have become realistic at moments in history when a large number of people supported them. It is for this reason that utopians should not be discouraged from formulating their proposals and thinking the unthinkable, unencumbered by the inhibitions and obstacles of political constraint that the defenders of the status quo devote to its elaboration.

THE BLOCS

In spite of the plea for the utopian exercise of institutional imagination, one would be ready to agree that the likelihood of any of these steps towards a global order, based on plurality and equality, being implemented is minuscule. Let us therefore consider a more probable scenario – the formation of blocs.

The multilateral system that emerged during the quarter century immediately after the Second World War has been undermined by the formation of G-3, G-5, G-7 and the economic summits. What we may see emerging in the future is something resembling the picture Orwell presented in *1984*: Oceania, Eurasia and Eastasia. Thurow has recently pronounced that GATT is dead, and that multilateralism will be replaced by blocs. But GATT may have nine lives, and the news of its death may be exaggerated.

The liberal world order that the US advocated after the war was never accepted by Europe and Japan. Germany opened its markets only in return for US troops and a defence guarantee against the USSR. In the 1980s even the US retreated from liberal trade, and the US, Japan, Germany, France and Britain withdrew from multilateral institutions.

If this trend is to continue we might see the formation of three blocs: Europe with its ex-colonies in Africa; the US, Canada and Mexico (the three NAFTA countries) with the Caribbean Basin and parts of Central and South America; with Japan, the Pacific Rim Tigers and ASEAN countries forming the East Asian bloc. Some members of these blocs may reach out to other blocs, such as Caribbean countries to the UK, ex-French colonies to France, Europe to Eastern Europe and Russia, and so on. This could serve to weaken the bloc formation.

It is not clear whether there is uniform support for bloc formation. Singapore and Malaysia, for instance, are keen to preserve a multilateral, open trading system and maintain a strong US presence, and they are suspicious of a yen bloc. Similarly Japan's attempt at regional bloc formation could be a reaction to fears that there might be a retreat from GATT-led free trade, and that it might be excluded from its two main export markets, the US and Europe.

There are, however, good reasons for an East Asian bloc. Apart from the growth of trade among these nations, Japan has become a big market for Asian manufactures, rather than an exclusive importer of primary products. In addition the yen is playing a more important role in the international capital market and other countries' foreign exchange reserves. Japanese interest rates are low and savings are high. Lately

Japanese foreign investment in the region has significantly increased. The East and South-East Asian economies are becoming increasingly vertically integrated.

Much will depend on what form these blocs take: whether for example Europe will be an open, outward-looking community, part of a global order, or a highly regulated, bureaucratic bloc. As early as 1954 Francois Perroux, in his *L'Europe sans Rivages*, painted a global, cosmopolitan vision (though not one of *laissez-faire* or even free trade), which must be contrasted with that of an enlarged, exclusive, inward-looking superstate. If Perroux's vision comes true, blocs can be seen as a step towards an integrated global system. Since a global system can not be achieved at once, regionalism may lead the way to it.

This solution need not be as horrifying as Orwell painted it. It is second best compared with the multilateral, pluralistic solution, but it could produce a well-working system. The bloc system would permit standards of living to be maintained within each bloc, and trade between blocs would probably be managed through market sharing and cartel agreements.

A faster rate of growth within each bloc, fostered by homogeneous attitudes and institutions, could lead to more trade between blocs, even though the ratio of trade to GNP might be lower for any given level of income than in a more open, though more slowly growing world economy.

COORDINATION AMONG OLIGARCHS

A third scenario is that of the US, Japan and Germany (with the cooperation of France, Britain, Italy and Canada) together deciding to rule the world. Fiscal and monetary coordination between the three, five, or seven plus any additional coopted powers (China, India or Brazil) would be required. This would not be easy to achieve.

There are authors who oppose coordination between governments and advocate competition. But competition in the market place and even reduced government intervention in trade policy call for international cooperation – cooperation to refrain from intervening. Free trade is not the same as *laissez-faire*, but it needs to be enforced.[11]

There are drawbacks to such a system. First, its exclusivity, like that in the interwar period, may encourage aggression. Second, some areas might be left out. This is a matter for concern, even if it does not lead to aggression (for example, it is not clear what would be the role for South Asia, where India is a potentially important country in a global economy; or what would be the role of Russia among the ex-communist countries of Eastern Europe).[12]

Some interesting normative questions arise from the bloc scenario. Apart from the question of the nature of the blocs and their policies, there is the question of their optimum number and optimum size.

At the same time it is also important to remember that coordination of policies can be ineffective (because similar policies can be substituted for those agreed upon), or even harmful. This is the case if the coordination is based on false analysis or wrong predictions (or if there is disagreement on issues such as whether deficits affect interest rates); or if coordination gives rise to countervailing private power (such as trade unions pushing up wages); or if coordination removes constraints on bad, politically convenient policies (such as inflation); or if it diverts attention from domestic reforms in the expectation that others will act (such as the US expectation that Germany and Japan will expand sufficiently to make reduction of its deficit unnecessary). But remember, coordination does work, though often only in response to a crisis.

The oligarchic solution has the drawback that the interests of nonparticipants are only incidentally served. A response to oligarchy could perhaps be the creation of, for instance, a Group of Non-Five, which could include all members of the IMF and GATT that are not members of G-5. Its objectives could be the restoration of multilateralism in trade, payments, development and so on. This group could even lobby for representation in G-5 and its summits.

BALKANISATION

A final scenario would be the fragmentation of the world into numerous sovereign states. The splitting up of the Soviet Union, Yugoslavia and Iraq provide the model, and the World has witnessed a transition from zoo to jungle. After having been looked after moderately well, but deprived of freedom, there is now a free for all world without security. About 5000 ethnic, religious or cultural groups in the world aspire to nationhood. Perhaps the world needs to create an organisation of non-state nations.[13]

CONCLUSION

The problem that the world is facing is how to adjust to a world in which the power of the dominant economy – the US – has declined, but without replacing it with a new dominant leader, be this a single country or a group of countries. The call for new global institutions must not be taken as a call for more international bureaucracies, but for institutions with rules, procedures, norms and values, as well as organisations that would replace a regime of dominance and dependence by one of pluralism and equality.

Notes

1. In the Caribbean island Montserrat, anyone with US$3700 can buy a licence to operate a bank.
2. One does not have to subscribe to the thesis of Paul Kennedy's book, *The Rise and Fall of Great Powers*, to see that America was weakened by its large military expenditure.
3. There is no clear correlation between economic performance and the proportion of GNP spent on defence. In 1937 Britain was spending 5.7 per cent against Japan's 28.4 per cent, the USSR's 36.4 per cent and Germany's 23.5 per cent, yet Britain's economy was one of the weakest. In 1985 South Korea spent a higher proportion than any NATO country except the US and Greece. Sweden, a successful economy, spent about as much as most NATO countries (3.0 per cent). Singapore and Taiwan, both highly successful economies, spent even more than South Korea (6.8 per cent), while the economically weak countries of Eastern Europe spent far less (see Phillip Towle, 'Last Days of the American Empire', *The London Review of Books*, 19 May 1988, p. 8).
4. For example acid rain from the US falls on Canada. If the damages are greater than the benefits to the US, Canada could offer compensation to the US for relinquishing the emission of sulphur dioxide, and still be better off than it would be by accepting to have acid rain; or, if the benefits are greater than the damages, the US could offer compensation to Canada for accepting to have acid rain and still be better off than it would have been, had it been prevented from inflicting the damage.
5. In some cases of individual action people do act according to Kant's categorical imperative rather than adopt self-seeking behaviour, but nations are less prone to moral action.
6. Even Margaret Thatcher, the archpriestess of free markets and state minimalism, in a speech to the UN in New York on 8 November 1989 recognised that in order to avoid global warming and coastal flooding, countries that emit carbon dioxide and other atmospheric heat-trapping would have to act together, that restrictions would have to be obligatory and that their application would have to be carefully monitored. Any

one country acting by itself would be put in a competitively disadvantageous position by having to bear the higher costs of protecting the environment (*The New York Times*, 9 November 1989, p. A17).

7. J. K. Galbraith (1961) *The Great Crash of 1929* (London: Penguin), p. 20.
8. J. M. Keynes (1931) *Essays in Persuasion* (London: Macmillan), pp. 176, 178.
9. Peter Drucker has expressed doubts. He has argued that recent advances in technology have weakened or even broken that link, as well as those between employment and production and between finance and trade. But the fact is that the volatility of commodity prices in line with swings in manufacturing activity suggests that the link still exists.
10. Only a few years ago nobody anticipated the dramatic events that were to take place in Central and East Europe, the Soviet Union, China and South Africa.
11. The silliness of attempting to follow national policies without regard to others is illustrated by a remark attributed to (possibly apocryphally) a distinguished American adviser to presidents: 'Let others worry about their exchange rates, and we will worry about ours!'
12. During the Gulf crisis the Belgian foreign minister, Mark Eysken, remarked that the EC was an economic giant, political dwarf and military worm. New threats from Islamic fundamentalism and age-old German–Russian geopolitical tensions may call for a partnership between the US and the EU that would run against and overcome the lines of the economic alignments.
13. Such as the Kurds, Armenians, Palestinians, Basques, Scots, Welsh, Cornish, Quebequois, Cree Indians, Catalans, South Tyroleans, Tibetans, Tamils, Australian aboriginals, Northern Irish Catholics and many others. There currently exists the Unrepresented Nations and Peoples Organisation (UNPO), whose Charter was signed in The Hague on 11 February 1991.

3 Globalisation and Macroeconomic Management

Zoran Jašić

'Globalisation' is used today as a catchword, although many are not fully aware of its meaning and content. Globalisation has become a new philosophy in the running of day-to-day business worldwide. Reducing the time taken to reach distant places has become a global challenge. As twenty-four-hour decision making occurs around the world, those who can not adjust to the speed required face the threat of being left behind in the slippery street of the global village, where even to stay where you are, you have to keep moving.

Globalisation as a process, reflected through different manifestations and the ever-increasing interdependence of the world economy, requires the methodology of analytical segmentation. Lately, globalisation as a multidimensional term has become the subject of many studies in sociology,[1] culture,[2] economic development,[3] politics and economics. For sociologists globalisation means global civilisation or a global culture (the global village). For politicians globalisation involves power in terms of defence strategies and alliances as a reflection of economic power. For modern economics globalisation is closely connected to the concept of increasing interdependence through the advance of technology, especially in countries that are moving towards an information-based economy,[4] where the driving forces behind globalisation have changed during the course of time. In the 1950s and 1960s globalisation was used when referring to international trade; in the 1970s and early 1980s, the term was linked to the rapid integration of financial markets. Recently direct foreign investment and the new multinational organisations have been stimulating the process of globalisation. Extrapolations of present trends suggest that during the remainder of the 1990s, transborder investment flows will grow at double the rate of trade flows.[5]

Globalisation affects the real spheres of economic development – the allocation of resources in different sectors, as well as in the financial sphere, which in turn results in complex interactions in the development of a national economy. Around the world financial markets are synchronised, and transactions are managed through increasingly sophisticated telecommunication and computer networks. This has given rise to speculative activity on the money and capital markets.

The forces at work in globalisation are closely connected to improvements in technology, which in turn determine global trends. The multinationals of the developed countries set these global trends, and the developing countries try to follow them.

In terms of macroeconomic management, globalisation does not mean the smooth movement of capital and labour in a borderless world, as is sometimes conveyed through sweeping changes in informatics and telecommunication. A technical, superficial, narrow understanding of globalisation in an economic sense must be understood rather as a gradual proces of increasing pressure by multinational companies towards increasing efficiency.[6] In that sense Charles Oman is right in looking at globalisation as a centrifugal process and a microeconomic phenomenon:

> One of the effects of globalisation is thus to reduce the economic distance among countries and regions as well as among the economic actors themselves. Another effect results in reducing the effective policy sovereignty of national governments *vis à vis* the market, internally as well as internationally. Third effect of globalisation is a tendency to disrupt entrenched oligopolies effectively changing the *rules of the game* in the struggle for competitive advantage among firms within, as well as between and among countries.

In terms of technology the process of globalisation leads to a shift in core technology. The industries involved in producing electronics equipment, chemicals, plastics, petroleum and cars have given way to those involved with microelectronics, biotechnology and new materials. The characteristic features of new technological changes are increased energy consumption, savings in materials, employment innovations resulting from miniaturisation, and so on. The results are superior quality production, less input costs, shorter production time and so on. The role of information technology in the development of modern techniques of production is very significant. Knowledge input and investment in human capital are vital for this development.

As far as consumption patterns are concerned, globalisation results in a shift from mass consumption in an era of mass production – as a reflection of economies of scale – to a highly differentiated consumer style of consumption.

Table 3.1 Analysis of the globalisation of the world economy

	Level of analysis	
Phenomena	*Macroeconomic*	*Microeconomic*
Economic development and trade phenomenon	*State (national) level* Centrifugal forces contribute to free movement of human resources, finance, goods, services between countries, regions and economic actors. *Economic grouping level* Integration of nations as regional blocks – TRIAD (EU, NAFTA, AFTA). *Developing-country level* Attitude towards the inflow of foreign capital and know-how.	*Multinational level* Development and application of global rules (technology and management) sensitive to host country. *Host-country level* Local enterprises and institutions attract foreign investment as precondition of macroeconomic management.
Financial phenomenon	*Global financial infrastructure* IMF, World Bank, IFC MIGA, EBRD, GATT (WTO). *Developed countries* Coordination of financial policies with G7, OECD, G24, international taxation. Coordination of international investors, global capital market and electronic banking (GLOBEX). *Developing countries* Growth of financial discipline and infrastructure.	*Companies developing global links* Attention to problems of transfer pricing, repatriation of profils, formation of local links, establishing licensing arrangements for foreign – local joint ventures and subsidiaries.

Source: Jašić (1988).

Table 3.2 Guidelines for global competitiveness

Objectives	*Means*
1. Help European firms adapt to globalised interdependent situation.	Capitalise on community's strengths. Develop policy of industrial cooperation. Establish strategic alliances. Target measures to ensure competitive markets.
2. Promote competitive advantages of knowledge-based economy	Reform tax policies re-disincentives and efficient use of resources. Develop policies for 'non-physical' investment (training, research, technical assistance. Streamline/rationalise rules and regulations. Review public support of industry to enhance value-added and employment growth. Launch European 'quality' policy.
3. Promote sustainable development of industry	Increase/coordinate R & D for clean technology. Develop incentives for diffusion of R & D results into products and processes.
4. Reduce time-lag between pace of change and adjustments in demand.	*Demand-side measures* Facilitate revival of world consumption. Promote new markets. *Supply-side measures* Encourage structural adjustment by supporting privatization. Underpin dynamism of SMEs. *Supply-and-demand measures* Facilitate partnerships between large firms and subcontractors. Improve interface between producers and users. Establish collaboration networks, develop competitive activities groups.

Source: Adapted from *Global Economic Prospects and Developing Countries* (Washington, DC: World Bank, 1993), p. 67.

Table 3.1, summarises the main elements of macroeconomic management in a globalised world economy and shows the intersection of the main features of macroeconomic management in developed and developing countries. By distinguishing between the macro and micro levels of decision making, the table shows the complexity of the phenomenon of globalisation.

Table 3.2 gives examples of how developed countries are going ahead with the implementation of the globalisation process in terms of the objectives and policies of global competition.

GLOBALISATION IN DEVELOPED COUNTRIES

In developed countries the major impetus towards globalisation is closely linked to new trends in technological development, which in turn cause changes in organisation and management at all levels of the decision making process.

The Ford Motor Company's organisational theory – international mass production based on the utilisation of economies of scale – is shifting towards the new capabilities of economies of scope. The scope approach refers to the flexible application of CAD/CAM methods by organising and controlling production. At the level of multinational companies, depending upon the production sector, the application of the scope theory contributes to greater flexibility in production design and mix, rapid responses to market shifts, and increased control and predictability. These economies contribute to efficiency by stimulating the application of new technology that improves a firm's competitiveness by allowing variation of the products produced rather than increasing volume.[7]

In terms of the market, globalisation shifts from the world market to the three leading regional groupings: NAFTA, AFTA and the EU. In K. Ohmae's terminology,[8] these market blocs correspond to TRIAD and include the US, Japan, South East Asia and Europe. The converging demand pattern, as a common denominator of these markets, accelerates the diffusion of technological knowledge throughout the TRIAD blocs. The emphasis is on shorter life cycles for new products in all three major markets at the same time so as to avoid losing markets.

In order to facilitate the diffusion of the positive effects of globalisation in developed countries towards the rest of world, there is an ever-increasing need for coordination of their economic policies.

Economic policy actions, particularly those of larger countries, create quantitatively significant spill-over effects or externalities for other countries, and a global optimum requires that such externalities be taken into account in the decision making calculus.[9] Wallich sees international coordination of economic policies as '. . . a significant modification of national policies in recognition of international economic interdependence.'[10]

An interesting approach to the necessity of coordination of macroeconomic policies is that of James Tobin, who says:

> the coordination of macroeconomic policies is certainly not easy; maybe it is impossible. But in its absence, I suspect nationalistic solutions will be sought – trade barriers, capital controls, and dual exchange rate systems. War among nations with these weapons is likely to be mutually destructive. Eventually, they, too, would evoke agitation for international coordination.[11]

GLOBALISATION IN DEVELOPING COUNTRIES

In the increasingly interdependent and competitive international economy of the 1990s, the process of attracting direct foreign investment has become the strategic instrument that determines the position of a particular developing country. Numerous conditions govern a country's ability to attract investment, but political and social stability are crucial.

Macroeconomic management in this critical area of development policy concentrates on setting up institutions to provide foreign investors with information that is relevant to their investment decisions, in particular information on:

- the taxation of profits, customs regulations, the repatriation of dividends, and the availability of tax havens;
- accessibility to foreign markets;
- the basic characteristics of the labour market;
- the availability of skilled personnel;
- the quality of education at all levels;
- the country's health standards;
- the availability of infrastructural services in computer technology, telecommunication and transportation;
- the country's ecology.

Also of crucial importance to foreign investors are the quality and speed of procedures in the evolution and implementation of different phases of project cycles. Depending on the nature of a particular project, (segments of infrastructure) macroeconomic management must provide additional information that is critical to the final outcome of the cost–benefit analysis of the project's viability.

A developing country's institutional set-up is extremely significant for macroeconomic management in the area of attracting foreign investment. The country must provide accurate and clear indications as to its capacity to absorb foreign investment. In that context two factors deserve special mention. First, the organisation of the country's education system. Particularly in smaller countries, the approach to education must be to promote a life-long educational philosophy in order to provide the human capital that is required for sustained development. The second critical factor is management of environmental projects that have global effects. Management's task is to deal with the costs of environmental protection and to find solutions to developmental problems.

In developing countries macroeconomic policy, which is the core of development policy, helps decision makers to find a balance between the financial factors that influence development and those that affect the accumulation of capital, which in turn are based on factor endowments, the implementation of appropriate technology, the possibility of economies of scale, and the quality of the education system, including adequate research and development institutions. R. Dornbusch rightly stresses the constraints put on poor countries.[12]

The long-established and widely accepted view regarding the strategic importance of financial factors in economic development, advanced by the Stanford School (John Gurley, Edward Shaw and Ronald McKinnon), has recently been challenged by R. Dornbusch and A. Reyenoso (1989), who opt instead to analyse the role of finance in a complex context of factors that determine the position of small countries in the increasingly hostile environment of the world economy:

> Finance does not matter for the mobilization of resources, but this ordinarily accounts for little in changing growth rates. The more important fact is macroeconomic: poor finance leads to inflation and external bottlenecks, which in turn bring about restrictive macroeconomic policies that slow down growth and investment. A protracted period of poor macroeconomic policy in turn casts a shadow over the future, because it slows down or diverts abroad supply of capital and the incentives to invest and innovate in the home economy.

CONCLUSION

The leading role in globalisation is being played by the developed countries. By using economies of scale and scope, the multinationals, as leading actors, are contributing to the process and are receiving the political support of both developed countries and developing countries that are seeking foreign direct investment. In addition, the multinationals are accelerating the acceptance of international accounting standards, such as the use of a dynamic approach to the balance of payments and so on.

These organisations are increasingly becoming the main actors in the globalisation process and are enabling the transfer of technology – through direct foreign investment and know-how – to the developing countries. However the multinationals are looking for macroeconomic management techniques in order to utilise more effectively the spill-over effects that are generated through direct investment in the developing countries. Therefore macroeconomic management is the core of development policy in these countries.

Notes

1. According to R. Robertson: 'It must also be emphasised that although . . . what I call a flexible model of globality in synchronic terms, as a one-shot, basically contemporary image of what is involved in thinking about the theory and practice of globality, the model is in fact applied diachronically. It is intended to take strongly into account changes in each of the four major components (societies, individuals, international relations, and human kind) in tandem with shifts in the relations between them. Such considerations are dealt with intermittently. . . . Globalisation is a process bound up with diachronic perspective. Yet it should be clear that my model of the global circumstance is both multidimensional and much more global than is usually meant by socio-scientific and other connotations of that word. Hence the extended discussion of the problematics of the model. Multidimensionality refers in the present context to a mode of grasping the basics of what I sometimes call the global human condition, basics which at one and the same time take into account the most general feature of life in relatively recent history and the growing concern with the connections between different conceptions thereof. We can again see that globalisation involves comparative interaction of different forms of life' (see R. Robertson, 1992, pp. 26–7).
2. 'As the general process of globalisation proceeds there [are] concomitant constraints upon such entities to *identify* themselves in relation to the global human circumstance. In addition, globalisation also yields new actors and *third cultures* such as transnational movements and international organisations – that are oriented, negatively or positively to the global human circumstance' (Robertson, op. cit., p. 61).
3. See John Friedman's theory of centre and periphery systems in which major centres are called core regions and all others peripheral. Core regions

consolidate their dominance over the periphery. He identifies six self-reinforcing feedback effects:

- The dominance effect (the steady weakening of the peripheral economy by net transfers of natural, human and capital resources to the core).
- The information effect of an increase of potential interaction within the growing core.
- The psychological effect of innovation success, facilitating more innovation.
- The modernisation effect, causing transformation of social values and behaviour.
- The linkage effect, or the tendency of innovation to breed new innovations.
- The production effect, dealing with attractive reward structure for innovation and growing economies of scale specialisation.

For more detailed discussion on feedback effects and Friedman's theory see H. Brookfield (1975), p. 120.

4. For example: informatics becomes an invisible part of economic and social life; communications are based on electronic highway for multi-media information delivery, with all services liberalised; human capital benefits through diffusion of informatics literacy throughout workforce; information services are deregulated as industry globalises; in the legal system informatics changes rules of legal procedure; and finally, the economic impact of an information-based economy is that the organisations become information driven and realise the benefits of informatics investments. All this contributes to faster productivity growth through diffusion of knowledge. For more detail see *Turkey Towards an Information Based Economy* (Washington, DC: The World Bank, 1990), p. 8.
5. See W. Michalski, 'Support Policies for Strategic Industries: An Introduction to the Main Issues', in *Strategic Industries in a Global Economy: Policy Issues for The 1990s* (Paris: OECD), p. 8.
6. See Oman (1994), p. 33.
7. See Rugman, Lecraw and Booth (1986), p. 371.
8. See Ohmae (1992), pp. 19–21.
9. See J. A. Frankel, M. Goldstein and P. A. Mossan in W. Goth (1988), p. 150.
10. See H. C. Wallich, 'Institutional Cooperation in the World Economy', in J. Frankel and M. Mussa (eds), *The World Economic System: Performance and Prospects* (Dover, Mass.: Auburn House, 1995), pp. 85–99.
11. See James Tobin (1987) 'Agenda for International Coordination of Macroeconomic Policies', in Paul A. Volcker *et al.*, *International Monetary Cooperation: Essays in honour of Henry C. Wallich* (Princeton: Princeton University Press), p. 61.
12. 'The poorer a country and the more adverse the conditions it faces in terms of resources availability, export prices, or world market access, the more important it is to implement good policies precisely to minimise the severe costs of an unfavourable environment. Rich countries

can afford to waste the resources; poor countries can not. Rich countries may be able to neglect saving and investment (at least for a while) poor countries can not' (Dornbusch, 1993, pp. 2, 65).

References

Annemieke, J. M. R. (1987) 'The Crisis in Fordism and the Use of a New Paradigm', *Futures*, vol. 10, no. 2 (April).

Austin, J. E. (1990) *Managing in Developing Countries – Strategic Analysis and Operating Techniques* (London: The Free Press).

Brookfield, H. (1975) *Interdependent Development* (London: Methuen).

Brookfield, H. (1993) 'Growth, Competitiveness, Employment: Challenges and Ways Forward into the 21st Century' (White Paper), *Bulletin of the European Union* Supplement 6/93 (Brussels: CEC).

Dornbusch, R. (ed.) (1993) *Policymaking in the Open Economy: Concepts and Case Studies in Economic Performance* (New York: The World Bank and Oxford University Press), EDI Series in Economic Development.

Dornbusch, R., F. Leslie and C. H. Helmers (1988) *The Open Economy – Tools for Policymakers in Developing Countries* (Oxford: Oxford University Press).

Dornbusch, R. and Reyenoso, A. (1989) 'Financial Factors in Economic Development', *American Economic Review*, 72 (2).

Frankel, J. A., A. Ralin and E. Sadka (1991) *International Taxation in an Integrated World* (Cambridge, Mass.: MIT Press).

Goth, W. (1988) *Economic Policy Coordination* (Washington: IMF).

Guitian, M. (1992) *Rules and Discretion in International Economic Policy* (Washington, DC: IMF).

Jašić, Z. (1988) *The Globalisation of World Economy and Transfer of Technology for National Development*, mimeo, Lecture at the University of Kualalumpur (Malaysia).

Jašić, Z. (1988) 'Management of the Third World Debt', in H. W. Singer and Soumitra Sharma (eds), *Growth and External Management* (London: Macmillan).

Haque, I. (ed.) (1991) *International Competitiveness* (Washington: The World Bank), EDI Seminar Series.

Oman, C. (1994) *Globalisation and Regionalization: The Challenge for Developing Countries* (Paris: OECD).

Ohmae, K. (1992) *TRIAD Power: The Coming Shape of Global Competition* (New York: Free Press).

Premchand, A. (1993) *Public Expenditure Management* (Washington, DC: IMF).

Robertson, R. (1992) *Globalisation – Social Theory and Global Culture* (London: Sage).

Robson, P. (1980) *The Economics of International Integration* (London: Allen and Unwin).

Rugman, A. M., D. O. Lecraw and L. D. Booth (1986) *International Business* (Singapore: McGraw Hill).

Tobin, J. (1989) *Policies for Prosperity: Essays in a Keynesian Mode* (edited by P. M. Jackson) (Cambridge, Mass.: MIT Press).

Tobin, J. (1991) *Strategic Industries in a Global Economy–Policy Issues for the 1990s* (Paris: OECD International Futures Programme).

Tobin, J. (1993) *Global Economic Prospects and the Developing Countries* (Washington, DC: World Bank).

Wells, Louis T. Jr. and A. Wint (1993) *Marketing a Country* (Washington: World Bank).

4 Does Fiscal Policy Matter?*

James Tobin

Strange proposititions are commonplace in macroeconomic commentary these days; the world has been turned upside down. The federal government is about to increase real defence spending over the next several fiscal years by 9 per cent annually, to cut personal income tax rates by 10 per cent both this year and next, and to phase in drastic reductions in taxation of business investments in equipment and structures. Similar budgets in the past have invariably made the economy more prosperous, creating jobs and lowering unemployment, speeding the growth of production, raising profits. Consider, for example, 1940–41, 1950–52 and 1966–69.

But this time the budget prospects are widely regarded as a bad omen. Many forecasters, with or without formal models, would lift their estimates of the strength and longevity of recovery from the current recession if the budgets for fiscal years 1983 and 1984 were revised by cutting spending or raising taxes, or both. They would be more optimistic not just about prices and interest rates but about employment and real activity.

It is a puzzle. Suppose the news was that the hundred largest corporations were planning to borrow and spend US$100 billion more than previously thought, say on investment projects resulting from R & D breakthroughs. Would that be regarded as a minus in the economic outlook? Suppose then that they announced cutbacks in these plans, would that be regarded as a plus?

Policy makers, politicians and pundits, businessmen, bankers and brokers, speak with many voices about the effects and dangers of federal deficits. Economists too. 'Deficits and public debt are the culprits for inflation.' No they aren't – they aren't inflationary unless they are monetised, and the central bank can and should resist political pressures to monetise. 'Government borrowing raises interest rates and preempts saving that would otherwise finance private capital formation.' No it doesn't – rational taxpayers will save enough extra to buy the government bonds, as a hedge against future taxes or inflation; the real burden of government is its draft on the nation's resources, no matter how financed. 'Tax cuts mean bigger deficits, but stimulate aggregate demand, employment and output.' No, they're just inflationary.

No, they raise interest rates and do nothing. No, if they are well designed they provide such strong 'supply-side' incentives that tax revenues will actually increase.

FISCAL STIMULUS, MONETARY POLICY, AND CROWDING OUT

The question as to whether fiscal policy matters refers to macroeconomic outcomes: output and unemployment, prices and inflation, investment and growth. Obviously government budgets are major determinants of the allocation of the nation's resources among various uses and of the distribution of wealth, income and consumption. But it has been alleged that pure fiscal policy – pure in the sense that variations in government expenditure and tax revenue are fully absorbed in non-monetary debt – have no significant systematic short-run macroeconomic consequences. At the same time, fiscal policies may affect the division of output between consumption and capital formation, a division of importance for the future growth and level of the economy's capacity to produce.

It is frequently said that government purchases of goods and services, using resources that could be employed for other purposes, is the true and sufficient measure of its impact and burden on the economy. What that impact is, in what degree it is a burden, obviously depends on the nature of the government's activities, on the public consumption or investment provided. These are the difficult agendas of politics at all levels – federal, state, and local. Objection can be raised against the prevalent idea, unfortunately encouraged by economists, that the size of the government relative to the economy can be rationally discussed and debated without reference to the functions the government is performing and to the circumstances of the day. Economic calculus does not suggest that a perceived need for increased defence expenditure, or a national decision to socialise health care for the aged and the indigent, must be met wholly from other public outlays.

The major issues concern the financing of a given programme of public expenditure. At one extreme is the Ricardo–Barro equivalence theorem, which says that the mix between taxation and borrowing makes no difference. That is, interest rates, prices, current consumption, investment, employment and output are the same however large the government budget deficit. Private agents regard debt issues as postponement of taxes, are indifferent to such postponements and buy bonds as the perfect, riskless way to provide for future tax liabilities. According to the theorem, deficit spending is impotent – it cannot absorb savings in times of slack and excess unemployment – and innocuous. Increased supplies of bonds generate their own demands; they do not raise interest rates or crowd out private demands for resources or saving. Increased government purchases may both directly and indirectly employ otherwise idle resources, or displace other uses of resources already employed. But these effects are independent of their financing.[1]

Although there are grains of truth in the theorem, there are not enough for policy makers to take it seriously. Nor is there convincing empirical evidence that the rate of national saving is independent of the amount of government saving, a proposition that contradicts 'Denison's Law' and the findings of David and Scadding that *private* saving is a constant share of national income.

The other extreme position is that substitution of government borrowing for taxation has no effect on prices and inflation, or on output and employment. In short, it has no effect on aggregate demand – but it does alter the composition of national output and generally raises real interest rates. Here government borrowing does absorb private saving, and this is why it completely 'crowds out' other claims for saving. There are two scenarios of 100 per cent crowding out, and they may coincide. One is monetary crowding out. The path of output is independently determined by monetary policy, whether or not unemployed resources are available for a higher path. The second is resource crowding out. Whatever the monetary policy, if the economy is producing at capacity, demands for goods and services by the beneficiaries of tax reductions or transfers can be met only by displacing other demands. If monetary policy is not accommodative, then the mechanism of displacement is the real interest rate. To the extent that it is accommodative, the mechanism may be saving forced by inflation.

The extent of crowding out, and the kinds of demands displaced, depend on the nature of the tax cuts (or increased transfers) that lead to the borrowing. Contrary to Barro and Ricardo, in a world where current tax reductions have value to taxpayers and therefore make a difference, they almost inevitably lead to some increase in consumption. But supply-side tax reductions may be slanted towards investment, so that the rise in real interest rates mainly crowds out investment. The result is the substitution of the kinds of investment favoured by the tax incentives for other kinds, for example business equipment and structures benefiting from accelerated cost recovery for residential investment or capital projects of state and local governments. In a world of floating exchange rates the nation's current account surplus, its net accumulation of foreign assets, is a prime victim of crowding out. The mechanism evident in the US in the past is that high home interest rates attract foreign funds, appreciate the local currency, and make exports less competitive and imports more attractive.

Monetary policy could conceivably be made with a target path of real output and employment, to which the Central Bank would try to hold the economy by adjusting its instrument settings. If this path were considered sacrosanct, independent of the economic objectives of the fiscal policy makers, then full crowding out would occur even though in the eyes of many observers resources would be available to accommodate the demands of the government and its beneficiaries without displacing any other demands. Another way to put it is in terms of saving: the funds to finance the public borrowing could be generated from the incomes associated with expanded production and employment. No rise of real interest rates would be required, and no crowding out would occur, if the monetary authority were to accommodate the expansion. This was the essence of the quarrel between Keynes and the Treasury in 1929. The debate, with all the old misunderstandings and confusions, recurs again and again. Today it seems hardly accurate to blame the federal budget for high real interest rates and for threatening massive crowding out. Rather, *monetary policy* has crowded out private investment with high real interest rates. The resulting recession has added US $60–75 billion to the deficit, absorbing some of the saving that might have gone into the monetarily displaced investment. Most of that saving has simply vanished, lost along with wages and profits in the recession.

Generally monetary policy does not take a real output path as target but some nominal quantity, thought to be closer to its jurisdiction and grasp. As the Federal Reserve has staked its credibility on M1 targets, presumably it is prepared to allow a variety of outcomes – paths of output, prices, interest rates – without changing those targets. It is hard to believe that the Federal Reserve would ever expect or want 9.5 per cent unemployment or 9.5 per cent real interest rates, or that Federal targets and reserve supplies would be appreciably different if by chance unemployment were only 8.5 per cent. The Federal Reserve is unwilling to do anything to bring about a better economic performance, while quietly hoping for good luck with velocity.

It makes sense, therefore, to ask what the effects are of fiscal stimuli, given the Federal Reserve's targets for monetary aggregates. The standard textbook answer is, or used to be, that the paths of output, prices and real interest rates will all be higher. A forecaster should show a stronger 1983 recovery if federal taxes are not raised and defence spending is not slowed down, just as he would if he learned that the Fortune 500 companies were, in an onset of confidence, going to raise in the securities market US$50 billion more than previously thought and spend it on new plant and equipment. In both cases the first-order effects are more spending on goods and services, and in both cases the second-order brake is the limited supply of bank reserves. (Actually a government purchase-driven expansion is slightly less dependent on monetary accommodation because federal cash balances are not included in Ml.)

It is probably true that the LMl curve is steeper than it used to be. Nominal interest rates are so high, and have been high for so long, that little marginal economy in cash management may be induced by further increase. (The spread of interest-bearing NOW accounts, included in Ml, works in the other direction.) More important is what might be called the Akerlof–Milbourne effect, namely that the elasticity of demand for money with respect to transactions volume is very low in the short run. When business picks up, it can be handled. Later adjustment to more comfortable cash, liquidity and debt positions raises interest rates.

Does the longer-run LM curve actually slope the 'wrong' way? A few years ago this proposition seemed to be implied by complaints that the textbook treatment of fiscal stimulus ignored the wealth and portfolio effects of repeated additions of public debt. Over time, it was argued, these would gradually move the short-run LM curve to the left, raising interest rates and eventually overcoming the spending effects of the fiscal policy. The trouble with this argument is that it is hard to see why the demand for money is so high if income has not risen but interest rates have. The rise of interest rates induces people to hold more wealth in the form of government bonds, but why should they demand more money too?

MEASURING THE MACROECONOMIC IMPACT OF THE BUDGET

The deficit or surplus is commonly taken as the relevant measure of fiscal stimulus, even by economists who know better – witness the controversy over the budgets for financial year 1983 and subsequent years.

For most purposes, the first thing we want to know about the budget

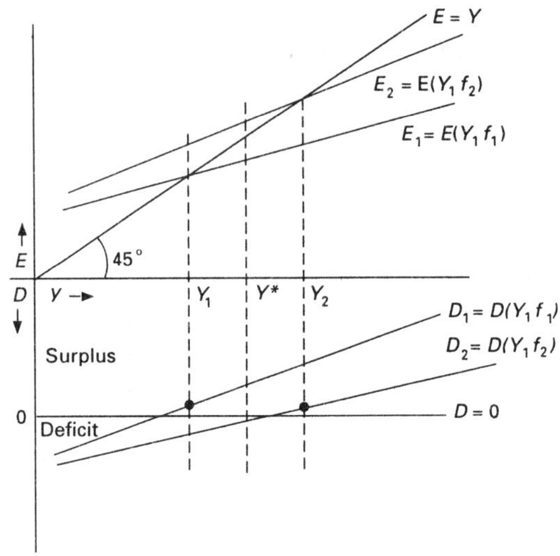

Figure 4.1 Excess demand and deficit schedules for two budget programmes

programme for a year is how it affects aggregate *excess* demand for goods and services, $E - Y$. Now this is a schedule, not a number. Aggregate demand E is a function of Y, of the variables describing the fiscal programme f and of other variables x: interest rates, prices, asset stocks, expectations. The relevant comparison of one fiscal programme f_1 with another f_2 – that for the previous year or an alternative for the year at hand – is the shift of the schedule: $E(Y, f_1, x) - E(Y, f_2, x)$. Such a comparison is illustrated in Figure 4.1, ignoring or taking as constant the variables x. E_1 and E_2 are aggregate demand functions for the two fiscal programmes f_1 and f_2. Their deviations from the 45° line $E = Y$, positive or negative, are the schedules of excess demand. The government deficit is a function of the same variables $D(Y, f, x)$, also illustrated in Figure 4.1 for programmes f_1 and f_2.

Is there a single number that tells the macroeconomic impact of f_1 compared with f_2? Certainly the predicted actual deficit does not fill the bill. In Figure 4.1, for example, Y_1 and Y_2 are the incomes predicted from the ex post requirement $E = Y$, but $D(Y_2, f_2) - D(Y_1, f_1)$ tells us almost nothing of interest. This would be true *a fortiori* if the indicated shift of E, say from one year to the next, arose from differences in x instead of f, especially if those differences had little or no effect on the D function.

The concept of the high employment deficit (HED) was invented decades ago in order to eliminate the endogenous response of the deficit to Y. In Figure 4.1, Y^* is the assumed 'high employment' level of Y; $D(Y^*, f_1)$ and $D(Y^*, f_2)$ are the corresponding HEDs. Actually any reference Y^* in the range of normal experience will do for the purpose, whatever the rate of employment or unemployment to which it corresponds. The high or full employment tag may have confused politicians and public and aroused their suspicions. The idea that the budget should be balanced at Y^* and the idea that it need not, should not ever, be balanced for $Y < Y^*$ are normative propositions quite separable from the analytical objective of correcting for endogeneity. In any event, for comparisons of budget programmes over time, presumably the reference Y^* should grow at the economy's trend and the HED should be expressed as a fraction of Y^*.

Although HED corrects for the Y-endogeneity of the deficit, it is not the contribution of the budget programme to excess demand $E - Y$. In Figure 4.1 this comparison, as between f_1 and f_2, would be illustrated in the upper panel as $E(Y^*, f_2) - E(Y^*, f_1)$. Though this is generally positively correlated with $D(Y^*, f_2) - D(Y^*, f_1)$, it is not the same thing. But it is $E^* - Y^*$, not D^*, which tells how much spending must be increased or decreased by non-fiscal policies or events (for example by monetary measures affecting investment and saving) if Y^* were to be realised along with the fiscal programme. Thus it is $E^* - Y^*$ that is relevant to the much-discussed issue of crowding out.

Differences between the two comparisons arise, of course, because the various fiscal instruments affect aggregate demand and deficits differently. One example is related to the famous balanced budget multiplier theorem. An increase of a dollar in government purchases accompanied by a lump-sum increment of tax revenues will leave D^* – and indeed the whole D schedule – unchanged. But it will raise E^* and the E schedule uniformly by $\$(1 - b)$ where b is taxpayer's marginal propensity to spend. Government purchases of goods and services have a bigger multiplier than taxes, in absolute value.

More generally, items on the two sides of the budget – purchases of different goods and services, taxes of different types, transfers to different beneficiaries – vary in their multipliers. Tax cuts or transfers benefiting liquidity-constrained low-income households are virtually the equivalent of direct purchases, while liquid high-income beneficiaries will save significant fractions. Grants-in-aid to state and local governments, to the degree they are fungible (in other words directly or indirectly available for whatever purpose the recipients choose) may induce only partial spending; the recipient governments will augment their surpluses and lower their own taxes.

These considerations suggest the use of an adjusted deficit, AHED, in which various categories of outlays and receipts bear weights proportional to their multipliers, normalised to the multiplier for direct government purchases of goods and services.[2] This weighted measure would approximate $E^* - Y^*$ more closely than D^* does. The required adjustments, and the procedures for making them were pointed out long ago in Gramlich's doctoral dissertation.[3] Yet they have still not made their way into Office of Management & Budget (OMB) and Congressional Budget Office (CBO) documents, or into official and public debates on fiscal policy.

PROSPECTIVE FEDERAL BORROWING REQUIREMENTS: THE CURRENT DISCUSSION

Weighting adjustments will be crucial in assessing the potential crowding out effects of the federal deficit in prospect over the coming years. Clarity in approaching this confused and confusing discussion is best served by separating two issues. The first of these is the path of real output, Y, the economy will or should follow over the next few years, and how it depends on fiscal and monetary policies. This is the more important issue.

The second issue assumes the Y path as given and asks how much room the fiscal programme would leave for non-federal investment. This question, which can be asked and answered comparatively for various budget proposals, is one for which the adjusted high employment deficit (AHED) analysis is designed. To avoid misunderstanding, let it be left open at this point whether and how private investment will be forthcoming in just the amounts to fill the room left for it.

Alarmists about crowding out see huge federal debt issues coming on to the securities markets, commandeering saving that would otherwise flow to corporations, other businesses, farmers, home purchasers, state and local governments, and other borrowers. They look at prospective deficit numbers unadjusted, and include also off-budget and agency borrowing. As the Administration correctly points out these alarms are crude because they ignore increases in saving and in supplies of funds to buy securities or to replace borrowing – byproducts of the same fiscal programme that generates the deficits.[4] Some outside observers agree. Albert Wojnilower, for example, says that deficit-reducing proposals will lower the supply of saving to the capital markets almost as much as they lower federal demands. In short the proper concern is, as argued above, $E - Y$, not D. In this context, several features of the budget and prospective federal borrowing requirements deserve comment.

In principle budget accounting eliminates capital transactions and off-budget borrowing. Selling more oil leases adds to cash revenue, but unless the buyers are liquidity constrained the transactions do not reduce $E^* - Y^*$. The buyers will in effect borrow in the market what the government does not borrow, while maintaining their demands for goods and services. They may indeed increase borrowing and demand by undertaking investments to develop their new leaseholdings.

Although many analysts add net off-budget borrowing to the budget deficit, this procedure exaggerates crowding out. Here the government is acting as an intermediary, relending to eligible non-federal borrowers, who will not be in the regular capital markets. Some of them would not have been there anyway, or would have borrowed less. The government is accommodating them at rates below what private lenders would have charged. The intermediary operations add to net demands on the markets, but by only a fraction of the gross federal borrowing they entail.

Accelerated capital recovery and other tax concessions increase the cash flow of businesses. What the government is borrowing, businesses need not. The balance of aggregate demand and supply is worsened only to the extent that stockholders enjoy increased dividends or that capital gains raise their consumption.

Debt interest has become a major budgetary outlay, more than 10 per cent of the total budget, 2.5 to 3 per cent of GNP. As interest rates have risen beyond expectations, upward revisions of net interest outlays have significantly worsened the budget outlook. But it is by no means clear that interest payments have the same stimulative or crowding out effects as, for example, defence purchases. While some pensioners may simply spend whatever interest flows they receive, at the other extreme there are younger savers who accumulate in illiquid retirement accounts whatever interest they earn. Those who believe that the incentive effects of higher real interest rates dominate the income effects should not regard a government budget as expansionary because those rates entail higher outlays.

The 1982 Economic Report echoes many other economists in applying inflation accounting to the federal budget and eliminating interest outlays that merely compensate creditors for inflation. This procedure is relevant for calculations of stimulus and crowding out if savers rationally and automatically buy enough bonds to maintain their holdings in real value – indeed to increase them *pari passu* with the growth of the economy. Unfortunately there is not much recent evidence of such behaviour. Households have allowed real wealth to decline absolutely and relatively to real incomes, without much sign of saving extra to make up for real capital losses suffered in the past.

FEDERAL DEBT DYNAMICS

The significant fact about the longer-run budget outlook is that if the parameters of the federal budget are not changed, the federal debt will grow relative to the economy for the first time since the Second World War. Crowding out, a worry of little operational significance at present, could become important in more prosperous years ahead.

The dynamics of the debt are as follows. Let d_t be the ratio of the debt to GNP, r_t the net real interest rate on the debt, g_t the growth rate of real GNP, and x_t the primary deficit, that is, the deficit exclusive of interest cost, in ratio to GNP. Then,

$$\dot{d}_t = x_t + (r_t - g_t)\, d_t$$

For given constant values of the parameters r, g and x, the equilibrium d^* is $-x/(r - g)$, and

$$(d_t - d^*) = (d_0 - d^*)e^{(r - g)t}$$

The debt ratio d converges to d^* if r is smaller than g, but diverges otherwise.

In Table 4.1 calculations are shown for various periods of postwar history. Estimates of r allow for the degree of monetisation of deficits and for an assumed 25 per cent recoupment of debt interest by federal taxation. Although the systems are all stable, we are currently close to the edge of instability, with real interest rates so high relative to growth that the debt ratio might rise even if the primary deficit x were eliminated. As the final column shows, realistic CBO budget estimates for 1982–7 give values of d^* that are much higher than the current values of d and therefore presage a steady and fairly rapid increase in the debt/GNP ratio.

Table 4.1 US fiscal and monetary policy and federal debt dynamics, 1952–87

Fiscal year period (number of years)	*1952–7 (6)*	*1958–66 (9)*	*1967–74 (8)*	*1975–9 (5)*	*1980–1 (2)*	*1982–7 (6) Administration budget message*	*1982–7 (6) CBO baseline*
Federal debt: % of GNP, beginning and end of period	64.8–48.5	48.5–35.7	35.7–23.4	23.4–26.5	26.5–27.6	27.6–24.5	27.6–38.0
Federal deficit (+) or surplus (–), excluding interest: % of GNP, avg.	–0.58	–0.47	+0.28	+1.38	+0.80	+0.43	+2.58
Share of debt monetised: %, range	10.5–11.3	10.7–16.6	16.6–24.0	24.0–18.1	18.1–15.7	15.7–12.3	15.7–8.0
Share of deficit (including interest) monetised: %, avg.	0	50	46	12	6	6.5	2.6
Growth of real GNP: % per year, avg.	2.8	3.4	3.8	3.5	0.9	4.4	3.1
Inflation of GNP deflator: % per year, avg.	2.2	1.9	5.2	7.2	9.1	5.2	6.4
Treasury 90-day bill rate: % per year, avg.	2.1	3.2	5.8	6.7	12.8	8.8	10.4
Real net interest rate on debt: % per year, avg.	–0.7	–0.7	–2.8	–2.8	–0.1	0.9	1.7
Real GNP growth less real net interest rate	3.5	4.1	6.6	6.3	1.0	3.5	1.4
Hypothetical equilibrium debt/GNP ratio: %	–16.6	–11.5	+4.2	+21.9	+80.0	+24.1	+184.3
Trend of debt/GNP ratio:							
Actual, beginning of period	64.8	48.5	35.7	23.4	26.5	27.6	27.6
After five years	51.9	37.6	27.1	23.0	29.1	27.0	38.1
After ten years	41.1	28.6	20.8	22.7	31.6	26.6	48.0

YES, VIRGINIA, THERE ARE LAFFER CURVES

The now famous Laffer Curve shows the relationship between tax revenues and the tax rate, allowing for endogenous response of the tax base to the tax rate. In the spirit of its populariser, I take the response to be variation in *supplies* of factors of production in taxable employment and assume that aggregate demand adjusts or is adjusted to assure full utilisation of the supplies. I derive a Laffer curve based on labour supply only, taking the stock of capital as fixed. In a subsequent memorandum I derive a long-run Laffer curve, allowing for adjustment of the capital stock as well. These are theoretical calculations, designed to exhibit the strategic behavioural parameters and their roles in determining the shapes of the curves. I do, however, allow myself the luxury of some calculations based on plausible empirical values of the parameters.

The curve has been used to justify cuts in tax rates on the ground that they will actually raise tax revenues. In principle, the curve has a maximum somewhere between zero taxation and 100 per cent taxation. This obvious fact does not justify the assertion that tax cuts in the US in 1981, or in any other economy, will raise revenues. That depends, of course, on where we are on the curve relative to its maximum.

In any event, it is not clear why maximisation of tax revenues should be anyone's social objective. Milton Friedman, who favours tax reduction in all economic weather, says he certainly hopes it will not raise revenues.[5] Economists will generally agree that there is welfare loss in raising distortionary taxes beyond the point of maximum revenue. A political reason for stressing the claim that tax cuts pay for themselves is to disarm opponents who are fearful of enlarging government deficits.

A related supply side argument for tax reduction concerns inflation. The notion that an induced expansion of supply will lower prices is of course a simplistic fallacy of aggregation, refuted by J. B. Say a century and a half ago. Say's law may have its own problems, but the point is undeniable that additional supplies in aggregate also induce additional demand. A sensible question may be phrased in the following way. Does the additional supply generate additional national saving at an unchanged interest rate? If so, this can be used either (1) to relieve inflationary excess-demand pressure, if any, by elimination of abnormal or above-natural utilisation of resources, or (2) to finance extra investment, with the monetary authority letting interest rates fall as needed to employ the extra saving. In either case, the relevant calculation is to relate full-employment national saving, or potential investment, to the tax rate. This will produce a second Laffer curve for national saving, which is probably more interesting and relevant for policy than the first.[6]

Note that national saving is private plus government saving, or minus government dissaving. If we are at the maximum of Laffer Curve I, a tax cut leaves government saving unchanged. Since it presumably increases private saving, it increases national saving. So the peak of Laffer Curve II is at a lower tax rate than that of Laffer Curve I. Note also that an increase in private saving does not necessarily mean an increase in national saving. Failure to remember this elementary point is the main and distressingly prevalent fallacy in current public discussion of tax reduction as stimulus to saving and investment. A tax reduction can increase government dissaving by more than it raises private saving; in this case we are on the low-tax side of the maxima of both curves.

DIGRESSION TO THE DEMAND SIDE

There are the Keynesian demand–side answer to the two questions. Assume that tax revenues $\overline{TR}$ are a linear function of national product Y:

$$\overline{TR} = T_0 + TY \tag{4.1}$$

Assume consumption depends positively on income, negatively on tax revenues:

$$C = c_0 + c_1 Y - c_2 \overline{TR} \tag{4.2}$$

Recall the national product identity:

$$Y = C + G + I \tag{4.3}$$

where G is government purchase of goods and services and I is private investment. The three equations together give the multiplier equation:

$$Y(1 - c_1 + c_2 T) = c_0 + I + G - c_2 T_0 \tag{4.4}$$

$$\frac{\partial Y}{\partial T} = \frac{-c_2 Y}{1 - c_1 + c_2 T}; \quad \frac{\partial \overline{TR}}{\partial T} = \frac{Y(1 - c_1)}{1 - c_1 + c_2 T} \tag{4.5}$$

The multiplier is positive for government spending and tax reduction if $1 - c_1 + c_2T > 0$. Given this condition, tax reduction increases or leaves unchanged tax revenues only if $c_1 \geqslant 1$, an empirically unlikely value even if induced 'consumption' is reinterpreted to include some investment. In general, the model suggests that lowering tax rates increases Y but lowers tax revenue. As for national saving, equation 4.4 simply says that private saving plus government saving is equal to investment.

$$(Y - \overline{TR} - C) + (\overline{TR} - G) = \mathrm{I} \tag{4.4a}$$

If investment is a constant, independent of income, then tax reduction simply substitutes private saving for government saving.

A somewhat different question relates to the supply of saving at full employment. If equations 4.4 and 4.4a are interpreted in reverse, fixing Y at its full employment level Y^* while letting I be endogenous, then tax reduction unambiguously reduces investment in favour of consumption:

$$\frac{\partial I}{\partial T} = c_2 Y^* \tag{4.6}$$

This review of the Keynesian model is relevant because Kemp–Roth proponents have cited the 1964 Kennedy–Johnson tax cut as a precedent. Sober supporters of this legislation at the time and sober reviewers of the experience have not claimed that it paid for itself. The main rationale was demand stimulus. The 1962 revenue act had introduced the Investment Tax Credit, and the Treasury was liberalising depreciation guidelines. These measures were intended to stimulate investment demand in the short run and to increase the economy's capital stock and potential output in the long run.

DERIVATION OF LAFFER CURVES

To return to the Laffer Curves, assume that production is Cobb–Douglas in capital stock, fixed in the short run, and labour:

$$Y = K^{\alpha} N^{1-\alpha} \tag{4.7}$$

The pretax marginal product of labour and the pretax wage are equal to $(1 - \alpha)K^{\alpha}N^{-\alpha}$, and the wage bill is $(1 - \alpha)Y$ or $(1 - \alpha)K^{\alpha}N^{-\alpha}$. A proportional income tax at rate T collects revenues of $TY = TK^{\alpha}N^{1-\alpha}$. Labour is supplied in response to the after-tax real wage w, with elasticity of $1/\beta$:

$$N = (aw)^{1/\beta}, \ N^{\beta} = aw \tag{4.8}$$

where a is an arbitrary scale parameter.

The aftertax wage bill is:

$$Nw = \frac{1}{a} N^{1+\beta} = (1 - T)(1 - \alpha) K^{\alpha}N^{1-\alpha} \tag{4.9}$$

Therefore, letting $u = 1 - T$, we have:

$$\log N = \frac{1}{\beta + \alpha} \log u + \frac{1}{\beta + \alpha} \log (1 - \alpha) aK^{\alpha} \tag{4.10}$$

Tax revenues are given by:

$$\log \overline{TR} = \log (1 - u) + (1 - \alpha) \log N + \log K^{\alpha}$$

$$\log \overline{TR} = \log (1 - u) + \frac{1 - \alpha}{\beta + \alpha} \log u + \text{constants} \tag{4.11}$$

We are interested in the response of tax revenues to the rate $T = 1 - u$:

$$\frac{\partial \log \overline{TR}}{\partial T} = \frac{1}{T} - \frac{(1 - \alpha)}{(\beta + \alpha)(1 - T)}$$

$$\frac{\partial \log \overline{TR}}{\partial T} = \frac{\beta + \alpha - T(1 + \beta)}{T(1 - T)(\beta + \alpha)} \tag{4.12}$$

This is the slope of Laffer Curve I. Clearly it is positive until $T^* = \frac{(\alpha + \beta)}{(1 + \beta)}$, where $\overline{TR}$ is a maximum, and negative for higher Ts.

For Laffer Curve II, assume that wage earners consume a fraction c_w of their after-tax wages $u(1 - \alpha)Y$ and capitalists consume a fraction c_k of their after-tax profits $u\alpha Y$. Investment is the difference between production and the sum of public consumption G, assumed constant, and private consumption:

$$I + G = Y[1 - c_w u(1 - \alpha) - c_k u\alpha]$$
$$= K^{\alpha}N^{1-\alpha}[1 - c_w u(1 - \alpha) - c_k u\alpha]$$

$$\log(I + G) = (1 - \alpha)\log N + \log[1 - c_w u(1 - \alpha) + c_k u\alpha] + \text{constants} \tag{4.13}$$

$$\frac{\partial \log(I + G)}{\partial u} = \frac{(1 - \alpha)}{(\beta + \alpha)u} + \frac{-c_w(1 - \alpha) - c_k\alpha}{1 - u[c_w(1 - \alpha) + c_k\alpha]}$$

$$\frac{\partial \log(I + G)}{\partial u} = \frac{(1 - \alpha) - u(1 + \beta)(c_w(1 - \alpha) + c_k\alpha)}{u(\beta + \alpha)[1 - u[c_w(1 - \alpha) + c_k\alpha]]} \tag{4.14}$$

This slope is zero, and $I + G$ is a maximum when $u = u^{**}$:

$$u^{**} = \frac{1 - \alpha}{(1 + \beta)[c_w(1 - \alpha) + c_k\alpha]} = 1 - T^{**} \tag{4.15}$$

Suppose, for example, that $\alpha = \frac{1}{3}$, $c_w = 0.8$, $c_k = 0.4$. Let the elasticity of labour supply with respect to the wage be $\frac{1}{3}$, so that $\beta = 3$. Empirical evidence suggests that this is an implausibly high response of labour supply. Then $u^{**} = \frac{1}{4}$, $T^{**} = \frac{3}{4}$. In other words, so long as T is less than 0.75 we know that a tax cut diminishes the supply of national saving for private investment.

A fortiori, it will diminish tax revenues. Indeed, with the same parameter values, the slope of Laffer Curve I is zero at $T^* = 0.833$.

Figure 4.2 (p. 67) shows the two Laffer Curves and Figure 4.3 (p. 68) shows the derivation of Laffer Curves.

Notes

* This chapter is a seminal analysis of lessons to be learned from the US experience of the late 1970s and early 1980s. The chapter was presented by the laureate in 1982 at the Research Center of Stanford University, California. Due to its relevance even today it is being published here with the permission of the contributor with some minor style changes (Editor).

1. See Tobin, James, *Asset Accumulation and Economic Activity* (Oxford: Blackwell, 1980) ch. 3.
2. Gramlich, E. M., 'The behaviour and adequacy of the US federal budget', *Yale Economic Papers*, vol. 6, no. 1 (1966), pp. 98–159.
3. It is important not to use HED, adjusted or not, for the wrong purpose. If

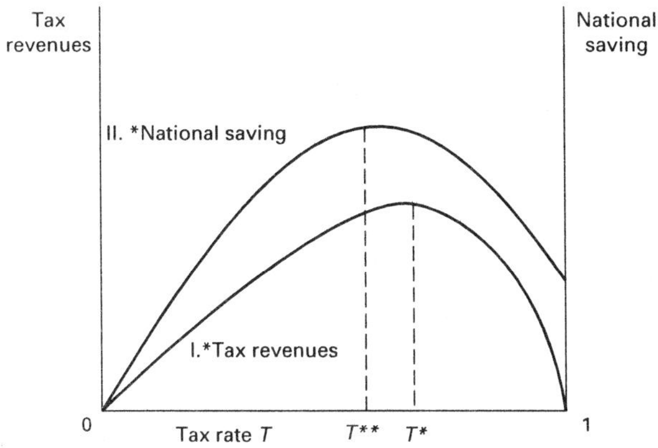

α = capital share of ouput $\frac{1}{\beta}$ = labour supply elasticity

c_k = marginal propensity to consume capital income
c_w = marginal propensity to consume labour income

$$T^* = \frac{\alpha + \beta}{1 + \beta}; \quad T^{**} = 1\frac{1 - \alpha}{(1 + \beta)(c_w(1 - \alpha) + c_k\alpha)}$$

For $\alpha = \frac{1}{3}$, $\beta = 3$, $c_w = 0.8$, $c_k = 0.4$, T^* would be $\frac{5}{6}$ and T^{**} $\frac{3}{4}$.

Figure 4.2 Laffer Curves

the economy is not at Y^* when a new budgetary programme is introduced, but at Y_1, the measure of fiscal stimulus needed by a forecaster is $E(Y_1, f_2) - E(Y_1, f_1)$ not $E(Y^*, f_2) - E(Y^*, f_1)$. A tax cut that would total US \$100 billion if the economy were at full employment may only be a stimulus of US \$50 billion to an economy in recession. This is obvious in Figure 4.1, but some reduced-form tests of the efficacy of fiscal and monetary policies have used HED as the measure of fiscal stimulus.

4. The Administration, though sympathetic in spirit with supply-side theories of the beneficial consequences of tax rate reductions for the economy and the tax base, never committed itself literally to the view that the US was on the inefficient slope of the Laffer Curve. But the Treasury did argue that the savings generated by tax cuts would be enough to buy debt securities covering the resulting deficit. This argument envisaged that supply-side tax incentives would move the economy to a higher output path. A Laffer Curve can be constructed for taxes plus savings and it is quite unlikely that we are at its peak or on the wrong slope.
5. *Newsweek*, 23 February 1981.
6. Norman Ture, under-secretary of the Treasury, is reported to say that the Kemp–Roth tax bill may not pay for itself in tax revenues but it will generate enough taxes plus savings to finance the government without crowding out any private investment. I interpret him, therefore, to be talking about Laffer Curve II.

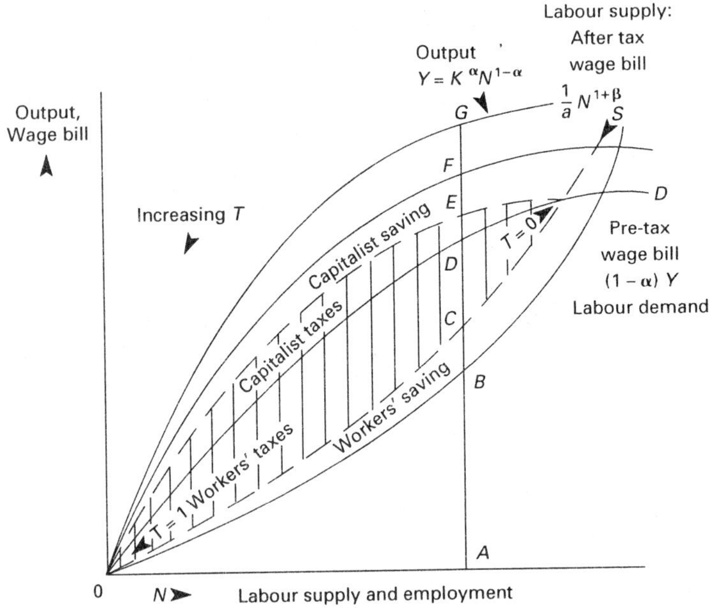

AB: Workers' consumption
BC: Workers' saving
CD: Workers' taxes
DE: Capitalist taxes
EF: Capitalist saving
FG: Capitalist consumption
BF: Taxes and saving available for government purchases and private investment (G + I)
CE: Tax revenues

Employment is determined for each tax rate *T* such that labour supply *S*, measured by $\frac{1}{\alpha}N^{1+\beta}$ plus taxes is equal to labour demand *D*, measured by $(1-\alpha)Y$. Here both *D* and *S* are in terms of wage bills. The vertical distance in the shaded area is tax revenue, from capitalists and workers combined.

Figure 4.3 Derivation of Laffer Curves

5 Domestic Stabilisation and the Balance of Payments*

James Meade

The purpose of this chapter is to consider the general principles to be followed by countries adopting national policies for the domestic stabilisation of their economies and in conducting their external financial relationships with other countries. The term domestic stabilisation refers to a level of high and stable economic activity – full employment – to be maintained and combined, if not with exact stability of some stated price index, at least with only a moderate, steady, nonexplosive rise in the general level of prices – to be called the control of inflation.

The countries to be discussed here are those aiming at full employment and the control of inflation by means of demand-management and incomes or wage-fixing policies. These are countries that are adopting orthodox Keynesian domestic policies, or fiscal and monetary policies designed to expand total money expenditure on goods and services provided employment is below some high predetermined full-employment level. If necessary, this policy will be combined with a centralised incomes policy that controls money rates of pay so as to prevent the high level of demand from leading to a run-away inflation of money costs and prices. This chapter will also cover those countries that are adopting New Keynesian policies.

To explain New Keynesian policy we must consider the recent experience in all countries, and in particular the United Kingdom, which has thrown doubt on the wisdom of expanding total money expenditure so long as employment is below some high and predetermined full-employment level. This policy has been found, in fact, to imply a threat of runaway price–cost inflation. The problems and implications of meeting this threat by an effective, centralised incomes policy are so acute that Orthodox Keynesianism must be stood on its head. In other words, demand-management policies should be used to maintain a steady but restrained rate of growth of the total flow of money expenditure on the products of labour, and thus on the services of labour, in order to control inflation. Against this background of a steady but moderate rate of growth in the total money earnings of labour, employment should be maintained by introducing into each sector of the economy methods of wage fixing suitably devised to promote the level of employment in that sector rather than to obtain the highest possible monopolistic reward for a limited number of people in that sector. This is New Keynesianism.

This view does not imply acceptance of strict monetarism, and the position adopted here differs from that of strict monetarism in three important respects. First, the direct objective of financial policy should be to control the flow of cash expenditure rather than the stock of money, since the relevant stock of liquid assets is Protean in its ability to change its form and in any case is to be regarded only as an indirect means of controlling the level of total expenditure. Second, fiscal and not just monetary measures are needed to achieve the desired stabilisation. Third, stabilisation through financial policy is enough and wage-fixing arrangements can be left to look after themselves. At any rate in the United Kingdom, a radical reform of wage-fixing arrangements is a necessary feature for the achievement of full employment against the background of a steady, controlled, moderate rate of growth in the total level of money demand for labour.

In the present state of development of national and international economic and financial institutions it seems clear that the primary responsibility for stabilisation policies of the kind outlined must remain in the hands of the national authorities. Accordingly this chapter assumes that each national government is devising its own national financial policies and its own wage-fixing institutions in such a way as to promote employment and control inflation.

It is not the purpose here to argue the toss between Orthodox Keynesianism and New Keynesianism. The assumption is that, by one or other combination of wage-fixing arrangements and of demand-management policies, a country has succeeded in controlling inflation, while maintaining a high and stable level of employment.

A CLOSED ECONOMY

Before turning to the international aspects of the problem we must analyse in a little more detail the implication that would arise in a closed economy. Demand-management policies, whether they be used by Orthodox Keynesians for the maintenance of full employment or by New Keynesians for the control of inflation, can be implemented either by monetary policy (which we will call interest-rate policy) or by fiscal policy (which we will call tax-rate policy). Which of these two, or what combination of the two, should one use for the management of demand?

My personal belief is that demand-management policies should be as finely tuned as possible. In this respect there is much to be said for placing the main emphasis on the tax rate. Changes in the rate of interest resulting from tighter or more relaxed monetary policies are likely to have a rather delayed action. It is probably true that interest rates can be changed more promptly than can tax rates, but their effect on expenditure by causing people to revise their plans and programmes for capital investment in new plant, machinery, housing and so on is likely to be much delayed. If short-run, reasonably fine-tuned control is desired, it is probably essential to search for suitable fiscal reforms that will enable certain tax rates to be varied reasonably frequently and promptly. Changing national insurance contributions and VAT might be a suitable way of influencing consumer expenditure.

If the rate of tax is to be used as the primary weapon to stabilise expenditure, what, if any, is the role to be played by the interest rate? At this point another domestic character enters the stage to play the third role, namely the budget balance. The analysis can best be made by considering one illustrative situation. Suppose that, at a particular rate of interest, it is found necessary to slash the tax rate to a very low level in order to prevent expenditure from falling below the desired level. The result is an excessively large budget deficit. Because borrowing for private investment is insufficient, the government has to mop up by borrowing part of the private sector's savings at the full-employment level of real incomes to spend on current governmental consumption. The cure for this situation is an expansionary monetary policy with a reduced rate of interest, which gradually leads to increased private investment. As this happens, in order to prevent expenditure from rising above the desired level, the tax rate must be raised so as to restrain private consumption, with the result that the budget deficit will be reduced.

In what follows the budget balance will accordingly be referred to as the third target for macroeconomic policy. This, however, does not imply that target should necessarily be a zero deficit or surplus. A budget surplus is a form of public saving that supplements private saving, and in conditions of full employment it may be judged desirable that there should be such a supplement to private saving, because insufficient weight is being given privately to the needs of future generations – or alternatively that a budget deficit of a certain size is desirable because the level of private savings is considered to impose an excessive burden on the current generation. The budget-balance target would be a zero deficit or surplus only if the authorities had no desire – in conditions of full employment – to add to or subtract from private saving. We shall talk of a country having a budget-surplus problem if, in the interests of short-term demand management, the authorities are having to run a budget surplus at a higher level, or a budget deficit at a lower level, than they would otherwise desire; and conversely for a budget-deficit problem.

One may summarise this strategy for the short-run stabilisation and control of the closed economy as follows:

1. The rate of tax and the rate of wages should be used in combination to maintain full employment and control inflation.
2. If the rate of tax that is required to maintain the desired level of expenditure is so low as to result in a persistent budget-deficit problem, the rate of interest should be reduced in order gradually to stimulate private investment, which will alleviate the need for such excessively low rates of tax; and vice versa to avoid a persistent budget-surplus problem.

If one were not concerned with the relative speeds with which the rate of interest and the rate of tax are likely to affect expenditure, what has just been said would amount to no more than the familiar proposition that, in devising demand-management policies, one should use tax policy if one wants primarily to influence private consumption expenditure, and interest rate policy if one wants primarily to influence private investment expenditure. All that has been added is the view that in the short run it is more important to prevent undesirable booms or slumps in total money expenditure than it is to keep investment and consumption in any optimal relationship to each other, and that as an instrument for controlling money expenditure, tax-rate changes are probably more prompt in their effects than are changes in interest rates.

It is time, however, to turn to an examination of the international implications of these proposals; and this, it will be found, greatly reinforces the desirability of relying on tax-rate changes rather than interest-rate changes when controlling a country's money expenditure.

A SINGLE OPEN ECONOMY

This analysis of an open economy will start by considering a small country in relation to much of the rest of the world, the latter having a set of tax rates, wage rates, price levels, incomes and so on that will not, to any appreciable degree, be influenced by what goes on in the small economy in question.

The rules given for a closed economy can be summarised as using (1) the tax rate and the wage rate to control employment and inflation and (2) the interest rate to control the budget balance. For the open economy we can add one 'target', namely equilibrium in the balance of payments, and one 'weapon', namely the rate of foreign exchange. At first glance it may appear reasonable to assume that the rules just given for a closed economy should remain unchanged and that the exchange rate should be used as an instrument for maintaining equilibrium in the balance of payments, being depreciated in order to expand exports and contract imports in the case of a balance of payments deficit, and being appreciated to cope with a balance of payments surplus.

But can the effect that changes in the rate of interest have on the balance of payments be neglected in this way? When discussing this basic question the term 'balance of trade' will be used to denote a country's balance of payments on the current account; that is, the excess value of a country's exports of goods and services over its imports of goods and services. A surplus on the balance of trade so defined is the same as the country's foreign investment, since it measures the net amount of the country's real resources that are being used to increase its net holding of foreign assets. It also measures one element of expenditure on the country's goods and services, the total of which it is the object of short-run domestic financial policy, and in particular tax policy, to keep on a moderate, stabilised growth path or control in the interests of full employment.

Here, a surplus in the country's balance of payments should be taken to mean an inflow of foreign exchange reserves, or transactions in official intergovernmental or inter-Central-Bank financing with similar effect. This occurs when the country's balance of trade exceeds any outflow of capital funds on autonomous or private accounts. A country's balance of trade will be determined by such factors as its money income, money prices and money costs relative to foreign money income, money prices and money costs, adjusted for the foreign exchange rate. The international flow of capital funds will be determined by other factors, such as the expected yield from different forms of asset at home and abroad, the yields being determined among other things by the rates of interest at home and abroad and by expected changes in the foreign exchange rate, as this will affect the home-currency value of assets denominated in terms of foreign currency. The problem of maintaining balance of payments equilibrium is the problem of matching a country's balance of trade (which is determined by one set of factors) with the international flow of capital funds (which is determined by another set of factors).

A rise in a country's domestic interest rate may be expected to cause a large, temporary inflow of funds as fund holders at home and abroad adjust their existing portfolio holdings in favour of the higher-interest-rate country. Once the portfolio adjustment had taken place this large shift of funds would cease; it would, however, be succeeded by a permanent but smaller improved flow as the continued savings of fund-holders at home and abroad were attracted in newly adjusted proportions to the higher-interest-rate country. From this one may conclude that if a country's domestic rate is gradually raised the gradual change in existing portfolios will cause a continuing flow of funds to the country concerned, and that when the rise ceases to take place and a higher rate has been established there will result a continuing increased flow out of current savings.

In view of these considerations it is impossible to neglect the effect of a country's interest rates on its balance of payments. This is an important reason why – for purposes of domestic demand management of total money expenditure on the country's products – stress must be laid on the use of fiscal policy (tax-rate policy) rather than on the use of monetary policy (interest-rate policy). Both rate of tax and rate of interest will, of course, affect the balance of trade by affecting the level of total expenditure on goods and services. But we are not concerned with that effect except insofar as there may be some difference in the import contents of tax-controlled and interest-controlled expenditures, since we are assuming that, whatever policy weapon is used, it will be used to the extent necessary to maintain the total money demand for the country's products at the desired target level. But the interest rate will have the additional direct and immediate effect on the balance of payments of affecting the international flow of capital funds. The rate of tax will have no such effect.

If, then, wage-rate policy and tax-rate policy are to be used domestically on Orthodox Keynesian or New Keynesian lines to maintain full employment and control inflation, we are left with two weapons – namely interest-rate policy and exchange-rate policy – to achieve two targets: a balanced budget and equilibrium in the balance of payments. The purpose of this chapter is to consider the appropriate use of these two weapons to achieve these two objectives against the background of successful use of wage-rate policy and tax-rate policy in avoiding unemployment and inflation.

A country may be facing a budget-deficit problem or a budget-surplus problem as a result of using tax-rate policy to prevent the level of money demand for its products from falling below or rising above the desired level. At the same time it may be facing a balance of payments deficit or surplus as a result of its balance of trade falling below or rising above the outflow of capital funds. Or it may be facing any combination of these two sets of problems, which gives four possible cases.

Two of these cases present no analytical difficulty. Consider a country with a budget-surplus problem. The closed-economy rule was to raise the rate of interest so as to reduce domestic investment and make it desirable to cut the rate of tax in order to promote an offsetting increase in consumption. If the country also has a balance of payments deficit, the rise in the rate of interest (effected to relieve the budget-surplus problem) will attract funds from abroad and thus relieve the balance of payments deficit. So long as the country has a budget surplus and a balance of payments deficit, the closed economy rule of using the rate of interest to deal with the budget-surplus problem need not be modified.

Conversely, so long as a country is faced with a budget deficit and a balance of payments surplus, lowering the rate of interest to relieve its budget-deficit problem will cause an outflow of funds, which will relieve its balance of payments surplus.

Problems, however, arise in the two remaining cases where the country has either a deficit problem or a surplus problem simultaneously on both budget account and balance of payments account. If the country has a deficit problem on both counts, the closed economy rule that calls for a reduction of the rate of interest to relieve the budget-deficit problem would encourage the outflow of capital funds and intensify the balance of payments deficit. A country's budget-deficit problem will be referred to as being intractable if it has not at the same time a surplus in its balance of payments, that is to say, so long as a reduction in the rate of interest needed to relieve its budget-deficit problem would create a new, or intensify an existing, balance of payments problem. Conversely a country's budget-surplus problem will be said to be intractable so long as it is not combined with a balance of payments deficit.

Let us consider the case of a country with a deficit problem on both its budget balance and its balance of payments. An obvious possibility would be to depreciate the exchange rate. If the immediate effect of the depreciation was to shift demand at home and abroad away from foreign goods and towards the country's goods on such a scale that the balance of trade improved, all would be well. The balance of trade represents the country's real investment of current resources abroad. This increase in the net demand for the country's goods for investment abroad would enable the rate of tax to be raised to induce an offsetting reduction in the country's consumption expenditure. The increased foreign investment would relieve the country's budget-deficit problem as well as its balance of payments problem.

If the exchange-rate variations worked promptly in this fashion the rules of the game would be simple. A country with a deficit or a surplus problem in both the budget and the balance of payments simultaneously should make use of the exchange rate so as to relieve its balance of payments problem, and this will work in the right direction to relieve its budget problem. A country with a surplus problem on the one count and a deficit problem on the other should make use of the rate of interest so as to relieve its budget balance, and this will work in the right direction to relieve its balance of payments problem.

We now return to the country with the intractable budget-deficit problem. Suppose that it does reduce its interest rate in order to promote domestic investment and relieve its budget-deficit problem, in spite of the fact that it will create or intensify a deficit on its balance of payments. Suppose that it lets the exchange rate find its own level as a means of dealing with this intensified balance of payments problem. What will happen?

In fact the resulting depreciation of the currency reduces the country's money prices and costs relative to those in the rest of the world. While in the long run this will almost certainly have the desired effect of improving the country's balance of trade, it is likely to do so only with considerable delay as trade is gradually diverted into the more profitable channels. Indeed the immediate effect may be perverse and the well known J-curve may display itself. Before the channels of trade are diverted as a consequence of the changes in relative prices, the rise in the price of imports may cause a temporary deterioration in the balance of trade.

If this happens the exchange-rate depreciation will be intensified as the temporary worsening of the balance of trade is added to the adverse effect of low domestic interest rates on the international flow of capital funds. In fact the depreciation will have to go so far as to cause fund-holders at home and abroad to consider:

1. that the exchange rate has become grossly undervalued;
2. that the exceedingly favourable rate of exchange will gradually improve the balance of trade;
3. that the improvement in the balance of trade will cause an appreciation of the exchange rate from its present grossly undervalued level;
4. that the appreciation of the exchange rate is about to start; and
5. that the rate of appreciation will be sufficiently rapid.

The expected rate of appreciation is, of course, crucial. In comparing yields on assets at home and abroad it is the rate of interest at home plus the rate at which the home currency will appreciate in terms of foreign currency that must be compared with the rate of interest on foreign funds.

It is possible that a solution to the problem can be found in this way, but such a solution may not exist if the channels of trade do not respond, or respond only slowly, to changes in relative prices. In such a case the initial worsening of the balance of trade might be very great, so that the inflow of funds to be attracted by the expected exchange rate appreciation would have to be very large. Likewise the rate of the expected appreciation might not be sufficiently rapid to attract the large flow of funds needed.

This problem needs formal dynamic analysis, but what is quite certain is that violent swings in the exchange rate may well take place if the solution of freely floating exchange rates is adopted. This would lead to marked temporary changes in relative prices that would require subsequent reversal. In the example here it could lead to marked increases in the cost of living due to temporary excessive rises in the cost of imports and misleadingly high temporary boosts to the country's tradable products. Appropriate wage fixing and informed business planning would be much easier if the temporary collapse of the exchange rate were avoided.

This might be done to some extent by utilising the country's offiicial foreign exchange reserves. But if the problem were on a large scale and such reserves were inadequate, it would be inevitable that during the temporary strain on the balance of payments the interest rate would have to be raised to attract foreign funds in spite of any adverse effect on the budget-deficit problem. The exchange-rate adjustment will itself ultimately relieve the budget-deficit problem by increasing the country's foreign investment. The aim should, therefore, be to postpone the adjustment of the interest rate for as long as possible, if necessary by the use of foreign-exchange reserves; any adjustments of the interest rate that may be needed on budget-balance grounds being made later, as and when the exchange-rate adjustment develops its favourable effect on foreign investment. The ultimate requirement on budget-balance grounds may in fact turn out to be no fall, or even a rise, in interest rates as foreign investment grows.

This suggests that the basic principles for the open economy should be on the following lines. Let the rate of interest always be adjusted so as to help maintain equilibrium in the balance of payments so long as the change is also in the direction needed to relieve any budget deficit or surplus problem. If, however, there is an intractable budget deficit or surplus problem, seek ultimate adjustment of the exchange rate, and ease this process of adjustment by relying as much as possible on the use of foreign-exchange reserves rather than on interest-rate changes as the means for dealing with the immediate balance of payments problem.

The final result of using the interest rate to cope with tractable budget-balance problems and the exchange rate to cope with intractable budget-balance problems on the principles just outlined, would be that the country, as well as preserving full employment and controlling inflation by means of its domestic fiscal and wage policies, would also be in balance of payments equilibrium. At the same time total savings (private and public) will be at the desired level and will be being used to finance domestic and foreign investment in proportions determined by relative yields at home and abroad as capital funds flow in search of such yields.

This strategy involves use of the exchange rate to set in motion a change in the country's total investment, both domestic and foreign. But this does not imply that there is no day-to-day exchange-rate problem with regard to the short-run balance of payments equilibrium. The price level of the country's products will be the outcome of the rate of change in the country's output per head, and in the wage rate set by incomes policy or resulting from the rate of growth that has been set for the total money demand for labour, depending on whether an Orthodox Keynesian or New Keynesian policy has been adopted. There is no *a priori* reason to believe that the country's price and cost levels will be moving exactly in line with those in the rest of the world. The structural adjustment that may be needed to control the country's balance of trade, and therefore its foreign investment, is not in fact an adjustment of the exchange rate itself. What is needed is an adjustment of the country's domestic price and cost levels relative to those of the rest of the world after conversion at the current rate of exchange; in other words, an adjustment of the real terms of trade between the country's own products and the competing products of the rest of the world.

This suggests that exchange-rate policy should be considered at two levels. First, the day-to-day adjustment of the exchange rate through an exchange equalisation fund should be conducted in such a way as to keep constant a competitiveness index of the country's products *vis-à-vis* the competing products of the rest of the world. Second, from time to time there should be structural adjustments of the level at which the competitiveness index should be stabilised, competitiveness being increased if greater domestic and foreign investment were needed to relieve an otherwise intractable budget-deficit problem, and *vice versa*. Exchange-rate adjustments of the kind needed to alter the competitiveness of a country's products in overseas markets will be referred to as 'structural exchange-rate adjustments'.

MANNA FROM HEAVEN

Application of the principles just outlined can be illustrated by means of a parable. The title 'Manna from Heaven' rather than 'Oil from the North Sea' has been chosen in order to emphasise a certain element of the miraculous, namely that the country enjoying this bounty of nature is successfully applying the domestic policies I have advocated; that is to say, it is suffering neither from inflation nor from unemployment since it has a set of appropriate domestic fiscal and wage policies.

Imagine, then, that the bounty of heaven starts to pour into the coffers of the country's Treasury – an annual supply of manna, a primary product for which there is an insatiable overseas market. Taken by surprise the Treasury simply sells the manna abroad. The impact effect is thus straightforward. There is an added annual budget surplus and an added positive balance of payments taking the form of an annual addition to the country's foreign-exchange reserves equal to the value of the annual supply of manna from Heaven.

In this parable the labour and capital needed to gather up the manna is negligible, and those who do find it have to pay all but a tiny part of it in tribute to the government. Thus the authorities are faced with no immediate need to change their demand-management or wage-fixing policies in order to maintain full employment and control inflation.

All that has happened is an increase in the budget surplus that is matched by an increase in the authorities' holdings of foreign exchange reserves as the manna is sold abroad. In the rest of the economy money expenditure, prices, wages and incomes remain unchanged.

So far the effect would be that the citizens of the fortunate country were saving and investing abroad the whole of the community's income from manna. The anomaly of this situation might even be intensified if the monetary authorities felt compelled on balance of payments grounds to ease monetary conditions and reduce interest rates to help to restore equilibrium to the balance of payments by encouraging an outflow of capital funds to match the export of manna. Any such reduction in the interest rate might have some effect in stimulating domestic investment; and in order to prevent this from causing an unwanted inflation of total money expenditure on the products of the country's labour, the rate of tax might have to be raised and the budget surplus further increased in order to encourage some offsetting reduction in consumption.

This would indeed be an anomalous outcome. Even if the flow of manna were not expected to be permanent, it would be anomalous that the citizens as consumers should enjoy no benefit from the bounty, and much more anomalous that they should actually be asked to tighten their belts. If the flow were expected to be temporary, it would be reasonable to save some part of it. One possible target would be to use the temporary flow of manna to finance a permanent rise in consumption levels. This would involve saving enough so that, when the flow ceased, the yield on the additional capital wealth of the community would be sufficient to maintain in perpetuity the initial higher level of consumption.

It would thus be natural for the authorities to decide that the supplement to the country's savings that was represented by the uncorrected budget surplus was excessive. The country is thus faced with an intractable budget surplus problem. It would be desirable to raise the rate of interest to discourage investment at home. This would allow taxes to be reduced so that citizens could spend more on consumption out of their post-tax incomes and devote less resources to domestic investment since their foreign investment had grown so greatly. But any rise in the rate of interest would worsen the balance of payments problem and add an additional inflow of capital funds to the large surplus in the balance of trade (inclusive of manna).

According to the rule book, this intractable budget surplus problem should be remedied by a structural appreciation of the country's currency so as to reduce the competitiveness of the country's products other than manna, thus reducing the country's balance of trade in products other than manna. This reduction would have to go far enough to cause a net reduction in total domestic and foreign investment in such products. This would make room for a reduction in taxation in order to stimulate an offsetting rise in the consumption of such products. The balance-of-payments problem would be relieved when foreign disinvestment in products other than manna offset foreign investment in manna; and the budget-surplus problem would be relieved as tax rates were reduced to stimulate consumption to offset the net reduction in domestic and foreign investment in products other than manna.

Such are the basic features of the story, which has been related simply to illustrate the operation of the rules advocated here. Any such domestic structural change as that resulting from a rich stream of manna from heaven would, of course, bring with it many other important economic problems. In particular, the necessary shift of resources from production of exports and import-competing goods other than manna to production of the additional goods and services the citizens would purchase when their tax burdens were reduced would involve changes in relative prices and incomes and problems of structural unemployment, all of which important disturbances would somewhat impair the benefits of the gift from heaven. On the other hand, another set of changes would increase the benefit to the country concerned at the expense of the rest of the world. The country's terms of trade, insofar as tradable products other than manna were concerned, would be improved as a result of the appreciation of the exchange rate and the reduction in the required competitiveness of its tradable products. The country would obtain more imports per unit of its remaining exports other than manna. But the scale and precise nature of all these disturbing and beneficial price and structural adjustments would depend essentially upon the particular economic structure and conditions of the country heaven had chosen for its bounty; but that is not the subject matter of this chapter.

AN INTERNATIONAL ORDER

So far we have dealt with rules that are appropriate for a single, relatively small country in a large world in which the other countries are operating a miscellany of other policies, with their price levels, rates of interest, total levels of demand and so on all given as exogenous variables to the decision makers in the single country under examination. But the question must be raised as to whether the system could be successfully generalised. If every country in the free-enterprise world operated the set of policies proposed for the single small country, would the system work without appropriate modification of existing international institutions?

The answer is, perhaps, that principles of international cooperation in the setting of exchange rates and interest rates could be devised that would make the generalisation of the system effective and in the interests of all participants. Here there is room only to sketch these principles with a very broad brush. For this purpose we shall suppose a two-country world made up of countries Delta and Sigma, Delta having a balance of payments deficit and Sigma, therefore, a balance of payment surplus. The principles deduced from this two-country world could be readily applied, with suitable modifications, to a many-country world, and one can think of Delta as standing for a group of countries with balance of payments deficits and Sigma as standing for the corresponding countries with balance of payments surpluses.

Each of the two countries, Delta and Sigma, may have a budget-surplus problem, *S*, or a budget-deficit problem, *D*. Thus ΔS means that country Delta has a balance of payments deficit problem and a budget-surplus problem.

Four possible states of the world economy are expressed in the following taxonomic schema:

	Country Delta	*Country Sigma*
State 1	ΔS	ΣD
State 2	ΔD	ΣS
State 3	ΔS	ΣS
State 4	ΔD	ΣD

By considering these various states of the world economy one can deduce the general outlines of the principles for international monetary and financial cooperation in a world in which all countries are using domestic fiscal and wage policies to maintain full employment and avoid inflation.

State 1 is a case in which if both countries adjust their interest rates – upwards in Delta and downwards in Sigma – so as to relieve their budget-balance problem, then this will also relieve their balance of payments problem. Both are faced with what I have called tractable budget-balance problems. This is a clear case for both countries using interest-rate policies to look after their own domestic and international positions.

State 2 is the case where both countries are faced with intractable budget-balance problems and is thus the reverse of State 1. In State 1 the country with the balance of payments deficit was having to fight a domestic inflation of money expenditures by undesirably high tax rates, while the country with a balance of payments surplus was having to slash taxes to fight domestic deflation. Tighter money in Delta and easier money in Sigma was the obvious answer. But in State 2 easier money in Delta would be needed to fight deflation but would make the balance of payments worse; and the tighter money that would be needed in Sigma to help to fight inflation would make the balance of payments still worse.

In this case the rule book previously devised for the single country instructs Delta to depreciate and Sigma to appreciate its currency, Delta relying as little as possible on a rise in interest rates and Sigma as little as possible on a fall in interest rates as a means of looking after the balance of payments. In due course the change in the exchange rate should move the balance of trade in Delta's favour; the increase in Delta's foreign investment and the decrease in that of Sigma would then relieve both countries' domestic demand-management problems as well as the problem of the balance of payments between them.

The rules devised for a single country are thus appropriate in this case also, and indeed would – by obvious international cooperation – be made even more effective than in the single-country case. During the process of adjusting the channels of trade resulting from the exchange-rate adjustment, the balance of payments problem would, as we have seen, continue and could indeed be intensified. To avoid the temporary use of interest-rate adjustments, which are undesirable on budget-balance grounds, Delta will need, and Sigma will have the means, to finance the temporary disequilibrium in the balance of payments. This is the case where official arrangements for financing international balances of payments is most desirable and also in the interest of both parties.

Whereas in State 1 both countries have tractable and in State 2 both have intractable budget-balance problems, States 3 and 4 are cases where one country has a tractable and the other an intractable budget-balance problem. I suggest that in such cases the international rule book should put the onus of responsibility in the first place on the country with the tractable budget problem to initiate action by adjusting its interest rate.

Let me illustrate this by considering State 3, leaving the reader to apply the corresponding analysis to State 4.

In State 3 both countries have to fight undesirable domestic inflationary pressures by adopting excessively high tax rates, but Delta has a deficit on its balance of payments with Sigma. Suppose that Delta raises its interest rate sufficiently to restore equilibrium to its balance of payments by attracting capital funds from Sigma. Sigma will continue, presumably, to have a budget-surplus problem since neither its domestic nor its foreign investment is yet affected.

When the rise in interest rates in Delta has had its effect on domestic investment, Delta's initial budget-surplus problem may have been converted into a budget-deficit problem. In essence this returns the countries to State 2, in which both have intractable budget-balance problems since Delta cannot lower its interest rate nor Sigma raise its interest rate without provoking a reemergence of the balance of payments disequilibrium between them.

An alternative possibility is that the rise in Delta's interest rate will leave the country in a budget-surplus position. In this case what is needed is a further rise in interest rates in both Delta and Sigma, preserving the interest-rate differential needed to maintain equilibrium in the balance of payments, but raising the whole structure of interest rates so as to reduce the budget-surplus problem in both countries.

Such interest-rate adjustment might to all intents and purposes solve both domestic and international problems. But at some point, with interest-rate differentials sustained in order to maintain equilibrium in the balance of payments, one of the countries may solve its budget-surplus problem long before the other. With interest-rate differentials that preserve equilibrium in the balance of payments, there may be no absolute level of the whole structure of interest rates that will at once satisfy budget-balance in both countries, so that one will have a budget-deficit problem and the other a budget-surplus problem.

Once more the world will be back to State 2, where both countries have intractable budget-balance problems. An adjustment of the exchange rate is needed to increase the balance of trade and foreign investment of the country with the budget-deficit problem and decrease the foreign investment of the country with the budget-surplus problem. But it should be noted that one cannot deduce from the original State 3 position that, as the rule book for the single country would suggest, whether Sigma should be the one to appreciate its currency. We cannot tell which country will ultimately be left with the intractable budget-deficit problem and which with an intractable budget-surplus problem when the appropriate adjustments of interest-rate differentials and structures have been made.

This analysis suggests that, for a world order in which countries are making successful use of fiscal and wage-fixing policies to maintain full employment and control inflation, the following five guidelines for international cooperation in monetary and foreign-exchange policies would be appropriate.

Guideline 1

All countries with tractable budget-balance problems should use domestic monetary and interest-rate policies so as to maintain equilibrium in their balance of international payments. If this rule is effectively observed, any remaining balance of payments problems will be associated with intractable budget-balance problems and the world economy will be in State 2.

Guideline 2

The first guideline might, however, solve all balance of payments problems but leave all countries with a budget-deficit problem. A second guideline should, therefore, be that when the world economy is suffering, not so much from balance of payments problems, but from a general need to use fiscal policies to fight the threat of inflation of money expenditure, there should be cooperation to tighten national monetary policies so as to raise the whole structure of interest rates without affecting the differentials needed to preserve balance of payments equilibrium. The reverse applies if the world-wide problem is a fight against deflation of money expenditure.

Guideline 3

This concerns exchange-rate policy and states that there should be international cooperation for normal, continuous, gradual exchange-rate adjustment to maintain international trade competitiveness as domestic policies for the control of inflation lead to some moderate divergences in the development of national money price and cost levels.

Guideline 4

If guidelines 1, 2 and 3 are observed, the remaining problem will be that of individual countries facing intractable budget-balance problems.

Structural exchange-rate adjustments should be made to increase the competitiveness of the products of those countries with intractable budget-deficit problems and/or decrease the competitiveness of those countries with intractable budget-surplus problems, and should be confined to such cases.

Guideline 5

Where structural exchange-rate adjustments are made under guideline 4, cooperative arrangements should be made for the official financing of the balance of payments of such deficit or surplus countries, while the exchange-rate adjustment is working out its effect on the balance of trade.

Note

* This chapter is reprinted here with the permission of the author and is based on a lecture given at the Institut für Wirtschaftsforschung-Hamburg in 1980. Some minor editorial changes have been made [Editor].

6 Incomplete Markets in Foreign Exchange and Asymmetric Financial Integration

Pan A. Yotopoulos

'Getting the prices right' is the basic tenet of the development strategy of less developed countries and for restructuring the former Soviet Bloc economies. The main policy instrument for development and structural change is liberalisation of the market for goods, labour and finance in order to align relative domestic prices more closely with international ones. The link between domestic and international prices is the exchange rate, which should be set at the market-clearing level through liberalisation of the foreign exchange regime.

This chapter[1] introduces a systematic asymmetry that exists between developed countries (DCs) and less developed countries (LDCs) that makes for an incomplete foreign exchange market in the latter. This market incompleteness is the result of reputation asymmetries, as opposed to information asymmetries that have featured prominently in the analysis of other incomplete markets. Under conditions of market incompleteness the free-market price of foreign exchange is not Pareto optimal and intervention is warranted. Moreover, there is the challenge that intervention may not be successful.

The first section of this chapter presents an endogenous growth analysis that employs a novel index of the real exchange rate, which forms the foundation for the interpretation of market incompleteness in LDC currency markets. The second section explores the implications of market incompleteness for the financial integration of DCs and LDCs. The final section presents a summary and the conclusions of the chapter.

AN ENDOGENOUS GROWTH MODEL OF INCOMPLETE MARKETS

Real Exchange Rates

Appropriate exchange-rate policies have always been considered crucial instruments in fostering economic development. However a more careful distinction between the nominal exchange rate (NER) and the real exchange rate (RER) will help in deriving some alternative conclusions about the impact of exchange-rate parities on trade and development.

The NER is formed in the market of tradables, which is a subset of GNP and it is expressed in terms of units of domestic currency per unit of foreign currency. The equilibrium value of the nominal rate is defined as the rate that satisfies the intertemporal budget constraint, which means that the discounted sum of a country's current account is equal to zero. In other words, in the long run the NER balances the trade account (tradables) appropriately considering also capital movements. The RER, on the other hand, considers both tradables and nontradables and is expressed as the price of tradables in terms of nontradables (Edwards, 1989). Its equilibrium value is the rate that both clears the nontradable goods market in the current period and maintains equilibrium in future periods. As such the RER satisfies the equimarginal principle; that is, the marginal product of domestic resources in producing tradables and nontradables is equal – in other words, the same opportunity costs are incurred when producing one unit-value of tradables or one unit-value of nontradables.

Intuition suggests that NER and RER, while clearly covariant, may not fully correspond, especially in LDCs. Since the two rates are formed in different markets, there is no need for an equilibrium NER to coincide with an equilibrium RER. For the purposes of this research, it is not necessary to know the equilibrium value of either the nominal or real exchange rates. An index of RER will suffice for drawing conclusions as to whether the nominal rate is more likely to be undervalued in one country than in another. The value of the RER index has been computed from micro-data produced by the International Comparisons Project, or ICP.

The most common applications of the project have emphasised purchasing power parity and expenditure comparisons among countries. The familiar expression that gives purchasing power parity (PPP) for Country I as the geometric average of the *k* GDP-exhaustive commodity categories is as follows:

$$PPP^I = \prod_{i=1}^{k} \left(\frac{P_i^I}{P_i^W} \right)^{Q_i^I / \sum_{i=1}^{k} Q_i^I} \tag{6.1}$$

where P_i^I and P_i^W are the prices of the *i*th homogeneous commodity for Country *I* and for the numeraire country (world), and *Q* represents the quantity weights.

Different aggregations of equation 6.1 can lead to alternative price indexes, such as the national price level of consumption or of government expenditure. In this application the focus is on the prices of tradables and nontradables, P_N and P_T, respectively:

$$P_T = \prod_{i=N+1}^{T} \left(\frac{P_i^I}{P_i^W} \right)^{Q_i^I / \sum_{i=N+1}^{T} Q_I^i} \tag{6.2}$$

$$P_N = \prod_{i=1}^{N} \left(\frac{P_i^I}{P_i^W} \right)^{Q_i^I / \sum_{i=1}^{N} Q_i^I} \tag{6.3}$$

where $i = N + 1, \ldots, T$ is defined for commodities that are nontradable in Country *I*, and $i = 1, \ldots, N$ is defined for commodities that are tradable. The PPP indexes in equations 6.2 and 6.3 are expressed in local currency per US (numeraire country) dollar.

The ratio of the prices of tradables to nontradables in equations 6.2 and 6.3 gives a pure number, an index of the real exchange rate:

$$\text{RER} = P_T / P_N \tag{6.4}$$

It still remains to be determined how to delineate the two subsets of commodities, $i = 1, \ldots, N$ and $i = N + 1, \ldots, T$. Tradability is certainly related to tradedness and could therefore be defined, based on the empirical–positivist rule of whether a particular good enters (international) trade or not. One could then define two mutually exclusive categories of *traded* and *nontraded* goods. But is any participation in international trade sufficient to mean that a good is traded? Empirically the issue is addressed by resorting to the standard definition of openness in an economy that involves the ratio of imports and exports to GDP. The binary classification into tradables and nontradables was made by adopting an arbitrary cut-off point of trade value (the sum of exports and imports) for a commodity group of 20 per cent of the total commodity expenditure in GDP. The arbitrariness of the criterion has been effectively blunted by distinguishing a large number of commodity groups and by weighting both prices and the participation of each individual commodity into tradability by actual expenditure weights.

Data for implementing the definition of the RER are derived from the basic commodity classification of the ICP. Nominal and real per capita expenditures, expressed in domestic currency per US dollar, are available at the level of the basic commodity classification (152 commodities). They were used to derive prices of tradables and nontradables in a flexible aggregation form. The data for the definition of tradability were taken from the United Nations *Yearbook of International Trade Statistics*, which provides in 5-digit SITC classification for each country the value of exports (fob) and imports (cif) in US dollars. The 5-digit classification was reaggregated to achieve concordance with the ICP data.

Table 6.1 presents the value of the RER for the benchmark countries of the ICP that were included in at least one of the phases II and III for 1970 and 1975, respectively (Kravis, Heston and Summers, 1982). It should be emphasised at this point that the RER is just an index, and it implies nothing about the equilibrium value of the real exchange rate. In fact, the value of the index changes as the cut-off point of tradability varies; but in a sensitivity-analysis test the ranking of the countries derived from the index does not change.[2]

The Endogenous Growth Model

The endogenous growth literature attempts to associate specific differences in development performance with a set of explanatory variables that extend beyond the neoclassical conventional inputs of production.

The usual measure of development performance in endogenous growth studies is the real rate of growth of per capita GDP, GRGDPC (Penn World Tables 5). By using benchmark-country data, the analysis covers the period 1970–5 with at most two observations for a benchmark country. The dependent variable in this study, therefore, was derived by fitting the logarithmic growth rate of the annual observations of real per capita GDP on time for each five years, centred on the benchmark year.

The substantial body of endogenous growth literature that has considered the intercountry variance in rates of growth has established two facts. It is not hard to devise econometric specifications in which sundry variables measuring economic policy are significantly correlated with economic growth. It is almost impossible, however, to dis-

Table 6.1 Index of real exchange rates, 1970 and 1975

Areas	*1970*	*1975*
Africa:		
Kenya	1.037	2.067
Malawi		1.138
Asia and Oceania:		
India	1.525	1.962
Japan	1.097	1.071
Korea, Republic of	0.971	
Malaysia	1.083	1.580
Pakistan		0.821
Philippines	1.688	1.523
Sri Lanka		1.593
Thailand		1.140
Europe:		
Austria		1.314
Belgium	1.112	0.902
Denmark		0.985
France	1.185	1.080
Germany	1.010	1.027
Ireland		1.031
Italy	1.112	1.293
Netherlands	1.331	0.972
Spain		1.157
UK	0.896	0.936
Yugoslavia		0.939
Central and N. America:		
Jamaica		1.279
Mexico		2.009
South America:		
Brazil		1.261
Colombia		1.737
Uruguay		1.126

Source: Yotopoulos (1995).

cover explanatory variables that are robust enough so that their estimated coefficients do not depend importantly on the conditioning set of information. Levine and Renelt (1992) reviewed forty one studies and found over fifty variables that correlated significantly with growth in various papers. But only one, the ratio of investment in GDP, had a robust coefficient in an 'extreme bounds' analysis (Leamer, 1983, 1985).

The innovation in this Chapter is that the RER is considered one of the crucial variables because it incorporates information about market incompleteness. The motivation is to control for the effect of the stylised endogenous growth variables while measuring the impact that the RER has on measures of development performance. The basic hypothesis is about development performance and exchange rate policies as reflected in the values of the NER and RER.

The presentation of the results of the analysis in Table 6.2 is organised in five groups so as to provide an immediate indicator of the robustness of the maintained hypothesis. The main variable of interest is the RER, which appears in group I. Group II adds an explanatory dummy variable, Dum*L*/*M* (=1), which distinguishes between low/middle- and high-income countries and thus describes more accurately the state of the world within which the RER operates. Group III contributes OPEN, the ratio of imports and exports to GDP, as a measure of the openness of an economy, and DIR, the share of a country's trade with OECD countries, to indicate the direction of trade. Both variables are of primary interest in describing the trade regime which complements the RER policy instrument. Group IV increases the number of explanatory variables to five by also including INV, the ratio of investment to GDP. It is the only variable that has proven robust in other endogenous growth studies. Group V increases the number of explanatory variables to ten by adding: GINFL, the average rate of change in inflation; GOVCONS, the average rate of government consumption expenditure in GDP; SECENRL, secondary school enrolment; and GPOP, the rate of growth of population. With a careful eye on the available degrees of freedom, the variables were chosen because they are among those most commonly used in endogenous growth studies, and because they do not measure the same phenomenon with the main variables of interest. By inspecting the change in the value of the coefficient of a certain variable across groups, the reader can draw conclusions about the robustness of each variable. All explanatory variables enter the regressions of the rate of growth of real GDP per capita (GRGDPC) independently and linearly.

The results in Table 6.2 report the longitudinal analysis for the sample of 37 observations (26 countries) for the years 1970 and 1975. The coefficient of the RER has the expected sign, is consistently significant and is robust, with negative values that range from −0.023 to −0.034 in all regressions reported in the test for the five groups of variables.

In group II the dummy variable conditions for the state of the world in which the growth–RER nexus becomes relevant. The coefficient of

Table 6.2 Cross-section/time-series regressions on growth, all countries, 1970 and 1975

Explanatory variables	*Group*				
	I	*II*	*III*	*IV*	*V*
Constant	0.055	0.058	0.096	0.063	0.077
RER	–0.023	–0.029	–0.034	–0.031	–0.033
	(–1.967)	(–2.108)	(–2.505)	(–2.295)	(–2.164)
Dummy low/middle		0.007	0.008	0.007	0.009
(Dum L/M = 1)		(0.825)	(0.929)	(0.865)	(0.597)
Openness (OPEN)			–0.028	–0.027	–0.023
			(–1.541)	(–1.488)	(–1.016)
Direction of trade (DIR)			0.053	0.049	0.041
(share of OECD)			(1.890)	(1.777)	(1.286)
Investment in GDP (INV)				0.112	0.089
				(1.663)	(1.113)
Rate of inflation (change)					–0.019
(GINFL)					(–0.468)
Gov. consumption in GDP					–0.001
(GOVCONS)					(–0.583)
Secondary enrolment (SECENRL)					–0.002
					(–0.053)
Population growth (GPOP)					0.104
					(0.126)
Sample size	37	37	37	37	37
Adjusted R^2	0.100	0.117	0.218	0.282	0.299
Standard error	0.023	0.023	0.022	0.022	0.023

Notes: The dependent variable is annual rate of growth of real per capita GDP for the five-year period centred on the year of observation. For definition of independent variables see text. Numbers in parentheses are t-statistics.

Source: Yotopoulos (1995).

DumL/M varies little as the other variables are introduced *seriatim*, but it is insignificant.

In group III the two trade variables are added. The coefficient of OPEN is consistently negative, albeit barely significant in one case. A positive sign on this variable has been elusive in endogenous growth studies (Edwards, 1993). The negative sign, however, was expected within the interpretation of incomplete markets. It signifies that by controlling for RER, less trade will transpire in comparison with free-market trade. The obverse of this observation is that the larger the volume of trade, the more likely it becomes that trade will reduce welfare: this is the case of comparative-devaluation trade. But there are certainly benefits from trade, as the DIR variable indicates – it has a significant, positive, and robust coefficient. The explanation is that once we control for RER and for OPEN, the clear benefit of trade arises from the technological spill-over of having more developed trading partners (proxied by OECD).

The INV variable enters in group IV and is initially significant. The coefficient of between 0.9 and 0.11 is very close to the modal values reported in other studies for the same variable (Levine and Renelt 1992). Among the variables added in group V, the coefficients for GINFL and GOVCONS have the expected negative signs, although insignificant. The latter is commonly ratiocinated as contrasting government consumption with government investment behaviour, but it is a far cry from a more appropriate variable that would have proxied 'Good Governance'. SECENRL and GPOP have proven as difficult to capture in this study as they have in the parallel literature. It is noteworthy that all the coefficients in group V, with the exception of RER, become unstable as the addition of new variables pushes against the limitation of degrees of freedom.

Is There an Incomplete Market in Foreign Exchange?

The theme that emerges from the previous analysis has as its foundation the negative relationship between the RER and GRGDPC, the rate of growth of real GDP. In the spirit of the endogenous growth literature, the observed variance in RER across countries becomes the explanatory variable of the intercountry variance in rates of growth. The link between the two is an intermediate variable, the NER. Devaluation of the NER is a policy intervention that generates high RERs through the immediate impact on the prices of tradables. The value of the RER index *per se* implies nothing about over- or undervaluation of the RER, let alone about its equilibrium value. Similarly, the index implies nothing about the equilibrium value of the NER. However, examined within an international cross-section, high values of the index are more likely than low values to be associated with high values of NER (an undervalued NER which means relatively high prices of tradables). The causality then goes from undervaluation of NER to low rates of growth of GDP. This is a novel (and controversial) position. Overvaluation of the NER is commonly considered endemic among LDCs and its devaluation is the orthodox policy instrument for delivering development stimuli, as for example with stabilisation and structural adjustment programmes (Krueger, 1980, Khan, Montiel and Haque, 1990). The unorthodox thesis advanced here is that undervalued NERs, or depreciated home currencies, are not only common in LDCs but are also causally related to low development outcomes.

Why should some countries, specifically LDCs, tend to have 'high' NERs that lead to high RERs? One can make the case that there is an inherent dynamic in these countries towards depreciation of the domestic currency: in a liberalised foreign exchange regime the market-clearing price of the NER tends to be 'high' and the domestic currency undervalued. Consider the intuition behind a basic asset value dynamics theorem that links hard and soft currencies in the free market.

Besides its role as a unit of account and a medium of exchange, a currency also serves as a store of value. The important distinction between hard and soft currencies is not convertibility; rather it is the fact that the former is broadly used as a store of value in an open economy, while the latter does not have that function. The store-of-value quality of hard currency is based on 'reputation', which means that there is a credible commitment for stability of relative 'international' prices *vis-à-vis* that numeraire. For soft currency there is not such a credible commitment, which means that a soft currency is expected to depreciate. In an open economy with free foreign exchange this expectation sets off a reverse Gresham's law: there is an asymmetric demand from citizens of the soft-currency country to hold hard currency as a store of value – a demand that is not offset by the citizens of the hard-currency country holding the soft currency as a store of value. The lack of reputation for the soft currency and the expectation that it will depreciate become a self-fulfilling prophecy. Thus a dynamic for spiral devaluations develops.

The implication of the asset value dynamics theorem is that the competitive equilibrium value of the NER tends to favour the tradable sector, as successive devaluations shift resources away from nontradables. Beyond a point, however, increased production of tradables constitutes competitive devaluation trade, as opposed to comparative-advantage trade. This 'trade bias' can result in misallocation of resources and Pareto-losses and is captured by the negative sign of the relationship between GRGDPC and the RER, as noted earlier. Two policy implications arise from the dynamic towards spiral devaluations in LDCs under a liberalised foreign exchange regime. On the supply side, where the high cost (in terms of domestic resources) of producing tradables leads to competitive devaluation gaming, the appropriate policy response is to increase efficiency in the tradable sector. If this succeeds, the competitive devaluation trade becomes once again comparative advantage trade. The downside of this option is that commonly in LDCs there are no quick-fix financial solutions for the problems of the real economy. It is difficult enough to increase efficiency, and especially so in the tradable sector.

The policy implication from the demand side for foreign exchange is more targetable but equally treacherous. If inherent asset-value dynamics tend to produce systematically a market-clearing NER that is 'too high', the remedy is to override the foreign exchange market. Rationing can achieve 'low' NERs and, on the strength of the causal relationship, can also induce growth. Rationing is tantamount to overvaluation of the NER – that is, relative to its free-market rate. The policy focus on an overvalued NER is consistent with the central hypothesis of this chapter that there is an incomplete market in foreign exchange. But operating with an overvalued NER does not necessarily imply overvaluation of the RER, which in principle is consistent with its 'equilibrium' because of the Ricardo Principle and the systematic relationship that exists between the prices of tradables and nontradables in the process of development. With the NER affecting the former more directly than the latter, there is no one-to-one correspondence between equilibrium NER and equilibrium RER. In LDCs, if the NER is at equilibrium, the RER is likely to be undervalued; and an overvalued NER is more likely to be associated with an equilibrium RER. Another way to explain the negative relationship between the RER and growth is that near-Pareto-optimality obtains, the closer the real economy is to equilibrium. Or, conversely, an undervalued RER (in the extreme case the RER that corresponds to the 'equilibrium' NER) extends the range of tradability into the area where exports (or import substitutes) are produced at high domestic resource cost – in relation always to the nontradables that could have been produced in their place. This is again an implication of the Ricardo Principle.

The systematic nature of the relationship between the NER and the RER at different levels of income implies that market incompleteness, and thus the need for rationing, abates as development occurs. The prices of nontradables increase relative to those of tradables, and eventually free-market, free-trade, laissez-faire policies can be allowed to determine the NER. The ailment of an incomplete market in foreign exchange has then been remedied.

IMPLICATIONS OF INCOMPLETE MARKETS FOR FINANCIAL INTEGRATION

Financial integration is predicated on opening the foreign account, and at a minimum it entails abolishing restrictions on capital movements and exchange transactions. It often also involves eliminating controls on interest rates and improving the competitive environment of financial institutions by deregulation and by facilitating the establishment of foreign banks. The objective of financial integration is to use the external sector as an anchor for stabilising the economy, for setting prices right and for increasing efficiency. Additionally, the monetary and exchange-rate policies of liberalisation are expected to lure foreign capital, thus further contributing to the improvement of the fundamentals of the economy. In this scenario the external account and the financial sector play a crucial role in the rehabilitation of the real economy.

As described above, financial integration constitutes the backbone of stabilisation and structural adjustment programmes that exist in most overindebted LDCs. The asset value dynamics theorem proposed earlier has definite implications that militate against attempting financial integration in the face of macroeconomic instability. This will be illustrated with the canonical case of LDCs where integration is attempted prematurely. In these circumstances, asymmetric financial integration involves heavy contractionary costs for the LDC economy. Symmetric integration, on the other hand, is properly sequenced only after the real economy has been stabilised and is launched into self-sustained growth. This case of financial integration under the proper circumstances will be illustrated with the example of Taiwan.

The Canonical Case of Asymmetric Financial Integration

The asset value dynamics theorem, when applied to LDCs, predicts that once restrictions on capital movements and exchange transactions are abolished, the portfolio demand increases for holding foreign exchange – and in the worst cases the transaction demand also increases. This puts pressure for depreciation of the home currency (devaluation of the nominal exchange rate). Devaluation in turn feeds inflationary pressures and leads to further depreciation of the domestic currency. The process can thus create a spiral for devaluation and for inflation. In fact integration in an environment of inflationary finance is a special case of financial integration under asymmetric reputation. In an unstable inflationary environment people anticipate future inflation by substituting large amounts of foreign exchange for their domestic money balances.

Two policy responses are available in an environment of asymmetric reputation: one is to give up on the foreign exchange rate as a policy control instrument and to surrender to the process of currency substitution; the other is to engage monetary policy in defending the exchange rate by using it as an anchor to stabilise the economy. Either policy involves heavy costs for an LDC.

In the first alternative, as inflation breeds devaluation which breeds further devaluation, currency substitution is needed to curtail inflation. In the extreme case of complete 'dollarisation', a currency board is established that holds interest-earning foreign exchange reserves against the domestic currency. As the practice has devolved, for instance in Argentina, it amounts to fixing both the exchange rate and the rate of inflation at its international level. As gradual dollarisation of the economy sets in, the balance of payments deteriorates. Loss of seigniorage revenues leads to a deterioration of the fiscal deficit and to a reduction in the base of the inflation tax. Moreover inequality in income distribution is likely to increase, as people in the higher income brackets are better able to substitute dollars for pesos, making the inflation tax even more regressive.

Of these various costs of dollarisation the seigniorage component is more readily measurable. In contrast to bank deposits and securities, notes and coins do not yield interest. They represent an interest-free loan extended by the public to the issuer, the Central Bank. The total interest earned on the amount of fiat money in circulation, minus the cost of minting and printing, is the yield of the loan. This yield increases as currency is destroyed or goes out of circulation, and also as its value is eaten away by inflation. Currency decay and inflation favour the borrower at the expense of the lender: the Central Bank's net worth increases, because its liabilities are reduced and its assets are not. The amount of revenue that is lost to the state by accepting the dollar in financing transactions and in denominating accounts can only be accurately known if the total stock of dollars in the country were known. In a wide range of cases, however, the one-shot seigniorage cost has been estimated at 8–10 per cent of GNP for full dollarisation. These are indeed large numbers relative to other sources of state revenues (Fischer, 1982, 1992; Melvin, 1988).[3]

Currency substitution is costly, as are the available measures for containing it. Barring foreign exchange restrictions, one alternative is to promote foreign currency deposits in the domestic financial system. This has the advantage of reducing the pressure on international reserves and on the exchange rate, along with improving the Central Bank's balance sheet in foreign assets if reserve requirements are imposed.[4] Attracting foreign currency deposits requires a contractionary monetary policy that drives up interest rates so that they appeal to foreign depositors. The contraction on the side of aggregate demand is a real cost to the economy, but it helps alleviate the pressure on the exchange rate. Differential interest rate policies that make domestic currency deposits more attractive to foreign investors can also help stem the dollarisation of the economy and thus reduce the pressure on reserves. The interest-rate differential can make the sale of debt instruments by the Central Bank attractive to holders of foreign exchange. Private investors then buy local currency denominated debt, which 'flushes out dollars' as the Central Bank defends the exchange rate. The 'premium' in this scenario is paid in terms of higher interest rates (that compensate for the risk of future depreciation of the currency) and thus more protracted contraction in the economy.

The contractionary effect of dollarisation discussed so far relates to aggregate demand. As demand consists of tradables and nontradables, however, it is only natural to impose contraction in the tradable sector as a result of the foreign exchange constraint. It is an entirely different story to impose the same contraction in dealing with the nontradable sector, where transactions do not (or should not) involve foreign exchange. This argument amounts to making the case for a higher rate of optimal inflation for LDCs, in proportion to the importance of their nontradable sector.

The macroeconomic prescription against spiral devaluations is to improve the fundamentals of the economy and to increase productivity. If this is possible, the problem is solved: the competitive devaluation trade will in time become comparative advantage trade. But in most cases this prescription is hard to administer: there are few quick fixes for the real economy, and that includes liberalisation. Therefore in many instances the pressure for adjustment is placed on the areas of employment and wages which has social and economic effects. Even worse, the prescription can provide only temporary relief. Even considering the possibility of an overbloated industrial sector, there is only a slim margin before an LDC faces recriminations from developed country trading partners about violating labour standards and workers' rights through low real-wage policies.[5]

Substantial capital inflow could have provided a neat solution to the problem. But experience with LDCs indicates that – apart from exceptional circumstances – most of the capital inflow consists of 'swaps' (repatriated capital flight) or of short-term capital that comes in at onerous terms: for the swaps, at fifty cents on the dollar and for the loans, at real interest rates that are higher than international interest rates and are creeping up. What is even worse, the short-term hot money is as quick to leave the country as it was fast in coming in. This means that in LDCs, both the exchange-rate risk and the political risk are higher, given observationally equivalent events. It is only a question of how long it will take for the confiscation of foreign currency deposits and the repudiation of debts; and thus the cycle starts again as soon as memories fade and the cast of characters changes.

This scenario applies in various countries as some examples indicate.[6] In Bolivia, foreign currency deposits were first allowed in 1973 and were confiscated in 1982. In Peru they were first allowed in 1978 and were forcefully converted to domestic currency in 1984. In Mexico foreign currency deposits existed between 1977 and 1982 and became especially important towards the end of this period, just before they were confiscated. In these countries, and specifically in Mexico, the recurrence of the process is impressive. Although people are forced to convert their deposits back at the official rate at a huge capital loss, when there is a change in government and credibility is perceived people will again deposit their currency into these instruments.

What has been described is a Sisyphean task: as you push the rock up the hill the pressure increases for it to tumble back down again. In the case of financial integration in LDCs, this pressure is the result of asymmetric reputation.

In the two scenarios outlined, the special circumstances have been emphasised as exceptions. In general, the propitious circumstances boil down to sequencing financial integration very carefully, but only after the macroeconomic house has been put in order. This is a very strict condition, rarely met in most cases of recent financial integration.

Taiwan: Financial Integration in Exceptional Circumstances

The exception of special circumstances qualified this sceptical analysis of the prospects for asymmetric financial integration. The case of Taiwan provides an apposite example of these special circumstances.

Stung from the experience of hyperinflation in the 1950s, since 1960 the authorities have resorted to draconian measures to combat inflation and secure price stability. The policy instruments used were fiscal and monetary with an exchange rate that was pegged and kept stable throughout the 1970s (Table 6.3).[7] The NT dollar was considered generally overvalued for most of the period (Kuo, 1983, Chs 10, 14). The fiscal policy was premised on curtailing government consumpiton expenditure while favouring savings and capital formation in the private and public sectors. On the revenue side the level of income tax was moderate, except for that imposed on agriculture in the earlier period when it was assigned the role of financing the industrialisation drive. The fiscal side produced a consistent surplus in the operating budget, averaging more than 1 per cent of GNP over the period.

The three components of monetary policy that will be examined here are interest rates, money supply, and the intersection of the two as it relates to the balance of payments and net foreign assets.[8] The criterion for evaluating the outcomes of monetary policy is the extent to which the growth of real GDP was accommodated and the rate of inflation was controlled.

Early on, Taiwan's interest-rate policy became the foundation of its monetary policy. The 'preferential interest rate deposit scheme' that has been in existence for more than forty years was intended to lure the private sector into a continuous increase in monetary savings. As shown in Table 6.3 the incentive was high interest rates that were consistently positive and became high when inflationary risks lurched. The rate of personal savings rose from 3 per cent of disposable income in 1952 to 21 per cent in 1980, and has remained at that high level ever since (Scitovsky, 1985). Real interest rates, averaging 6 per cent through the mid-1970s, are very high in comparison with the negative real interest rates that are stylised facts in comparable growth histories. Still, the average productivity of capital has been high enough so that the high interest-rate policy has not choked off investment and growth.[9]

The second component of monetary policy was based on the stable growth of the money supply to finance the vertiginal growth in real GDP, bordering on an average of 8 per cent per year. The annual increase in the demand for money for accommodating the rate of growth

Table 6.3 Taiwan: rate of growth of GNP and financial statistics, 1953–92

	Growth rate of real GNP (per cent)	*Inflation rate (per cent)*	*Growth in money supply (per cent)*	*Interest rate (per cent per annum)*	*Exchange rate (NTS per US$)*
Averages				–	–
1953–56	7.7	–	–	–	–
1957–63	7.5	–	–	–	–
1964–68	10.0	–	–	–	–
1969–74	10.2	–	–	–	–
1975–79	10.1	–	–	–	–
1980–89	8.0	–	–	–	–
1970	11.4	3.6	–	9.25	40.00
1971	12.9	2.8	27.20	8.50	40.00
1972	13.3	3.0	33.50	10.75	40.00
1973	12.8	8.2	45.40	12.00	37.90
1974	1.2	47.5	11.80	10.75	37.95
1975	4.9	5.2	24.70	9.50	37.95
1976	13.9	2.5	21.90	8.25	37.95
1977	10.2	7.0	34.40	8.25	37.95
1978	13.6	5.8	35.30	11.00	35.95
1979	8.2	9.7	10.20	11.00	35.98
1980	7.3	19.0	19.10	11.75	35.96
1981	6.2	16.3	13.80	7.75	37.79
1982	3.6	3.0	14.60	7.25	39.86
1983	8.4	1.4	18.40	6.75	40.22
1984	10.6	0.0	9.30	5.25	39.42
1985	5.0	–0.2	12.20	4.50	39.80
1986	11.6	0.7	51.40	4.50	35.45
1987	12.3	0.5	37.80	4.50	28.50
1988	7.3	1.3	24.40	7.75	28.12
1989	7.4	4.4	6.10	7.75	26.12
1990	–	–	–6.60	6.45	–
1991	–	–	12.10	–	–

Note: Interest rate is the rediscount rate of the Central Bank of China.

Sources: *The Central Bank of China, Financial Statistics*, Monthly and Annual issues; *Taiwan Statistical Data Book 1990*, Council for Economic Planning and Development, Republic of China.

was 16 per cent per year.[10] In addition, the requirements for financing foreign trade transactions, and those imposed by a significant increase in net foreign assets, resulted in vigorous growth of the money supply throughout the period.[11] Nevertheless, inflation was tamed through the combination of interest-rate policies and fiscal policies, along with the overvalued exchange rate that accounted for cheap imports of raw materials and intermediate products. With the exception of an interlude of double-digit rates around the years of the oil crisis, inflation stabilised below 5 per cent for most of the period (Table 6.3).

Real interest rates in Taiwan were higher than in the US. In an open economy the inflow of capital would have driven down interest rates. Similarly in the textbook case the overvalued currency would have contributed to capital outflow. In Taiwan foreign exchange controls were used to insulate domestic interest rates from external influences, whether during the period of the current account deficits, prior to 1976, or afterwards when the inflow of foreign assets was increasing. The exception was the financing of foreign trade that had from the beginning free access to foreign capital at interest rates that were lower than domestic rates. Other inflows of capital were strictly controlled, as were capital outflows. In the period of persistent current account surpluses, interest rates were nudged downwards and some capital outflows were countenanced, but both remained strictly controlled.

Despite the success that Taiwan had experienced in stabilising the domestic sector and in enjoying a consistent record of self-sustained growth, it approached liberalisation and financial integration gingerly, cautiously and late. Great effort went into building and diversifying the institutional structure for financial intermediation and for integration. A securities market had been started in the 1960s, a bond market was established in 1974, and a money market in 1976. The latter two were exempted from interest ceiling regulations, and they were intended to pave the way for interest-rate deregulation and to contribute to capital deepening by channelling financial savings from the informal market to capital formation. The success of the policies is best gauged by the fact that the value of money market instruments outstanding doubled in relation to the total banking loans (from 8.6 per cent to 15.6 per cent) in a period of only 18 months in the late 1970s (Kuo, 1983, p. 321).[12]

In 1978 with the preconditions met and the institutional structure established, a managed floating exchange rate was introduced. Liberalisation of the capital market followed in 1983.[13] Foreign capital transactions, however, continued to be closely monitored,[14] and strict oversight of the foreign exchange rate was maintained at least until 1989, when a 'liberalised' floating exchange-rate system was introduced. At the same time interest rates became fully liberalised.

CONCLUSIONS

In his 1974 Nobel Prize lecture Kenneth Arrow observed that the cross-country inequality in per capita incomes is hardly amenable to the neoclassical explanation of differences in physical and human capital endowments. Since then a veritable cottage industry has developed to explain the conundrum. The main branch of the endogenous growth literature focuses on the failure of the conditions under which the second fundamental theorems of welfare economics holds; that is, the presence of increasing returns, technological externalities and agglomeration effects. The other approach advanced in this chapter is via the dynamic version of the fundamental theorems of welfare economics and incomplete markets. In a non-Arrow–Debreu world, free market, free trade, laissez-faire policies do not lead to Pareto optimal outcomes. The success of the requisite intervention, however, is contingent on the existence of good governance.

This approach deals with the incomplete market and is cast within an endogenous growth framework. The strong empirical link between overriding foreign exchange (and trade) markets and the rate of growth of real GDP is preternatural, considering the fact that no variable for good governance has been introduced in the regressions. However the implications of the hypothesis of systematic market incompleteness in foreign exchange have been drawn for financial integration. Asymmetric integration is equivalent to the premature opening of the foreign account at an early stage of development when the market is still incomplete. It is associated with high costs for the LDC economy. On the other hand, as development proceeds and market institutions develop, liberalisation of the foreign account can be successfully phased in. The case of the proper sequencing of financial integration is illustrated by the example of Taiwan.

The scenario this chapter has presented is tentative and not unlike Arrow's predicament: if the scenario works in practice, does it also work in theory? Further empirical work by the author examines whether the pattern between RER and growth characterises the rest of the countries for which micro-ICP data exist. Moreover, the intuition about nominal exchange rate devaluation and the RER, and the direction of causality from the RER to rates of growth of GDP need to be better embedded in standard theory.[15]

The unorthodox diagnosis of market incompleteness in foreign exchange (and trade) and the policy prescription of intervention (which systematically decreases with the level of development) will certainly be contested. It has some grounding in pragmatism and was consistent with development policy long before the mainstream view switched towards indiscriminate liberalisation. Moreover the precondition of good governance is strict, and a country should seriously consider its implications before it moves 'back into the future' with intervention.

Notes

1. This chapter draws on the author's forthcoming book *Exchange Rate Parity for Trade and Development: Theory, Tests and Case Studies* (London and New York: Cambridge University Press).
2. Besides the criterion of 20 per cent value of exports plus imports in total commodity expenditure, the alternative cut-off points of 10 per cent and 30 per cent were also used for experimentation. The ranking of the countries with respect to the RER did not change materially.
3. The corresponding gain that dollarisation represents for hard-currency countries is estimated at 0.5–1 per cent of GNP.
4. This improvement, however, can prove illusory. As long as the foreign exchange holdings of the Central Bank represent foreign currency liabilities to commercial banks, they should not be treated as net foreign assets – but they are! See Ramirez-Rojas (1985, p. 661).
5. For a graphic presentation of this dilemma, see *The Economist* (London), 9 April 1994.
6. See the Symposium at the World Bank on 'Currency Substitution and Currency Boards' (January 1992).
7. There was a small appreciation of the NT dollar in 1973, and a general appreciating trend after the introduction of the float in 1978.
8. For a detailed account of the monetary policy of Taiwan, see Chiu (1992) and Liu (1992).
9. It is estimated that the net productivity of capital was 25 per cent in the 1960s, 20 per cent in the 1970s and 15 per cent in the 1980s (Fry, 1989).
10. The estimated long-run GNP elasticity of the real demand for money is 1.7 (Chiu, 1992).
11. The ratio of M2 (money and deposits) to GNP was 9 per cent in 1955, 56 per cent in 1975, and 136 per cent in 1990. The ratio of broad money to GNP approached that of Japan in just two decades (Lundberg, 1979).
12. With the exception of treasury bills, all other money market instruments (including bankers' acceptances, certificates of deposits and commercial paper) increased by multiple factors for a few years in a row, in comparison with total loans, which increased at the rate of 20 per cent (Kuo, 1983, Ch. 15).
13. For a detailed chronology of the policy interventions in the Taiwan economy, see Li (1988).
14. For example, there still remains an overall limit in foreign investment in Taiwan's stock exchange (effectively about 7 per cent of the market's capitalisation); no more than one tenth of a company's stock can be owned

by foreigners; and the Central Bank drags its feet in processing investment applications from foreigners (US$4 billion worth were still pending in mid-1994).

15. These issues are handled in Yotopoulos (1995).

References

Arrow, Kenneth J. (1974) 'Limited Knowledge and Economic Analysis', *American Economic Review*, vol. 64 (March), pp. 1–10.

Chiu, Paul C. H. (1992) 'Money and Financial Markets: The Domestic Perspective', in Gustav Ranis (ed.), *Taiwan: From Developing to Mature Economy* (Boulder, CO: Westview Press), pp. 121–93.

Edwards, Sebastian (1989) *Real Exchange Rates, Devaluation, and Adjustment* (Cambridge, Mass.: MIT Press).

Edwards, Sebastian (1993) 'Openness, Trade Liberalization, and Growth in Developing Countries', *Journal of Economic Literature*, vol. 31 (September), pp. 1358–93.

Fischer, Stanley (1982) 'Seigniorage and the Case for a National Money', *Journal of Political Economy*, no. 2 (April), pp. 295–313.

Fischer, Stanley (1992) 'Seigniorage and Official Dollarization', in Nissan Liviatan (ed.) *Proceedings of a Conference on Currency Substitution and Currency Boards*, World Bank Discussion Paper No. 207, pp. 6–10.

Fry, Maxwell J. (1989) 'The Rate of Return to Taiwan's Capital Stock, 1961–1987,' *Hong Kong Economic Papers*, vol. 28, pp. 17–30.

Khan, Moshin S., Peter Montiel and Nadeem U. Haque (1990) 'Adjustment with Growth; Relating the Analytical Approaches of the IMF and the World Bank', *Journal of Development Economics*, vol. 32 (April), pp. 155–79.

Kravis, Irving B., A. Heston and R. Summers (1982) *World Product and Income: International Comparisons of Real Gross Product* (Baltimore, Md.: Johns Hopkins University Press).

Krueger, A. O. (1980) 'Trade Policy as an Input to Development', *American Economic Review*, vol. 70 (May 1980), pp. 288–92.

Kuo, Shirley W. Y. (1983) *The Taiwan Economy in Transition* (Boulder, CO: Westview Press).

Leamer, Edward F. (1983) 'Let's Take the Con out of Econometrics', *American Economic Review*, vol. 73 (March), pp. 31–43.

Leamer, Edward F. (1985) 'Sensitivity Analyses Would Help', *American Economic Review*, vol. 75 (June), pp. 308–13.

Levine, Ross, and David Renelt (1992) 'A Sensitivity Analysis of Cross-Country Growth Regressions', *American Economic Review*, vol. 82 (September), pp. 942–63.

Li, K. T. (1988), *The Evolution of Policy behind Taiwan's Development Success* (New Haven: Yale University Press).

Liu, Christina Y. (1992) 'Money and Financial Markets: The International Perspective', in Gustav Ranis (ed.) *Taiwan: From Developing to Mature Economy* (Boulder, CO: Westview Press), pp. 195–221.

Lundberg, Erik (1979) 'Fiscal and Monetary Policies', in Walter Galenson (ed.), *Economic Growth and Structural Change in Taiwan* (Ithaca: Cornell University Press), pp. 263–307.

Melvin, Michael (1988) 'The Dollarization of Latin America as a Market-enforced Monetary Reform', *Economic Development and Cultural Change*, vol. 36 (April), pp. 543–558.

Ramirez-Rojas, C. L. (1985) 'Currency Substitution in Argentina, Mexico and Uruguay', *IMF Staff Papers*, vol. 32 (December), pp. 627–67.

Scitovsky, Tibor (1985) 'Economic Development in Taiwan and South Korea: 1965–81', *Food Research Institute Studies*, vol. 19, no. 3, pp. 214–64.

Yotopoulos, Pan A. (1995) *Exchange Rate Parity for Trade and Development: Theory, Tests and Case Studies* (New York and London: Cambridge University Press, forthcoming).

7 The Austrian–Australian Approach (AAA) to Internal and External Stability

Emil-Maria Claassen

Internal stability is associated with price stability and can also be called 'internal equilibrium'. As employment is not the issue here for the sake of simplicity it will be assumed that full employment exists within a classical quantity-theoretical model. External stability coincides with the traditional notion of 'external equilibrium' and will be interpreted either in the form of an equilibrated trade balance or an equilibrated current account balance for a net debtor country whose interest payments require a trade balance surplus. External stability could also be conceived as a 'sustainable' current account deficit that is financed by 'sustainable' capital inflows.[1]

The Australian model goes back to the late 1950s, when some Australian economists emphasised the distinction between tradable and nontradable goods for a 'dependent' Economy of the size of Australia.[2] Since the prices of tradables are determined outside the country (which is the assumption of purchasing power parity), the relevant notion for the real exchange rate is the relative price of tradable to nontradable goods ($q = P_T/P_N$) or the 'internal terms of trade'. The following extract recalls the two traditional concepts of the real exchange rate.

> There are two variants of the real exchange rate. The older variant is the 'purchasing power parity' real exchange rate. This compares the domestic price of a representative basket of goods and services with the price of the same basket at world prices converted into local currency. It is, in effect, a measure of overall competitiveness. It can be approximated by comparing changes in consumer prices or changes in labor costs. It does not distinguish between traded and nontraded goods, because it implicitely assumes that their prices move together.

> The other variant, which has recently come to be emphasized, compares the price of *nontradables* in the national economy (typically services and labor, whose prices can be proxied by the GDP deflator) with world prices of *tradables* (foreign wholesale price indexes, for instance, or the import and export price indexes for the national economy). For a small country that cannot affect the world price of traded goods, this variant provides a measure of the changing incentives to move in and out of production and consumption of nontradable and tradable goods. For instance, a depreciating real exchange rate raises the relative price of tradables, encouraging more production and less consumption of import substitutes and exports. This is the interpretation that is most useful to bear in mind when looking at the effect of changing trade and macroeconomic policies on the structure of incentives and on the current account of the balance of payments (World Bank, 1987, p. 101).[3]

Any external 'disequilibrium' can only be eliminated by combining expenditure-reducing policies with expenditure-switching policies, where the latter is brought about by a real depreciation in terms of a rise in q. The first section of this chapter presents a short summary of this traditional policy mix.

The Austrian approach – which could also be named the Dutch approach – refers to the deliberate policy choice of a 'fixed-fixed' exchange rate with respect to the German mark as the monetary stability anchor over the last fifteen years ($q = P_T/P_N = E_0P^*_T/P_N$, where E is the nominal exchange rate and P^*_T the foreign price level of tradable goods).[4] Austria – and the Netherlands – did better than any other member of the former European Monetary System by imposing an exchange rate margin around the central parity of ± 0.11 per cent instead of the traditional ± 2.25 per cent, and it never devalued in nominal terms. The necessity of a real depreciation in the case of an 'external disequilibrium' must be handled by a fall in P_N or by a lower rise in P_N than in P^*P_T with the policy tool of monetary restrictions. This issue will be dealt with in the second section ('Money Market'), while the third section ('Labour Market') describes the constraints on wage behaviour of the Austrian policy mix.

The AAA is conducted mainly in geometrical terms, and the model is applicable to any small open economy as there is no economic theory for countries A, B and C. The approach can be applied to an industrialised country as well as to a developing or post-socialist country.[5] The factual difference between both kinds of economies lies in the degree of capital mobility. For industrialised countries, capital mobility (or the substitution of financial assets) is good in that a current account deficit does not constitute an external constraint, at least for the short run. For the other economies it is likely that access to international credit markets is rather limited and that external stability is a concern even for the short run.

POLICIES FOR REDUCING AND SWITCHING EXPENDITURE

Since any trade-balance deficit corresponds to the gap between absorption, A, (expenditure on goods by domestic residents) and domestic production, y, (GDP), an equilibrium in the trade balance can only be attained if this gap disappears, either through an increase in production or through a reduction in expenditure. To the extent that production is given, the necessary or primary condition for external stability is reduction in expenditure. The issue of real depreciation arises only if the expenditure-reducing policy creates an excess supply in the domestic market for nontradable goods, which is generally the case. The excess supply can be eliminated by a fall in the relative price of N, defined as real depreciation, which switches domestic expenditure from T to N and domestic production from N to T.

The policy mix is summarised in Fig. 7.1, which is derived from Salter's (1959) exposition of the Australian model and is often used in the literature on tradable/nontradable goods; for instance Dornbusch (1975). The production possibility curve is illustrated by PP. The economy's production is assumed to be on some point of the production possibility curve, which reflects the assumption of full employment. The initial equilibrium point for production should be P_a where the income line y_1y_1 is tangent ('internal equilibrium'). However the absorption line A_1A_1 is higher and the corresponding consumption point is at C_a – which is actually the 'absorption' point. At C_a an indifference curve (not drawn) is tangent to the A_1A_1 line, whose slope indicates the level of the real exchange rate (q_1). The distance C_aP_a represents the trade-balance deficit. While the consumption of N corresponds to its production, there is an excess demand for T that is satisfied by international trade. The trade-balance deficit is identical to the excess of absorption over GDP ($A_1 - y_1$).[6]

There are three scenarios for attaining external equilibrium, and all three have in common the reduction of expenditure. Assuming that government reduces its expenditure ($-\Delta G$), the target of this restric-

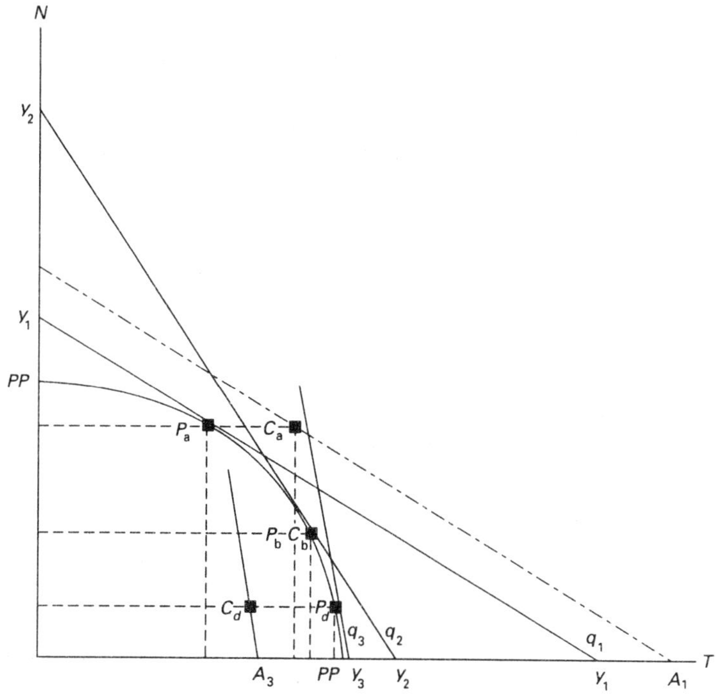

Notes: The trade-balance deficit is P_aC_a. The reduction in expenditures (A) plus real depreciation (q) produce an equilibrated trade balance (P_b) or a trade-balance surplus (P_d).

Figure 7.1 Policy mix for external equilibrium: expenditure-reducing and expenditure-switching policies

tive fiscal policy is to realise either an equilibrated trade balance ($TB = 0$) or a trade-balance surplus ($TB > 0$).

$-\Delta G = -\Delta G_T$ for $TB = 0$. Total absorption A_1 is reduced to the level of GDP (y_1). By assuming that the decline in expenditure concerns only the purchase of tradable goods, the consumption point of tradable goods (C_a) now coincides with the production point of tradable goods (P_a) *without any real depreciation*. The trade-balance deficit disappears. This rather 'academic' case illustrates the possibility that external equilibrium can be brought about without any change in the real exchange rate.

$-\Delta G = -(\Delta G_T + \Delta G_N)$ for $TB = 0$. The more realistic assumption is that government curtails its expenditure by the same amount as in the former case, but now on tradable *and* nontradable goods. Again, $-\Delta G_T$) directly improves the trade balance, while $-\Delta G_N$ creates an excess supply in the market for nontradable goods. The relative price of P_N has to decline from q_1 to q_2 and the consumption point, which is now C_b, coincides with the new production point, P_b, involving $TB = 0$.[7] The additional improvement in the trade balance results from the real depreciation, which provokes a higher domestic production of T at the expense of N for satisfying the switch in private consumption from imports to import substitutes.

$-\Delta G = -(\Delta G_T + \Delta G_N)$ for $TB > 0$. The reduction of public expenditure is stronger (from A_1 to A_3) for creating a trade-balance surplus under the hypothesis that the concerned country is a net debtor with respect to the rest of the world and that it desires to equilibrate its current account – or it is forced to do so in the absence of international credit to finance its interest payments. The new market value of GDP is y_3 and the production point is at P_d. Total absorption A_3 lies below GDP, implying the consumption point C_d. The distance C_dP_d represents the trade-balance surplus which is equal to the difference of y_3 (GDP) minus A_3 (GNP), reflecting the amount of net interest payments abroad. As a matter of course, the real depreciation rate is stronger (q_3) than in the former case.[8]

MONEY MARKET: INTERNAL STABILITY WITH ALTERNATIVE MONETARY ANCHORS

The real depreciation required for $TB = 0$ or $TB > 0$ can be realised by a nominal depreciation (floating exchange rates or nominal devaluation) or by a decline in the general domestic price level (fixed rates).

For a given money supply and interest rate, there is only one general price level that realises equilibrium in the money market. This precise equilibrium level of P_0 is represented by the rectangular hyperbola $LM(P_0)$ in Fig. 7.2. The equilibrium value P_0 can be accompanied by various combinations of P_T and P_N. P is defined as the geometrical average of P_T and P_N ($P = P_T^a P_N^b$) where a (b) represents the weight of tradables (nontradables) among all GDP goods. Any situation to the right of LM reflects an excess demand in the money market. The initial monetary equilibrium is at the intersection point A of the $0q_0$ ray (whose

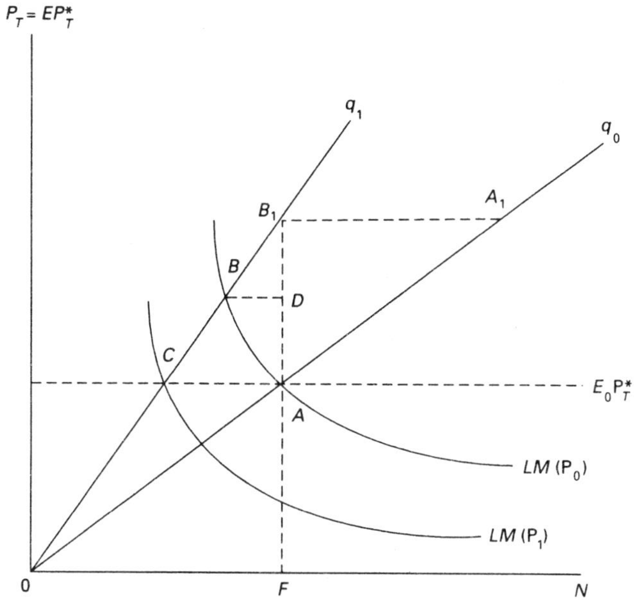

Notes: The slope of the $0q$ ray measures the real exchange rate. The rectangular hyperbola P_0 illustrates the equilibrium level of the general price level for different combinations of P_T and P_N. For the real exchange rate q_0, the monetary equilibrium is at point *A*. The monetary mechanism of a real depreciation (q_1) is as follows. Under floating exchange rates (point *B*) there is a nominal depreciation of *AD* and a decline of P_N which assures the maintenance of the price level at P_0. Under fixed exchange rates (point *C*) P_N has to fall, implying a decline in the price level to P_1, to be realised by a lower quantity of money.

Figure 7.2 Real depreciation under fixed and floating exchange rates

slope indicates the size of the real exchange rate) with the *LM* (P_0) schedule. A real depreciation is indicated by the rotation of ray $0q_0$ towards $0q_1$.

Floating Nominal Exchange Rates (or Devaluation)

There are two possibilities for a nominal depreciation that could bring about real depreciation. The first case concerns point *B* with a nominal depreciation rate of *AD*/*AF* (assuming $P_T^* = 1$). At point *D* the price level has risen via an increase in P_T. Consequently there is an excess demand for money, which pushes the price level downward. Since P_T cannot fall because it is linked to EP_T^*, only P_N can fall. A decline in P_N by the amount *BD* is necessary for equilibrating the money market. The rate of real depreciation is higher than the rate of nominal depreciation and results from an increase in P_T (via *E*) and from a fall in P_N.

The second case of the nominal depreciation is represented by point B_1. The nominal depreciation rate is AB_1/AF. Such a higher rate of nominal depreciation takes place when one operates with the assumption that prices of nontradable goods are rigid downwards. At B_1, the rate of real depreciation is identical to the rate of nominal depreciation. However the general price level (*P*) has to be higher. In order to create an equilibrium in the money market, the supply of money has to be increased so that the $LM(P_0)$ schedule shifts through point B_1. In contrast with the first case, the second case of nominal depreciation is inflationary.[9]

Fixed Nominal Exchange Rates

In such a regime the price level of tradable goods is not modifiable and it remains at the horizontal dotted line $E_0P_T^*$. The only possibility of bringing about a real depreciation is through a deflationary monetary policy that shifts the $LM(P_0)$ schedule towards $LM(P_1)$. This deflationary policy will only induce a fall in P_N since P_T remains constant (point *C*). Thus the relative fall in P_N will be stronger than the relative fall in *P* and *M*, respectively. If nontradable goods constitute one half of total goods ($b = 0.5$) and a real depreciation rate of 20 per cent is required for *q*, the general price level has to fall by 10 per cent. The rate of monetary contraction will be lower (10 per cent) than the rate of the real depreciation.

By comparing both nominal exchange rate regimes, one can come to the following conclusion as far as price stability is concerned. The point of departure is the necessity of a change in the real exchange rate. By comparing point *B* (floating rates) with point *C* (fixed rates), point *B* is realised with a constant price level (P_0) and point *C* with a variable price level (P_1). In this particular aspect, floating nominal exchange rates could more easily guarantee price level stability than fixed nominal exchange rates.

LABOUR MARKET: POLICY MIX AND WAGE BEHAVIOUR

As we have seen, real depreciation can be brought about in both exchange rate regimes, either by nominal depreciation under floating exchange rates, where the nominal anchor is the quantity of money, or by a fall in the general price level through a reduction in the quantity of money under fixed exchange rates, where the nominal anchor is the exchange-rate peg. However, whether ΔE or $-\Delta M$ results in a real depreciation depends crucially on the wage behaviour in the labour market.

From the point of view of labour demands by firms, the level of labour input is determined by the equalisation of the nominal wage rate (W) with the marginal product of labour (MPL) evaluated by its market price (P). This traditional formula of profit maximisation should hold in both production sectors, T and N:

$$W_T = P_T\, MPL_T \qquad W_N = P_N\, MPL_N \tag{7.1.}$$

Under product competition, prices should reflect marginal cost. With a fixed sector-specific capital stock in both production sectors, marginal costs are marginal labour costs, which are also called marginal unit labour costs:[10]

$$P_T = W_T/MPL_T \qquad P_N = W_N/MPL_N \tag{7.2.}$$

Floating Exchange Rates

Under floating exchange rates there is a rise in P_T ($\Delta P_T = \Delta E \times P^*_T$) and a fall in P_N for the maintenance of a stable general price level. Again, total domestic production remains unchanged (hypothesis of full employment) while its composition must be modified in favour of T. Assuming homogeneous labour qualifications between T and N, nominal wages are the same in both sectors ($W_T = W_N = W$), since otherwise labour migration would take place between both production sectors. However real wages (represented by the marginal product of labour MPL) are likely to differ as the consequence of different stocks of capital in T and N. Consequently, by using both parts of equation 7.2 we obtain the inequalities

$$P_T > W/MPL_T \qquad P_N < W/MPL_N \tag{7.2a}$$

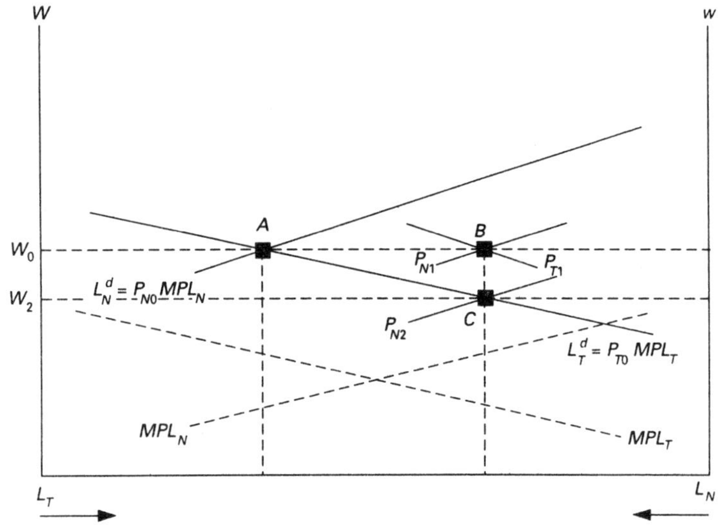

Notes: The initial equilibrium is at point *A*. Real depreciation increases labour input in *T* and lowers labour input in *N*. Under floating exchange rates, nominal wages remain constant (point *B*). Under fixed exchange rates, nominal wages fall (point *C*).

Figure 7.3a Labour market for *T* and *N*

In the *T* sector prices lie above marginal cost and in the N sector they are below marginal cost. More labour will be drawn from production sector *N* to production sector *T*, implying a lower MPL_T and a higher MPL_N, so that the equalities of equation 7.2 have been attained again.

The above argument can be understood more easily by consulting Figures 7.3a and 7.3b, which illustrate the labour market in terms of equation 7.1 for $W_T = W_N = W$. L_T^d, measured from left to right, represents the demand for labour in the production sector of tradable goods. Similarly, L_N^d, measured from right to left, is the demand schedule for labour in the production sector of nontradables. The initial equilibrium in the labour market is at point *A* with a low labour input in *T* and a high labour input in *N*. The real depreciation is necessary for producing more *T* with a higher labour input L_T at the cost of the labour input L_N. Under floating exchange rates, the value component

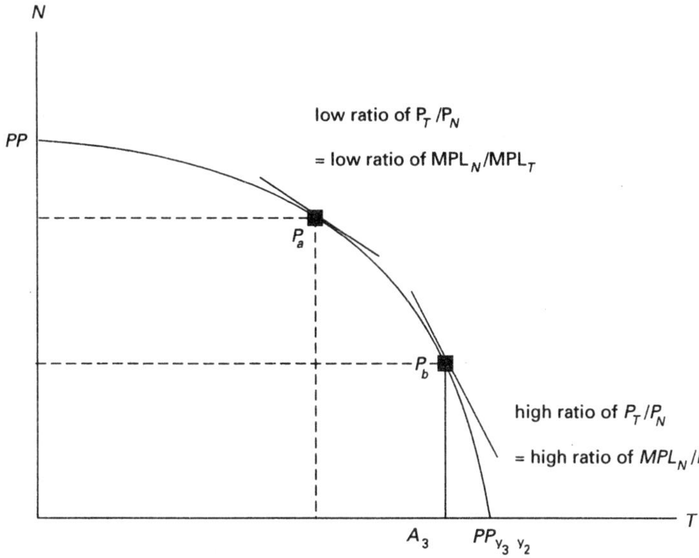

Notes: From the point of view of the supply side, the impact of the real depreciation on the production of *T* and *N* is the movement from P_a to P_b.

Figure 7.3b Production possibility curve

of the marginal product of L_T increases to P_{T1}, and, correspondingly the value component of the marginal product of L_N falls to P_{N1}, so that the general price level and the nominal wage level remain constant (point *B*).

Equation 7.2 can also be written in terms of the real exchange rate (for $W_T = W_N = W$):

$$q = P_T/P_N = MPL_N/MPL_T \tag{7.2b}$$

From the point of view of production cost, the real exchange rate has to correspond to the above ratio of labour productivities. A real depreciation involves a higher ratio of MPL_N/MPL_T, which is brought about by labour migration from *N* to *T*, as illustrated in Fig. 7.3b.

Fixed Exchange Rates

Under fixed exchange rates there is a decline from P_{N0} to P_{N2}, and consequently there is also a decline in P, which involves a fall in nominal wages from W_0 to W_2 (point C in Fig. 7.3a). With downward wage rigidities, unemployment could be avoided or attenuated in one or both of the following cases.

1. The anchor currency is slightly inflationary in terms of P^*_T. ΔP^*_T will be transmitted to ΔP_T. If the rise in P_T is equivalent to the decline in P_N that is required by the real depreciation from q_0 to q_1, there will be no necessity for a fall in P_N. As a matter of course, the general price level would rise and an accommodating monetary policy would be necessary. In terms of Fig. 7.2, the rise in P^*_T should be from point A to point B_1.
2. There is labour productivity growth that is not compensated for by increases in the nominal wage rate. In terms of Fig. 7.3a, both schedules of the marginal productivity of labour (drawn as dotted lines), MPL_N and MPL_T, have to shift upward by the distance of BC to the extent that this distance reflects the same productivity growth in both sectors.

One or both of these conditions are essential if the Austrian model of the Hartwährungspolitik is to be applied to other small, open economies whose priority is price stability.

Notes

1. The sustainable current account deficit could be defined by a net debt/GDP ratio that remains constant (D/y = constant). Consequently D can rise by the growth rate of GDP. However, in the long run the real interest rate (the foreign one, namely r^*) has to lie above the real growth rate (g). In that case, one part of the interest payments will be paid by the additional indebtedness, namely $\Delta D = gD$. The other part, $(r^* - g)D$ must be financed by a trade balance surplus. If the interest rate is equal to the growth rate, the total volume of interest payments will always be financed by an additional indebtedness and the debtor country will never reduce its debt. Under these conditions the creditor country will refuse to grant any additional credit.
2. For more recent descriptions of the Australian model (known also as the nontraded goods model, dependent economy model and Scandinavian model)

see Edwards (1989), Caves, Frankel and Jones (1990, chap. 19) and Burda and Wyplosz (1993, chap. 7).

3. World Bank Report (Oxford University Press, 1987), p. 101.
4. Instead of the German mark, Austria could have chosen another stable foreign currency, such as the Singapore dollar. The exchange rate has remained more or less equal to one Singaporean dollar for one German mark over the last twenty years. See Claassen (1992). However another criterion for the adequate choice of a foreign currency as monetary anchor is the trade weight. The transmission of P_T^* on the Austria level of P_T is stronger when the German mark is nominal anchor than in the case of the Singapore dollar.
5. For large countries such as the US, Brazil or Russia, the weight of foreign tradable goods in all other tradable goods is by far lower, so the exchange rate plays a less important role.
6. If, for instance, $(A_1 - y_1)$ is equal to the government budget deficit, the latter will provoke a trade balance deficit of identical size.
7. With respect to the demand side for nontradables, if real income is measured in terms of internationally traded goods, which is the value standard for small-open economies, real depreciation not only provokes the substitution effect in favour of nontradables (at the expense of tradables), it also produces the income effect, which is negative for the demand of both categories of goods.

   Total nominal income is $Y = P_T S_T + P_N S_N$, where S is supply. By dividing the equation by P_T and defining real income (y) as Y/P_T, we obtain $y = S_T + (P_N/P_T) S_N$. A decline in P_N lowers y; see the reduction of GDP from y_1 to y_2 on the horizontal axis in Figure 7.1. The substitution effect of a real depreciation increases the demand for nontradables and its negative income effect lowers it.
8. It should be mentioned that there is yet another price mechanism for the market clearing of nontradable goods, which would involve a lower real depreciation rate. The expenditure-reducing policy had created an excess supply of nontradables. To the extent that the concerned country is not integrated in the international financial markets, its interest rate (r) will not be strictly linked to the international one (imperfect capital mobility) and it will have some autonomy on r. Lower public expenditure in the sense of a reduction in the government budget deficit could produce a lower domestic interest rate. The subsequent negative crowding-out effect on private expenditure (higher private demand for T and N) would decrease the excess supply of N and require a lower real depreciation.

   There could be a very particular case where the interest rate mechanism produces a total (negative) crowding-out effect – lower public expenditure and, correspondingly, higher private expenditure – such that the gap $A_1 - y_1$ and also the trade balance deficit continue to exist. Fortunately this enigma can be solved. In the preceding period when government pursued a high budget deficit, implying a high domestic interest rate, the total (positive) crowding-out effect (higher public expenditure being compensated by lower private expenditure) would also have been in action such that total absorption remained equal to GDP with the consequence that $TB = 0$.

When there is complete capital immobility, the domestic economy works like a closed economy. Since the balance of payments coincides with the trade balance, any bond-financed budget deficit would be fully financed by domestic savings via a rise in the domestic interest rate (total crowding-out effect via the interest rate mechanism). The fall in private outlay for consumption and investment corresponds exactly to the rise in public expenditure. This model of an economy represents the ideal type of an open economy for the proponents of capital controls such as Liviatan (1980), Tobin (1982) and Dornbusch (1986) since real internal shocks would not be transmitted to foreign countries via the real exchange rate. Note that with Ricardian equivalence, this switch would take place without any rise in the interest rate.

9. We would like to mention also the case where a nominal depreciation-cum-excessive monetary expansion leaves the real exchange rate unchanged. Again, there is a nominal depreciation from A to B_1. However the money supply is not expanded to a quantity that produces the price level at B_1, but to a still higher volume of money realising the price level A_1. In that case the real exchange rate remains unaltered. Such a situation could emerge when wage earners in the production sector of nontradables evaluate their real wages also in terms of P_T. To the extent that they want to maintain their real wages, there will be higher nominal wage claims and the nominal wage costs increase in the sector of nontradables. The Central Bank increases the money supply beyond B_1 in order to avoid unemployment.
10. From the point of view of production costs, the real exchange rate can be reformulated as $q = (P_T/P_N) = (W_T/W_N)\ (MPL_N/MPL_T)$.

References

Burda, Michael and Charles Wyplosz (1993) *Macroeconomics. A European Text* (Oxford: Oxford University Press).

Caves, Richard E., Jeffrey A. Frankel and Ronald W. Jones (1990) *World Trade and Payments*, 5th edn (New York: Harper Collins).

Claassen Emil-Maria (1992) 'Financial Liberalisation and Its Impact on Domestic Stabilization Policies: Singapore and Malaysia', *Weltwirtschaftliches Archiv*, vol. 128, no. 1 pp. 36–67.

Dornbusch, Rudiger (1975) 'Exchange Rates and Fiscal Policy in Popular Model of International Trade', *American Economic Review*, December, pp. 859–71.

Dornbusch, Rudiger (1986) 'Flexible Exchange Rates and Excess Capital Mobility', *Brooking Papers on Economic Activity*, no. 1, pp. 209–26.

Edwards, Sebastian (1989) *Real Exchange Rates, Devaluation, and Adjustment: Exchange Rate Policy in Developing Countries* (Cambridge, MA: MIT Press).

Liviatan, N. (1980) 'Anti-Inflationary Monetary Policy and the Capital-Import Tax', *Warwick Economic Research Papers*, no. 171.

Salter, W. E. (1959) 'Internal and External Balance: The Role of Price and Expenditure Effects', *Economic Record*, vol. 35 (August), pp. 226–38.

Tobin, James (1982) 'A Proposal for Monetary Reform', in J. Tobin (ed.), *Essays in Economic Theory and Policy* (Cambridge, MA: MIT Press).

World Bank (1987) *World Bank Report 1987* (Oxford: Oxford University Press).

8 International Borrowing Strategy and Sovereign Creditworthiness

Ronald L. Solberg

The severe costs incurred by developing countries as a result of the debt crisis in the 1980s attest to the need for a systematic sovereign financial management strategy. This chapter offers a general set of financial axioms based on the cash-flow characteristics of foreign borrowing and is highlighted by examples drawn from the experience of the Baker-15 countries from 1972 to 1986. These financial guidelines support the efficient application of external financial resources to further structural transformation and other development goals.

Foreign borrowing can be used for a variety of expenditures: replenishing international reserves, repaying financial obligations and purchasing either imports or domestic goods and services to augment production, consumption or investment. An essential objective of foreign borrowing, however, is to supplement domestic savings to fund more investment and expand the productive capacity of the economy. Expanding the country's capital stock will increase the production of tradable goods which, in turn, can be sold abroad to establish the basis for a sustained rise in living standards while servicing the foreign debt borrowed to effect such an improvement. Recent successful examples of this growth-cum-indebtedness cycle are provided by Taiwan, China, Malaysia and the Republic of Korea, which after several decades of foreign borrowing as net debtors, became net creditors to the world in the 1980s.

Once a country has become a net debtor, its gross borrowing requirement (GBR) equals the sum of the current account deficit, the scheduled amortisation or principal repayments, the reduction of other external liabilities, the extension of overseas credit, capital flight and other financial asset acquisitions. The gross repayment source (GRS), defined as the sum of new external borrowing and international reserve usage, must be adequate to pay for these net expenditures so that payment arrears are avoided.[1]

In the early stages of a country's development, a plethora of investment projects coupled with a dearth of domestic savings virtually ensures a current account deficit. This shortfall means that debt service payments – interest and amortisation – cannot be financed from current export receipts; nor is a debtor country likely to possess abundant international reserves, which leaves external borrowing as the primary means of payment. Therefore the borrower must achieve a positive net financial transfer (NFT) by ensuring that gross loan disbursements exceed interest and principal payments. In effect, this capitalises interest and principal payments. The net financial transfer must be large enough to fund the remaining items which combine to account for the gross borrowing requirement.

A stable roll-over process wherein new loan disbursements exceed debt service payments is the first requirement needed to achieve a positive net financial transfer. Foreign borrowing must be large enough and sustained long enough to fund resource needs resulting from the growth-cum-indebtedness cycle.[2] These requirements must continue until a country eliminates its long-term constraint to creditworthiness by structurally transforming its economy so that its current account shifts from a secular deficit to surplus. If the GBR is allowed to become too large at any time during this extended period, then the stock of external debt will grow too quickly which, in turn, sends a signal to the financial markets that creditworthiness is declining. External credit rationing may result, forcing a negative NFT and a disruption to the development process. This was the experience of the Baker-15 countries during the 1980s.

Continued access to external financing is largely a function of the market's perception of the creditworthiness of the borrower. Once actual or perceived creditworthiness of the borrower has deteriorated, access to new borrowing is likely to be progressively restricted or even entirely curtailed. If other sources of external funding are unavailable and international reserves are inadequate, then a negative net financial transfer will result, signalling that the roll-over process has failed and the liquidity constraint is binding. Hard decisions must be made to allocate scarce foreign-exchange revenue to competing claims. Depending on the severity of the cash-flow crunch, the alternatives will require some combination of economic stabilisation, a less ambitious development plan and even arrears on debt-service payments.

A country's financial performance is determined by: (1) its economic 'profile' or the initial conditions that affect its vulnerability to economic shocks and circumscribe its policy options; (2) its past economic policy decisions; and (3) perhaps most importantly, its current policy stance. For example, when changes in the global financial environment increase the debtor's GBR, the country's policy makers should consider reducing the endogenous element of its external borrowings as a policy response. Moreover, the terms of debt repayment should be managed so as to minimise their volatility and ensure a positive financial transfer. If the GBR grows too quickly, whether due to economic policy errors or market shocks, there is a risk that access to external financing could be curtailed. To avoid the consequences of this cash-flow squeeze, a sovereign borrower should set external financial policies using a systematic strategy.

Sustained sovereign creditworthiness requires a strategy of external debt management involving a set of financial policies consistent with the objective of long-term development.[3] Since this set of financial policies must ensure that overseas financing is adequate in variety and amount to finance industrialisation, it should be formulated with an understanding of the mechanics of debt finance and the determinants of international lending to developing countries.

THE STOCK REQUIREMENTS OF EXTERNAL DEBT

Maturity Structure

Assuming a debtor country has unrestricted access to new credit along the full range of the yield curve, the choice of debt maturity will be determined by such issues as: the interest rate across the curve; the purpose for which the monies are used (for example trade finance, project finance, a bridging loan); and certain supply-side considerations, including the debtor's relationship with its creditors.

While a debtor should attempt to minimise the overall cost of its external borrowing, this should be done within the constraint of actively managing the maturity profile of its debt portfolio. Certain transactions like financing trade with letters of credit have standard maturities and are self-liquidating. For other transactions such as project finance, care should be taken to match the maturity of new borrowings with the gestation period of the investment being financed. A debtor is ill advised to utilise short-term maturities to finance long-term projects. The resulting maturity transformation can cause problems of illiquidity when roll-over or refinancing is attempted.

Despite attempts to correctly manage the debt's maturity structure, a bunching of the principal repayments can result from seasonality in borrowing requirements, a negligent borrowing strategy or resistance in the external capital markets. For example, when new borrowing at longer-term maturities is unobtainable in the quantity preferred, the debtor will be forced to issue short-term maturities (considered by most lenders to be inherently less risky than longer-term maturities) or to spend international reserves. None of these policy responses to tightened credit market conditions is particularly attractive. When the maturity structure of a sovereign's debt profile is shortened, debt service payments increase and the roll-over requirements rise.[4] Since a larger GBR results, the debtor's vulnerability to a liquidity crisis is heightened. Once bunching has occurred, it is advisable to use a preemptive strategy of timely refinancing to smooth out the principal repayments.

Currency Composition

Determining the currency denomination of new borrowing is an equally important decision for the sovereign policy maker. When a country issues foreign-currency-denominated debt, its effective cost not only equals the usual principal and interest payments but also includes the foreign-exchange translation gain or loss resulting from the change in the value of that currency relative to either the borrower's own currency or its export-invoice currency. This additional cost element of foreign borrowing can be a volatile and potentially large portion of the ultimate cost of foreign borrowing.

By the mid-1980s, after five years of consistent US dollar appreciation, many developing countries were issuing a higher portion of their external debt in currencies other than the dollar. This strategy was thought to be prudent since most non-dollar debt carried a lower interest rate; and it further held the prospect of being repaid in depreciated currency units, owing to the outlook for the continued appreciation of the US dollar which for many countries is their principal export-invoice currency.

When the value of the US dollar began its decline in February 1985, the dollar equivalent of a borrower's debt issued in non-dollar currencies (such as the Japanese yen and the German mark) increased commensurately. For example in 1986 the US dollar depreciated over 21 per cent against the Deutschmark and similarly against other key currencies. The World Bank (1988) reported that for the 109 countries in the Debtor Reporting System, total nominal debt increased by 7.6 per cent in 1986. Approximately 5.3 per cent of this increase was due to the translation loss associated with the depreciation of the dollar. This unanticipated increase in external indebtedness amounted to over US$50 billion for this group of countries in that year alone.

When a net translation loss occurs on the sovereign balance sheet, more than a mere accounting loss is sustained. Additional domestic resources are required to retire this larger liability; not because the debtor has issued additional debt and received more imported goods and services, but simply because of exchange-rate fluctuations.

To manage this risk, the currency composition of a country's debt service payments schedule should match the currency composition of its stream of foreign-exchange earnings. If this is not possible to achieve – resulting in residual currency translation risk – then the use of hedging instruments (for example currency swaps, options or futures) should be considered. Although a perfect hedging vehicle does not exist, these instruments can help reduce exposure to market risk. For stronger debtors, the loss resulting from the unhedged currency risk can be more easily absorbed. For other countries whose capacity to adjust is hampered by greater structural constraints, however, the use of hedging vehicles is an even more important strategy to mitigate this shock and reduce losses. The interested reader should consult Grumball (1987) for a full treatment of hedging and arbitrage strategies, using these and other derivative products.

Creditor Composition: Official versus Commercial

It is important to consider the creditor composition of external debt inasmuch as the terms of repayment for debt owed to official creditors are usually lower than those on debt owed to commercial creditors. According to the World Bank (1988) the average interest rate paid by all developing countries on new official commitments during 1980 to 1986 was 6.7 per cent. The average rate paid by all developing countries on new commitments from private creditors during the same period was significantly higher at 10.9 per cent.

Not only did the average interest cost of private debt exceed that of public debt, but the amortisation rate (or principal repayment) was also higher. This occurred because both the average grace period (that is, the number of years before principal repayment begins) and the maturity were shorter for commercial debt (4.1 and 9.6 years, respectively) than was the case for official debt (5.7 and 22.2 years, respectively).

Since policy makers should attempt to minimise total borrowing costs, credit lines from official creditors should be fully utilised before comparable forms of credit are drawn from private creditors. Recognising that the growth of official lending throughout the 1970s lagged relative to both the growth of commercial credit and international trade flows, new disbursements from this source were inadequate. While they have assumed a larger role during the 1980s and 1990s, official creditors may have been undercapitalised in the 1970s and even today remain constrained by the prohibition of leveraging asset growth off their capital base.

While the official creditor can offer credit to developing countries at concessional rates, many of the financial instruments required by a sovereign borrower for prudent external debt management are unavailable from this source. Moreover some of the credit extended by official lenders is compensatory, the disbursements of which is contingent upon debtor policy actions or performance criteria. Hence certain financial products and services may only be available from a private commercial lender or because of less stringent conditions may be more appealing. Therefore, while attractive from a cost perspective, credit from official sources remains insufficient both in terms of product mix, conditions and amount. It is for these reasons that a sovereign debt portfolio should be diversified by source of creditor.

External Debt Ratios

The stock of disbursed external debt measured against GDP and export revenue are both common indicators of sovereign creditworthiness. They are direct measures of leverage in the sovereign balance sheet, reflecting the country's past reliance on foreign borrowing. Owing to their use by commercial and official creditors, it is important that the debtor actively manages its GBR so that foreign borrowing and debt growth remain moderate. The more closely this goal is adhered to, the more likely it is that externally-perceived creditworthiness will remain favourable, ensuring continuous access to and an adequate supply of external credit.

It is preferable for the debtor to use the ratio of debt-to-exports rather than debt-to-GDP for its policy planning since the former indicator incorporates the export promotion bias in the debtor's development strategy – an element that is crucial to its creditworthiness. This was borne out during a critical period for the Republic of Korea, which, during the late 1970s and early 1980s had a higher level of disbursed debt and debt-to-GNP ratio than did the Philippines. Korea's debt-export ratio, however, was considerably lower than that of the Philippines.

Table 8.1 External debt of Baker-15 Countries (US$ millions, unless otherwise stated)[1]

	1972	*1973*	*1974*	*1975*	*1976*	*1977*	*1978*	*1979*	*1980*	*1981*	*1982*	*1983*	*1984*	*1985*	*1986*
Total debt:															
Total nominal debt (US $)	3650.0	4410.9	5570.6	6517.5	8264.4	10267.2	12442.6	15387.7	18855.2	22917.2	25546.6	27545.4	28656.2	30723.6	31863.1
% Change in total nominal debt	19.3	20.8	26.3	17.0	26.8	24.2	21.2	23.7	22.5	21.5	11.5	7.8	4.0	7.2	3.7
Total real debt[2]	76.4	67.6	54.4	66.3	79.9	82.0	100.5	101.5	100.0	127.7	151.3	170.9	226.2	286.0	372.6
% Change in total real debt	14.8	−11.5	−19.4	21.7	20.5	2.6	22.7	1.0	−1.5	27.7	18.5	12.9	32.4	26.4	30.3
Maturity profile:															
Medium and long-term debt (% of total debt)	71.9	72.1	71.9	71.3	70.3	70.3	74.8	73.5	72.4	71.7	73.1	78.7	80.8	81.5	86.6
Growth rate of medium and long-term debt (%)	18.4	20.8	22.2	15.5	27.2	29.8	38.0	23.6	19.1	20.7	14.0	18.4	7.1	9.2	12.8
Short-term debt (% of total debt)[3]	28.1	27.9	28.1	28.7	29.7	29.7	25.2	26.5	27.6	28.3	26.9	21.3	19.2	18.5	13.4
Growth rate of short-term debt (%)	23.0	19.3	25.8	18.7	35.0	31.1	11.9	35.3	36.3	27.0	7.4	−7.6	−5.2	5.9	−12.7
Creditor composition:															
Private nonguaranteed debt (% of total debt)[4]	54.3	53.3	51.5	49.2	47.7	46.8	42.9	45.1	48.3	50.8	47.8	38.1	33.1	27.1	20.1
Public debt (% of total debt)[5]	44.7	45.9	47.8	49.5	50.2	51.6	56.0	54.0	50.8	48.2	50.8	59.2	63.7	69.2	75.8
Use of IMF funds (% of total debt)	1.0	0.8	0.8	1.2	2.1	1.6	1.1	0.9	0.9	1.0	1.4	2.8	3.2	3.8	4.0

Debt burden:															
Total nominal debt (US $)	3650.0	4410.9	5570.6	6517.5	8264.4	10267.2	12442.6	15387.7	18855.2	22917.2	25546.6	27545.4	28656.2	30723.6	31863.1
International reserves (US $)[6]	784.7	1258.8	2000.1	1870.9	2203.3	2468.3	2944.5	4221.9	4618.6	3645.2	2707.8	2597.8	2597.2	3224.9	3119.7
Net debt (US $)[7]	2865.3	3152.2	3570.5	4646.6	6061.1	7798.9	9498.1	11165.8	14236.6	19271.9	22838.9	24948.2	25431.3	27320.6	28743.4
Total debt/exports	2.7	2.3	1.9	2.5	2.6	2.7	2.8	2.6	2.4	3.0	3.6	3.9	3.8	4.4	5.0
Net debt/exports	2.1	1.7	1.4	1.9	2.0	2.2	2.2	1.9	1.9	2.5	3.2	3.6	3.5	3.9	4.5
Short-term debt/imports in months)[8]	7.4	6.8	4.6	4.5	5.7	6.2	5.7	6.8	7.3	8.4	10.7	9.9	8.7	8.0	5.4
International reserves/ imports (in months)	5.1	6.1	5.7	4.8	5.7	5.2	5.4	5.6	4.4	3.4	2.5	3.5	5.4	5.6	4.8

Notes:

1. The numbers represent the arithmetic averages of the respective variables for the 'Baker 15' countries; Argentina, Bolivia, Brazil, Chile, Colombia, Cote d'Ivoire, Ecuador, Mexico, Morocco, Nigeria, Peru, Philippines, Uruguay, Venezuela, Yugoslavia.
2. The real debt has been computed as the nominal debt deflated by the unit value of exports, and indexed as 100 in 1980.
3. Short-term debt includes the use of IMF funds.
4. Short-term maturities are assumed to be entirely private nonguaranteed debt.
5. Public debt is assumed to consist only of medium and long-term maturities.
6. International reserves are defined as the sum of holdings of SDRs, reserve position in the IMF, foreign exchange, and gold valued at market price.
7. Net debt is equal to total debt minus international reserves.
8. Short-term debt does not include the use of IMF funds. Imports refer to imports of goods and services.

The debt-export ratio was the more accurate indicator of ability to repay, as borne out by their respective performances.

After the first oil shock increased the GBR of the Baker-15 debtors, their average debt-export ratio began to rise from a record low of 1.9 years in 1974. By 1978 external debt was equivalent to 2.8 years of export revenue, as shown in Table 8.1. This ratio fell back to 2.4 years in 1980 since real debt declined due to strong advances in the export prices of these debtors.

Developing country export revenue grew at a slower rate in 1981 and actually declined in 1982 and 1983 as many of the industrialised countries – their principal export market – fell into recession. During this period the real burden of external debt rose dramatically. Declining export demand and prices coincided with the developing countries' inability and, in some cases, unwillingness to cut back sufficiently on import expenditures. Consequently external debt grew more quickly than export revenue, and hence the countries' ability to repay declined. Payment arrears and rescheduling became commonplace.

Whereas the real external debt (adjusted for export prices) of the Baker-15 debtors increased only 31 per cent from 1972 to year-end 1980, it rose nearly fourfold from 1980 to 1986. In that year, the debt-export ratio stood at five years. This was significantly above the average ratio (1.7 years) for the Republic of Korea and Thailand, two borrowers that avoided debt difficulties.

Managing the growth of external debt is important not only to maintain access to the external creditor, but also due to the inherent analytics of compound interest. The stability of debt repayment in the longer run is dependent, *inter alia*, on the growth trend of nominal debt. Domar (1950) showed that the growth rate of new borrowing must eventually fall below the interest rate charged on the external debt, if the borrower is ever to become a net capital exporter (which is required to retire the debt successfully). If the rate of borrowing continues to exceed the average interest cost of external debt, then the country remains a perpetual borrower presumably ending in default.

Domar's analysis emphasises the internal mechanics of financial borrowing and suggests that a debtor should manage its foreign debt so that its growth rate eventually falls and remains below the prevailing cost of external funds (for example the market's risk premium plus LIBOR or US Prime). Achieving this goal is not as easy as it may seem, owing to the volatility of interest rates in key creditor countries.

His work provides a useful financial benchmark to assist in the management of foreign borrowing. However the secular growth trend of new borrowing is driven ultimately by structural change in the domestic economy – the production structure, savings behaviour, personal income and its distribution – and their linkage with sovereign solvency. This transformation underpins the secular decline in the GBR and the sustained reduction of the growth of new borrowing.

International Reserves and Net Debt

The uncertainty in anticipating the amount of required 'below-the-line' funding in the balance of payments is an important reason for a country's demand for international reserves. This uncertainty creates the need to hold excess international reserves to fund the overall balance: net foreign-exchange expenditures that were not funded by foreign borrowing and other capital transactions. Besides this precautionary demand for cash balances, other factors creating the need to hold reserves include transactions demand, speculative demand and real balance effects.

The conventional wisdom among sovereign credit analysts suggests that a country should hold foreign-exchange reserves equal to an amount equivalent to three months of average import expenditure on goods and services (that is, three-month import cover).[5] International reserves in excess of this amount will define, under many circumstances, a country's drawdown margin: the use of which would not erode the creditworthiness of the borrower. In certain cases, however, three-month cover may be either insufficient or excessive. For example, it may prove inadequate when a country is entering an economic recovery after a period of austerity-induced slow or negative growth. In this case, pent-up consumer and investment demand for imports may require additional reserves. This would be especially true if the debtor's growth is out of phase with its major trading partners, implying weak export demand and prices.

The amount of international reserves a sovereign debtor holds is adequate *de facto* if; subject to an unanticipated increase in the GBR, it is sufficient to supplement planned gross foreign borrowing to ensure a stable roll-over process. Since the size of the GBR will depend on the nature of the balance of payments shock and the policy response, the adequacy of international reserves also depends upon: the magnitude of the disequilibrium on the overall balance of the external accounts; the debtor's access to compensatory financing; its exchange-rate regime; and the effectiveness of the trade adjustment mechanism.[6]

During most of the 1970s these benchmark reserve levels were met, indeed exceeded, by the Baker-15 countries (see Table 8.1). Beginning in 1979, however, the confluence of numerous external shocks coupled with accelerating capital flight caused a reduction of net foreign-exchange earnings. As a result, import cover began to decline and reached a low of 2.5 months in 1982 before recovering. The growth of international reserves also did not keep pace with the growth of external debt. For the Baker-15 countries, net debt increased steadily throughout the 1970s both in value and *vis-à-vis* export revenue. It accelerated after 1980 for the reasons already mentioned.

Undiscovered Debt: The Importance of Monitoring and Allocation

The reporting of external debt and other relevant statistics on sovereign borrowers has improved significantly since the 1970s, particularly with the advent of the Institute of International Finance in Washington, DC. These improvements in debt monitoring also have been mirrored in many developing countries. With the help of the World Bank, other official agencies and private consultants, developing country governments have implemented computerised monitoring systems to track total foreign borrowing and various subcomponents, including the debt's composition by creditor, obligor, currency, maturity and interest-rate cost.

Not all debtor governments, however, have been equally rigorous in monitoring and regulating the growth of the country's external borrowing, particularly those obligations of public-sector enterprises, private companies and individuals. If the sovereign borrower is pursuing an aggressive growth-cum-indebtedness development strategy, complete autonomy regarding foreign borrowing by the non-sovereign sectors of the economy is unwise.

If the government wants to maintain control of foreign debt growth, the amount of new annual borrowing should be planned as a component of total credit growth in the economy. IMF financial programming techniques are an appropriate planning tool for this exercise.[7] First, the growth of money demand is estimated according to the outlook for economic growth and a money demand function. The required increase in money supply that is not expected to occur domestically defines the targeted amount of foreign borrowing.

Once the targeted foreign borrowing has been estimated, then a queuing or auction system could be implemented to allocate these scarce resources to their competing uses. With such a planning, monitoring and distribution system for external debt, the Ministry of Finance can minimise the unpleasant surprise of 'undiscovered debt'.

THE TERMS OF DEBT REPAYMENT

The Interest Rate

Fluctuations in global market interest rates can have a significant effect on the amount of debt service owed to external creditors. This interest rate risk arises from accumulating floating-rate debt and leaving unhedged the exposure to market interest rate movements. The vulnerability of the Baker-15 sovereign debtors to this risk increased steadily beginning in the early 1970s. As can be seen in Figure 8.1, the proportion of floating-rate debt to total debt increased from only 8.1 per cent in 1972 to almost 60 per cent in 1986. Since most syndicated loans were priced by quoting a risk premium or spread over either US prime or UK LIBOR, a price shock was directly transmitted to these sovereign debtors in the form of higher interest payments, once monetary policy was tightened in these major creditor countries.

In addition to these direct costs, rising interest rates abroad also had a deleterious indirect effect on these debtors. Tighter monetary policy abroad also reduced the economic growth in their major export markets, depressing both export demand and export prices for the debtor. This occurred in dramatic fashion to the Baker-15 debtors when real LIBOR (deflated by export unit value) jumped from negative 10.2 per cent in 1980 to positive 21.7 per cent in 1981 (see Figure 8.1). This huge swing in real LIBOR resulted from a sharp rise in nominal interest rates and a concurrent decline in export unit values.

An unanticipated increase in interest payments can also result from unhedged currency translation risk. The depreciation of the US dollar since February, 1985, has increased the dollar-equivalent amount of non-US dollar debt in a debtor's portfolio. Unless the exposure is hedged, this movement directly increases both interest and amortisation payments proportionate to the amount of total debt which is denominated in the appreciating currency. This risk is especially burdensome when no portion of the debtor's exports are invoiced in the appreciating currency, thus removing the natural hedge of matching the currency denomination of expenditures and revenues. The World Bank estimated that translation losses (due to accounting changes in debt valuation resulting from the US dollar depreciation) were equivalent to 42 per

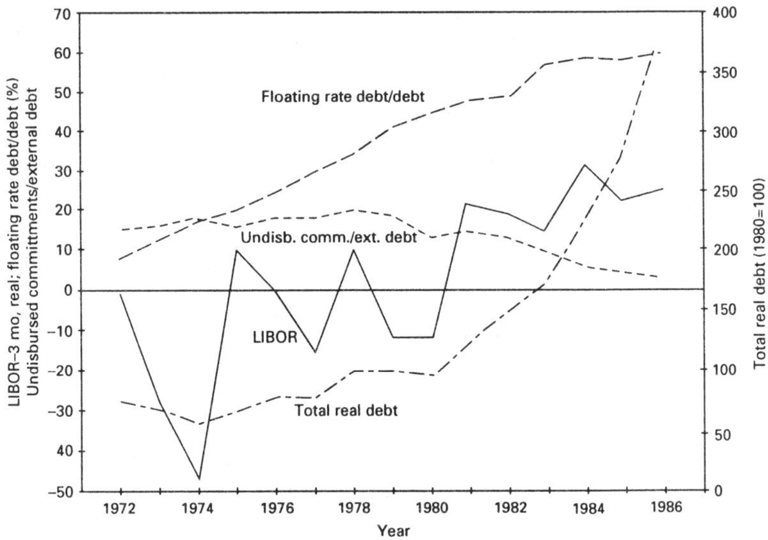

Figure 8.1 External financial shocks

cent of average outstanding debt for Turkey, Brazil and the Republic of Korea in the mid-1980s.[8]

Total interest payments for the Baker-15 countries increased progressively during the 1970s and 1980s. This was due to a number of factors, including higher debt levels, a rising proportion of floating-rate debt, the increasing share of debt owed to commercial banks, who lent at dearer terms than did public creditors, tighter monetary policy in the United States and other major creditor countries, inadequate debt relief and adverse currency movements (Solberg, 1988). As can be seen in Table 8.2, interest payments in 1985 were more than double those of 1979 and represented an eightfold increase over their level in 1975, a much faster rate than that for total debt.

In contrast with rising interest rates and payments, loan spreads actually declined for many debtors during the latter half of the 1970s and early 1980s, despite the rising risk of rescheduling. Freedman (1977) argues that this anomalous situation occurred because the growth of the capital markets was supply-led rather than demand-led during this period. Such an impetus to growth would tend to lower Euro-market interest rates relative to their respective domestic market rates. Whatever the reason behind the decline in the spread, it was dwarfed by the increase in the cost of funds.

The experience of the Baker-15 countries suggests that sovereign debtors should maximise the share of fixed-rate financing in their overseas borrowing programme. For floating-rate debt – whether syndicated general obligation debt or short-term cash instruments – the sovereign debtor is advised to hedge this interest rate risk by utilising a combination of FRAs and swaps. These instruments can be used to alter the country's liability structure from floating to fixed interest rates or from one currency's rate to another. When assessing the need for these derivative products, exposure management needs to be automated so as to easily monitor and assess issues of marking-to-market, netting, offsets, balance-sheet impact and profit/loss recognition.

The Amortisation Rate

When the choice of loan maturity is an endogenous policy variable, the sovereign debtor should choose its new debt so as to match its tenor, as closely as possible, with the gestation period of the investment project being financed. In this manner, refinancing the project is unlikely to be necessary and the uncertainty over both the future debt service cost and the availability of new credit to refinance will be minimised.

Table 8.2 shows that the average maturity of outstanding debt for the Baker-15 countries kept falling throughout the 1970s, as signified by an increasing amortisation rate (that is, principal repayments/total debt). The average maturity structure of their debt was shortened even further from 1979–81 by the increasing proportion of short-term debt to total debt (see Table 8.1). By 1980, principal repayments including the roll-over of short-term debt amounted to over 40 per cent of total debt. Such bunching of maturities was excessive and ill-advised since it increased their GBR, raised roll-over requirements and their vulnerability to a liquidity crisis. The amortisation rate (both short and long-term) has fallen since 1982, reflecting the lengthening of maturities from the numerous rescheduling agreements with official and private creditors and the extinguishing of debt through debt write-offs and debt-equity programmes.

Bunching of principal repayments – whether the result of seasonality of borrowing needs, poor financial management or credit rationing by the lender – should be avoided whenever possible and eradicated quickly once it occurs. When it occurs, a refinancing programme should smooth the amortisation schedule by issuing, if possible, longer-dated maturities and attracting non-debt creating or other equity flows. If access to

Table 8.2 Terms of debt repayment for Baker-15 countries ($US millions, unless otherwise stated)[1]

	1972	*1973*	*1974*	*1975*	*1976*	*1977*	*1978*	*1979*	*1980*	*1981*	*1982*	*1983*	*1984*	*1985*	*1986*
Interest rates:															
LIBOR 3 months (annual average)	5.4	9.4	10.9	7.0	5.6	6.1	8.9	12.1	14.2	16.9	13.3	9.7	10.9	8.4	6.9
% Change in LIBOR 3 months	−18.4	75.4	15.7	−36.2	−19.9	8.6	46.3	36.6	17.4	18.9	−21.2	−26.9	12.6	−23.2	−18.3
LIBOR 3 months, real (annual average)[2]	−1.2	−27.2	−45.8	10.8	0.4	−15.0	10.1	−10.4	−10.2	21.7	19.2	14.2	32.3	23.6	27.2
% Change in LIBOR 3 months, real	−125.3	−3902.6	68.5	−123.6	−96.5	−4094.2	−166.8	−203.6	−2.2	−313.1	−11.4	−25.9	127.0	−27.0	15.5
Interest payments (US $)	71.7	102.0	143.4	197.1	232.9	292.5	498.2	651.2	936.0	1133.4	1369.0	1338.2	1509.7	1667.7	1623.5
Interest payments/total debt (%)	2.1	2.4	2.5	2.8	2.8	2.8	3.5	4.0	4.8	4.7	5.1	4.5	5.2	5.0	4.8
Floating rate debt/debt (%)[3]	8.1	12.4	17.6	20.4	25.9	30.4	35.4	41.4	44.8	47.4	49.4	56.3	58.4	58.0	60.5
Amortisation rates:															
Principal repayments (US $)	154.3	218.9	258.7	298.9	363.2	508.4	838.9	1120.3	1003.1	1054.4	1015.9	873.3	822.3	866.4	879.1
Principal repayments/total debt (%)	5.1	6.0	5.9	5.4	5.6	6.2	8.2	9.0	6.5	5.6	4.4	3.4	3.0	3.0	2.9
Roll-over ratio (%)[4]	52.1	58.7	51.5	56.4	48.8	51.8	59.9	70.0	83.4	78.6	80.6	94.0	126.9	187.9	191.8
Principal repayments (including short-term debt) (US $)	1082.8	1352.3	1570.3	1778.4	2291.4	3002.6	3440.5	4837.3	6327.2	7722.9	8032.6	5781.1	4962.1	4617.3	3344.9
Principal repayments (including short-term debt)/total debt (%)	35.6	37.0	35.6	31.9	35.2	36.3	33.5	38.9	41.1	41.0	35.1	22.6	18.0	16.1	10.9

Debt service:															
Debt service payments (excluding short-term debt) (US $)	226.0	320.9	402.1	495.9	596.1	801.0	1337.1	1771.5	1939.1	2187.8	2384.9	2211.5	2332.0	2534.1	2502.6
Short-term debt (US $)[5]	928.4	1133.4	1311.6	1479.5	1928.2	2494.2	2601.7	3717.0	5324.1	6668.5	7016.7	4907.7	4139.9	3750.9	2465.8
Debt service ratio (excluding short-term debt) (%)	17.7	17.3	15.9	20.8	20.8	22.8	33.2	29.5	25.2	29.7	33.1	29.9	29.3	32.9	36.3
Debt service ratio (including short-term debt) (%)	83.6	71.8	53.5	67.9	73.2	80.0	90.2	88.9	88.4	109.1	127.2	96.8	79.9	80.7	74.1
Rescheduling:															
Incidence[6]	1	1	1	2	3	1	1	0	3	1	1	12	11	11	13
Net financial transfer (US $)	207.6	225.4	378.9	383.5	624.8	745.7	894.5	759.0	386.9	595.8	575.6	140.2	−494.0	−1185.8	−1197.6

Notes:
1. See Table 8.1, footnote 1.
2. The real LIBOR rate is equal to the nominal LIBOR rate minus the growth of the unit value of exports.
3. The debt figures in the denominator represent the public debt, only disbursed.
4. See Table 8.3, footnote (4) for definition.
5. Short-term debt does not include the use of IMF funds.
6. Number of countries to finalise a rescheduling agreement in each respective year.

new long-term credit is restricted, then compensatory finance and economic stabilisation measures aimed at reducing the trade deficit and GBR are required. If foreign exchange revenue and expenditures are still unbalanced and international reserves have been run down, then accumulating arrears and requesting a debt rescheduling is the ultimate policy option.

Arrears and Rescheduling

When international reserves are critically low and the debtor's GBR exceeds its ability to attract new external finance, then the roll-over process becomes unstable and the liquidity constraint becomes binding. If accumulated foreign debt is already large, then arrears on debt service payments are likely to become a forced alternative. From 1980 to 1982, the value of arrears doubled for the Baker-15 countries. By 1982 the limited set of policy options facing this group was reflected in the rising number of debt rescheduling requests lodged with both their private and official creditors (see Table 8.2). With notable exceptions, an IMF-sanctioned stabilisation programme and borrowing subject to policies of conditionality were usually required to secure debt rescheduling agreements from the commercial banks.

In the early part of the 1980s the amount of debt relief secured by the numerous rescheduling agreements was inadequate; total debt service payments were stabilised rather than reduced. With the advent of multi-year agreements, annual amortisation payments were lowered, while interest rates and payments rose through 1985. Many of these debt rescheduling agreements reduced total debt service payments by an amount less than the decline in new lending. Once the Baker-15 debtors began to run arrears, many became net exporters of both merchandise and financial resources although their external debt continued to grow. Inadequate debt relief caused 'debt fatigue'.

The continued payment of interest coupled with the reduction of new loan disbursements resulted in a negative net financial transfer beginning in 1984, as shown in Table 8.3. For some individual debtors, this resource outflow occurred even earlier. This outflow of financial resources imposed austerity, reduced the rate of economic growth and forced the government to rely largely on domestic resources. Faced with this shortfall of external funding, some countries exacerbated the macroeconomic imbalance by monetising their fiscal deficit and fueling price instability.

The costs of an interruption in the roll-over process, leading to a debt rescheduling, are clearly significant. These costs provide a strong incentive for debtors strategically to manage their foreign borrowing so that, when imbalances begin to occur, they explore alternative policy choices such as compensatory finance and stabilisation before running arrears and requesting a debt rescheduling.

THE FLOW REQUIREMENTS OF EXTERNAL DEBT

Net Financial Transfer

The multi-decade process of economic development and structural change requires the mobilisation of ever greater amounts of financial resources. Financial deepening in the domestic financial sector should provide a growing share of these needs. The purpose of foreign borrowing is to supplement these domestic resources and accelerate structural transformation. A net inflow of foreign savings is achieved when new loan disbursements exceed total debt service payments: a positive net financial transfer for the borrower.

Prudent application of these borrowed financial resources would include development-related investment, replenishing international reserves or funding export credits to promote exports. The use of foreign borrowing to fund imports of non-essential merchandise, services and financial assets (that is, capital flight) should be discouraged as these expenditures do not promote structural transformation or enhance creditworthiness.

The Baker-15 countries benefited from a positive net financial transfer from 1972–83. As shown in Figure 8.2, this net inflow of financial resources increased almost every year in the 1970s. In 1979, debt service payments grew more quickly than new disbursements, meaning that the net financial inflow began to diminish. By 1984, it actually became a net outflow.

The shortening of debt maturities coupled with rising interest costs meant that the net financial transfer was dwarfed by the amount of debt owed. Between 1972 and 1983 the cumulative net financial transfer amounted to approximately $6.0 billion, while the stock of debt outstanding grew from $3.7 billion to $27.5 billion. These numbers emphasise the importance of using borrowed funds productively so that they create a sound basis for repayment.

Table 8.3 External debt flow requirements for Baker-15 countries (US $ millions, unless otherwise stated)[1]

	1972	*1973*	*1974*	*1975*	*1976*	*1977*	*1978*	*1979*	*1980*	*1981*	*1982*	*1983*	*1984*	*1985*	*1986*
Capital flows:															
Disbursements (US $)	433.6	546.4	781.0	879.5	1220.9	1546.7	2231.6	2530.5	2326.0	2783.6	2960.6	2351.7	1838.0	1348.3	1305.0
% Change in disbursements	60.3	26.0	42.9	12.6	38.8	26.7	44.3	13.4	–8.1	19.7	6.4	–20.6	–21.8	–26.6	–3.2
Net capital inflow (US $)[2]	279.3	327.5	522.3	580.6	857.7	1038.2	1392.7	1410.2	1322.9	1729.2	1944.7	1478.3	1015.7	481.9	426.0
Net financial transfer (US $)[3]	207.6	225.4	378.9	383.5	624.8	745.7	894.5	759.0	386.9	595.8	575.6	140.2	–494.0	–1185.8	–1197.6
Roll-over ratio (%)[4]	52.1	58.7	51.5	56.4	48.8	51.8	59.9	70.0	83.4	78.6	80.6	94.0	126.9	187.9	191.8
Credit-based import capacity (%)[5]	15.0	8.4	10.7	10.4	14.3	20.2	15.9	12.1	7.9	6.6	8.1	1.5	–7.8	–16.0	–14.3
Capital flight:															
Unobserved capital outflow (US $)[6]	–51.7	41.2	154.8	177.2	230.2	33.5	49.3	–146.3	831.8	1683.9	1551.1	552.7	19.1	176.4	29.0
Adjusted net capital inflow (US $)[7]	331.0	286.3	367.5	403.4	627.5	1004.7	1343.4	1556.4	491.1	45.3	393.5	925.6	996.7	305.5	396.9
Adjusted net financial transfer (US $)[8]	259.4	184.2	224.1	206.4	394.6	712.2	845.1	905.2	–444.9	–1088.1	–975.5	–412.6	–513.0	–1362.2	–1226.6
Adjusted roll-over ratio (%)[9]	40.2	66.3	71.3	76.5	67.7	54.0	62.1	64.2	119.1	139.1	132.9	117.5	127.9	201.0	194.0

Market perception:															
External nominal debt growth (%)	19.3	20.8	26.3	17.0	26.8	24.2	21.2	23.7	22.5	21.5	11.5	7.8	4.0	7.2	3.7
Undisbursed commitments/ external debt (%)	15.2	15.8	18.5	16.3	18.5	18.8	20.7	20.0	12.8	15.1	12.9	9.3	5.9	'4.5	3.4

Notes:
1. See Table 8.1, footnote 1.
2. Net capital inflow is defined as disbursements minus principal repayments.
3. Net financial transfer is equal to net capital inflow minus interest payments.
4. The roll-over ratio is the ratio of debt service payments to disbursements.
5. Credit-based import capacity is defined as the ratio of the net financial transfer to merchandise imports.
6. Unobserved capital outflow is defined as the balance on errors and omissions whenever an estimate was unavailable from Lessard & Williamson (Capital Flight and Third World Debt, Institute for International Economics, Washington, DC 1988). A positive number represents capital flight or outflow.
7. An adjustment is made to include capital flight. Capital flight is subtracted from net capital inflow.
8. Capital flight is subtracted from net financial transfer.

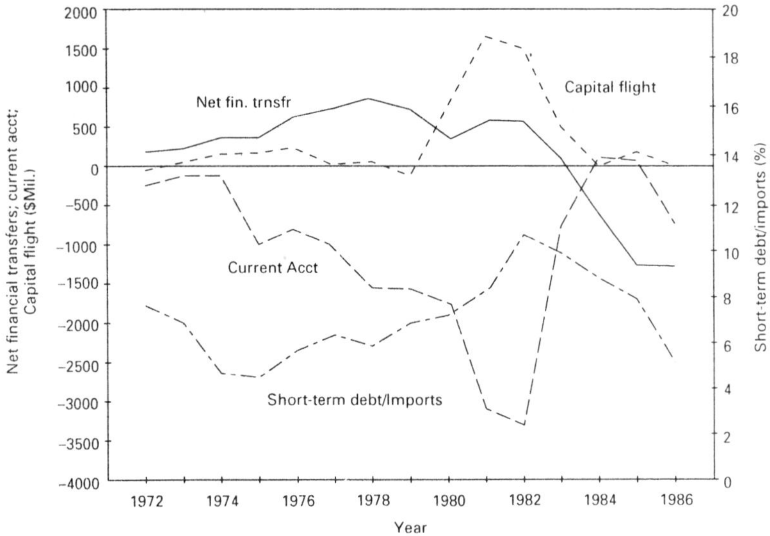

Figure 8.2 Financial flows

Credit-Based Import Capacity

The positive net financial transfer during the 1970s and early 1980s allowed the Baker-15 countries to increase their import capacity. Credit-based import capacity is measured by the ratio of the net financial transfer to merchandise imports. This ratio measures the positive or negative contribution of net financial flows to total imports. Although net external borrowing contributed positively to import capacity from 1972 through 1983, its share never exceeded a peak of 20.2 per cent in 1977 (see Table 8.3). Once the net financial transfer became negative in 1984, import capacity was reduced by an average of 12.7 per cent per annum through 1986.

Despite the large accumulation of external debt during this period, the expansion of import capacity was modest, particularly when the period after 1983 is included. From 1972 to 1987 the cumulative net increase in credit-based imports was only $2 billion, a mere $125 million per annum for all of the Baker-15 countries taken together.

The cost to the debtor from an unplanned reduction of import capacity will depend on the proportion of imports that are compressible and non-compressible. Since non-compressible imports (for example subsistence food requirements, fuel, raw materials and capital equipment) are essential to investment goals and basic economic development, a curtailment of these goods will lower the growth rate of the economy, reduce the standard of living and increase the probability of default. Compressible imports can be lowered without causing as many major dislocations to the economy.

Roll-Over Ratio

In the early stages of development the sovereign borrower faces weak export growth and a shortage of international reserves. This foreign-exchange constraint implies that interest and amortisation payments must be capitalised, paid by accumulating new debt. As long as the magnitude of loan disbursements is sufficient to cover debt service payments, then the roll-over ratio (that is, debt service payments/loan disbursements) will be less than unity or 100 per cent. In this case, the debtor is receiving a positive net inflow of financial resources, as was the case for the Baker-15 debtors from 1972 to 1983.

It is axiomatic that as a country's stock of outstanding external debt rises, so do its debt service payments. If new loan disbursements do not keep pace with rising debt service, then the roll-over ratio also will rise. The higher this ratio, the greater the magnitude of new capital inflows required to obtain a given net financial transfer (Dhonte, 1974). As the roll-over ratio approaches unity (100 per cent), the debtor's vulnerability to a liquidity crisis increases. If new loan disbursements from external creditors are suddenly rationed, for example due to an erosion of perceived creditworthiness, then international reserve usage and trade adjustment are the penultimate policy-response options before running payment arrears.

For the Baker-15 countries the roll-over ratio remained quite stable during the 1970s (see Table 8.3). This trend broke down beginning in 1979 with the confluence of numerous external shocks that raised debt service payments and diminished the growth of new disbursements. By 1984 the ratio exceeded 100 per cent, signalling that the roll-over process had become unstable. The negative net financial transfer forced them into austerity and slower economic growth, which was to last virtually the entire decade. If estimated capital flight is included as an additional financial expenditure, then the roll-over process broke down much earlier in 1980.

Capital Flight

Capital flight was an attendant problem and perhaps even a contributing cause of the debt crisis. 'Unrecorded' capital outflow, as measured by the deficit on the errors-and-omissions category in the capital account of the Baker-15 countries, became problematic in 1980 and continued to be a large drain on financial resources through 1983 (see Table 8.3). Although capital flight can result from political instability, economic imbalances were the motivation for much of the capital flight from the Baker-15 countries during this period.

Economic motivations of capital flight are intertwined with the market's assessment of changes in key financial prices or policies. The economic decision whether to invest in domestic or foreign assets is affected by (1) the outlook for the value of the exchange rate, (2) the relative return on fixed investment, (3) the relative return on financial capital, (4) relative cost of borrowing; and (5) the level of foreign borrowing or capital inflow.

Exchange rate overvaluation, which can result *inter alia* from a fixed exchange rate coupled with rapid price inflation, creates a strong incentive for both domestic residents and foreigners to reduce domestic asset holdings. The investor attempts to avoid windfall losses by lowering exposure to the overvalued assets before the anticipated currency depreciation. Cuddington (1987) found an overvalued exchange rate to be a significant factor underlying capital flight for Argentina, Mexico, Uruguay and Venezuela during the 1980s. Distortions in the value of the exchange rate will also affect decisions on fixed-capital investment and borrowing by changing relative rates of return and credit costs.

The rates of return on both productive capital and fiduciary investments in the debtor country relative to those respective rates abroad are also important factors in determining capital flows, whether unrecorded or not. Even though the debtor's real rate of return on productive investment may exceed the real rate of return abroad (at equilibrium prices), capital would be attracted abroad if the developing country maintains an overvalued exchange rate in excess of the investment return differential. In this case, foreign assets are undervalued in terms of domestic currency and the expected foreign rate of return expressed in local currency is artificially high. Moreover, it is unlikely that this exchange-rate value can be held indefinitely. This expectation creates a further incentive to shift capital abroad to avoid the windfall loss once the depreciation occurs.

Although intended to subsidise domestic investments, low (or negative) inflation-adjusted deposit rates, particularly in tandem with an overvalued exchange rate, can also create the incentive for capital flight. The relative rate of return on overseas financial assets will be artificially high when interest ceilings keep domestic deposit rates below those prevailing abroad. Ensuing capital flight will retard the growth of national savings and lower the rate of new investment.

Lutz (1966) has argued that market distortions in the relative cost of credit can result in an unwarranted increase in foreign debt. When the real price of credit abroad is lower than that at home and the currency translation risk is perceived to be minimal, then the local investor will borrow from foreign credit markets. If nominal interest rates are defined as the sum of the real rate of return on capital and the inflation rate, then an inflation-prone country can make its real borrowing costs equal to those of another country only by devaluing its currency by an amount equal to the amount of the inflation differential. By supporting an overvalued currency, however, a high-inflation country creates the incentive for rapid foreign debt accumulation, owing to the expectation that the real price of domestic credit will exceed that of foreign credit. In this case there will be a tendency for borrowers to demand more credit from abroad than is optimal. Thus foreign debt will increase more quickly than is justified by equilibrium prices of credit and foreign exchange.

The mere inflow of foreign savings increases the likelihood of capital flight simply by increasing the pool of total liquidity. Additional foreign borrowing may increase the supply of money relative to its demand, thus leading to a debit transaction either on the current or capital account. It was estimated that for every dollar that Mexico borrowed overseas from 1974–84, 31 cents resulted in capital flight. The use of foreign credit to acquire certain foreign assets such as export receivables or strategic direct investments can be appropriate. In general, however, the use of scarce external credit resources to fund the acquisition of foreign assets warrants close government scrutiny.

A debtor country is more likely to experience capital flight when it suffers from financial repression; that is, an overvalued exchange rate and low or negative inflation-adjusted interest rates. Hence the debtor country should keep both deposit and loan rates positive in real terms and maintain an exchange rate that is not grossly overvalued or undervalued according to measure such as relative purchasing power parity.

BORROWING IN INTERNATIONAL CAPITAL MARKETS

General Obligation Debt

During the 1970s and into the early 1980s, the most frequent form of developing country borrowing was that of general obligation debt arranged by syndicates of private commercial banks in the Euro-currency market. This form of financing was inexpensive and allowed the borrower a maximum amount of discretion in deciding on the application of these funds. Despite these advantages, the cost of these funds became more unpredictable in the late 1970s with the increased issuance of floating-rate debt and the rising volatility of key global interest rates. Moreover its continued supply ultimately was not assured. As many countries began to face payment difficulties and their creditworthiness declined, access to new commercial funds was restricted and in some cases entirely curtailed.

The resource flow during the 1970s financed a variety of expenditures, including development-related projects, fiscal expenditures, balance-of-payments needs and the roll-over of debt service payments. Not all the uses to which these funds were put, however, were as productive. Lack of control over how the money was spent and the absence of direct risk sharing between the borrower and lender suggest that large-scale syndicated commercial credits for developing country finance are not a completely appropriate vehicle for development finance. Since the structure of general obligation debt requires the borrower to repay the loan without regard to the return on the investment, or indeed, how the money was spent, the lender continues to have full recourse to the borrower for the repayment of principal and interest. For many developing countries during the 1980s this led to debt fatigue, wherein the dearth of new lending coupled with the overhang of past debt obligations and inadequate cash flow from past investments meant that most debt-troubled developing countries faced a severe foreign-exchange constraint.

The Debt Crisis

Since the syndicated lending by the private commercial banks virtually ended in 1982, their activity with debt-troubled developing countries since then has been limited to extending trade credit, foreign exchange lines, correspondent banking products, *a forfait*, leasing, swaps and other derivatives. The dearth of long-term financing from private commercial banks – what had been the primary source of funding during the 1970s – has meant that developing countries had to rely heavily on official financial flows during the 1980s.

After a lost decade during the 1980s for many of the developing countries, there are increasing signs that the debt crisis is over. The degree of financial recovery and independence which these countries exhibit represents a continuum; while many developing countries still face severe debt problems, other countries have begun to extricate themselves. They have done so through a combination of structural reforms, debt restructuring packages and better macroeconomic management. Improved sovereign creditworthiness, in turn, has lead to an expanding amount of new voluntary financing from overseas private markets, further supporting this incipient economic recovery. In some cases, this renewed access to the international capital markets has allowed developing countries to establish relationships with non-traditional creditors.

Product Diversification

Concurrent with this shift in creditor composition, the mix of financial instruments used by the developing countries for external funding has also evolved. International bonds, Euro-commercial paper and Euro-certificates of deposit and other debt instruments recently have grown in importance. It remains to be seen whether these new flows to developing countries are sustainable and expandable.

Equity and quasi-equity flows – foreign direct investment, limited recourse project finance, risk-based portfolio investment and equity linked bonds – have become more important sources of external finance for developing countries, especially as their financial condition has improved. Driven by the large number of debt-conversion programmes and buoyed by the repatriation of flight capital, foreign direct investment in developing countries has risen every year since 1985 and increased its share of total external financing. Equity portfolio investment too has expanded rapidly in the past decade, although the channels through which it has flowed have varied in importance.

While country-specific funds and multi-country investment funds were the primary vehicles for cross-border equity investment in developing countries during the 1980s, selective companies more recently have directly issued new equity in the bourses of overseas developed countries. Direct investment in emerging equity markets is another growing trend in the 1990s. In order to attract risk-based portfolio investment, a developing country must allow a relatively open flow of capital, and exchange and capital controls need to be lifted or minimised. Additionally, company disclosure requirements, accounting standards, regulatory oversight and settlement procedures need to be examined.

During the past several years a handful of developing countries have begun to use derivative instruments for purposes of hedging, arbitrage and perhaps speculation. Continued volatility of key commodity prices in developing countries' import and export baskets and a growing reliance on short-dated debt instruments will support ongoing demand amongst developing country counterparts for derivative instruments. Despite the recent introduction of derivative products to developing countries, their use remains a fraction of market potential, being hindered by issues of product cost, complexity and, in some cases, counterparty creditworthiness.

As these structural changes unfold in the international capital markets, developing country external financial strategy is becoming less concerned with managing existing external debt and more focused on financial resource management strategies that use the variety of foreign credits now becoming available. Given the hard-won battle to restore sovereign creditworthiness, it behoves the sovereign borrower to pursue a systematic financial strategy that supports sound economic policies and convinces lenders of the sustainability of these policies so that reentry to the international capital markets will gain further momentum.

FINANCIAL POLICIES FOR SOVEREIGN CREDITWORTHINESS

This review of the stock and flow characteristics of external debt and the determinants of international capital flows has served to highlight the short-term financial elements of sovereign debt service capacity. The following financial rules serve as a guide to help formulate external financial policies which maintain sovereign creditworthiness.

General Rules

1. Manage external assets and liabilities as a single portfolio.
2. To create a natural hedge, match the maturity profiles of the stock of external assets and liabilities.
3. Minimise the mismatch between the currency mix of external assets and liabilities.

4. Minimise the gap between external lending and borrowing rates by maximising deposit rates and minimising loan rates.
5. Avoid speculative money market techniques such as 'riding the yield curve': borrowing at short maturities and depositing at longer maturities.
6. Set priorities for managing external debt and international reserves based on longer-term strategic criteria rather than short-term speculative motives.
7. Ensure that the management of external assets and liabilities is responsive to unanticipated shocks to the balance of payments so that the gross borrowing requirement does not become unmanageable.

Financial Liabilities

1. Minimise the cost of borrowed funds within a given currency.
2. Minimise the cost of funds across currencies by comparing the foreign-currency loan rates adjusted for the expected exchange-rate translation gain or loss.
3. Plans for external borrowing should ensure that the tenor profile of a country's disbursed external debt does not exhibit an unnecessary bunching of maturities. Any lumpiness in this profile should be refinanced to smooth the maturity profile.
4. Contingent credit facilities should be arranged so that unplanned borrowing needs can be smoothly financed, minimising the need for trade adjustment or excessive reliance on international reserve usage.
5. The growth of new external borrowing should remain consistent with the stock of outstanding debt so that a sustainable roll-over ratio is achieved. When new loan disbursements exceed debt service payments, the net financial transfer is positive, precluding the policy dilemma of choosing between payments arrears and slower economic growth.
6. To ensure that the country reaches a limit to its external indebtedness and eventually becomes a net creditor, the growth rate of new borrowings must eventually fall below the external nominal cost of these funds. This suggests that a debtor's borrowing requirement, and thus its development plan, must be sensitive to changes in global trade, capital-market liquidity and the cost of external funds.
7. The floating-rate components of total external debt should be minimised or hedged so that the cost uncertainty resulting from global interest rate volatility is reduced.

8. Reliance on short-term external debt should not exceed a level equivalent to six months of merchandise imports.
9. Financial repression – negative real interest rates, and an overvalued exchange rate – should be avoided in order to reduce the incentives for capital flight and excessive external debt accumulation.
10. Diversify the list of external creditors to include private commercial banks, investment banks, bond investors, private suppliers, bilateral export-credit agencies and multilateral institutions. This diversity will minimise the likelihood that the supply of new external credit will become completely inelastic, forcing a *de facto* liquidity crisis.
11. External funding should also be diversified by product type. Direct foreign investment, fixed-interest bonds and other portfolio investment in many cases are preferable to general obligation debt inasmuch as they promote risk sharing by tying the timing and magnitude of the repayment to the rate of return of the investment itself.
12. Borrowers should use interest-rate and currency futures, swaps and other derivatives products to hedge the risk in their external balance sheet resulting from fluctuations of global interest and currency rates.
13. If a debt rescheduling is required, the terms that reduce debt service payments should reflect the severity of the underlying cashflow imbalance. An illiquid debtor will require a shorter restructuring of amortisation payments whereas deeper structural problems will require greater debt relief. By ensuring that the concessional element of the debt relief agreement is adequate, but not excessive, the problem of correlated rescheduling is reduced without promoting moral hazard.[9]

Financial Assets

1. Preserve capital.
2. Determine the tenor mix of international reserves by examining the liquidity requirements of foreign-exchange liabilities.
3. Match the currency mix of international reserves with the foreign-exchange requirements of merchandise, service and capital imports.
4. Maximise the rate of return on international reserves, subject to adequate safeguards for credit risk and subject to the maturity and currency requirements.

5. Maintain a stock of international reserves equivalent to or greater than three months of merchandise and service imports.
6. Avoid mercantilist policies such as accumulating excessively large international reserve levels, especially since the real rate of return on domestic fixed investment usually exceeds that on financial assets.
7. Minimise large fluctuations in the external reserve position.
8. Indicators measuring the strength of the debtor's foreign-exchange financial balance sheet – such as import cover, short-term debt, debt-export ratio, roll-over ratio – should be incorporated explicitly into the development planning targets and managed so that their values remain within acceptable ranges, thus avoiding a decline in externally perceived creditworthiness. This will help to ensure ample and continued access to external financing.
9. When conditions in the external financial markets limit a country's access to new medium- and long-term credit, macroeconomic adjustment and trade stabilisation, rather than heavy reliance on short-term debt or international reserve usage, should be the central policy response.

Notes

1. If international reserves are rebuilt instead of reduced, then they add to the gross borrowing requirement rather providing a repayment source. The Baker-15 countries rebuilt their international reserves in ten of the fourteen years from 1972 to 1986, recording a net drawdown of reserves in 1975 during the aftermath of the first oil shock and during 1981–3 at the onset of the debt crisis.
2. Given its prominence in the external financing of the Baker-15 countries during the 1970s, general obligation debt is the focus of this paper. Private and official transfers, foreign direct investment and other debt or equity flows were lesser used forms of foreign funding and thus are not the focus of this paper. For certain countries, however, reliance on private transfers (for example Turkey and India) or foreign direct investment (for example Singapore and Hong Kong) have been important elements of the external funding strategy. In some cases they were equally effective and may have been a less disruptive alternative to the successful use of general obligation debt (for example South Korea). In the 1990s international bonds, short-term cash instruments and portfolio investment are becoming increasingly important as funding vehicles.
3. For purposes of this chapter, long-term creditworthiness is distinguished from short-term creditworthiness. Successful completion of the growth-cum-indebtedness cycle wherein the country becomes a net capital exporter defines long-term creditworthiness. This requires myriad structural conditions to be met in key domestic areas such as institution building,

market liberalisation and reforms, investment policy, domestic savings mobilisation and stabilisation policies. These long-term issues are beyond the scope of this chapter, which focuses solely on short-term or financial conditions that underpin sovereign creditworthiness.

4. The roll-over ratio is defined as the ratio of debt service payments to loan disbursements. It is discussed in more detail in the section entitled 'The flow requirements of external debt'.
5. See Rawkins (1992) for further discussion of import cover as an element of assessing sovereign risk.
6. A country that allows the value of its exchange rate to float will require smaller reserves of foreign currency than would a sovereign debtor that sets a fixed parity. If supply constraints or demand elasticities are not too severe, a floating currency will allow a faster trade adjustment mechanism than that under a fixed exchange-rate regime. Since the magnitude and duration of the GBR would be reduced, the need for international reserves would be less.
7. See IMF (1981) and Swiderski (1992) for examples of financial programming techniques applied to the case studies of Kenya and Hungary, respectively.
8. As cited in a speech delivered by Yavuz Canevi, Undersecretary for Treasury and Foreign Trade, the Republic of Turkey at the Second Turkey-Japan Joint Economic Committee Meeting in Tokyo on 27 April 1988.
9. Moral hazard is the likelihood that the debtor will face a disincentive to repay its debt due to adverse relative prices (or costs) of debt repayment versus rescheduling.

References

Cuddington, J. (1987) 'Macroeconomic Determinants of Capital Flight: An Econometric Investigation', in D. Lessard and J. Williamson (eds), *Capital Flight and Third World Debt* (Washington, DC: Institute For International Economics), pp. 85–96.

Domar, E. (1950) 'The effect of foreign investment on the balance of payments', *American Economic Review*, vol. 40, pp. 805–26.

Dhonte, P. (1974) 'Quantitative indicators and analysis of external debt problems', mimeo (Washington, DC: IMF).

Freedman, C. (1977) 'The euro-dollar market – a review of five recent studies', *Journal of Monetary Economics*, vol. 3, pp. 467–78.

Grumball, C. (1987) *Managing Interest Rate Risk* (New York: Quorum Books).

IMF Institute (1981) *Financial Policy Workshops: The Case of Kenya* (Washington, DC: International Monetary Fund).

Klein, T. (ed.) (1992) *Managing External Debt in Developing Countries* (Washington, DC: World Bank).

Lutz, F. (1966) 'Money rates of interest, real rates of interest, and capital movements', in W. Fellner, F. Machlup and R. Triffen *et. al.* (eds), *Maintaining and Restoring Balance in International Payments* (Princeton, NJ: Princeton University Press), pp. 161–66.

Rawkins, P. (1992) 'The Analytics of Country Reports and Checklists', in R. Solberg (ed.) *Country Risk Analysis: A Handbook* (London: Routledge), pp. 27–51.

Rojas-Suarez, L. (1991) 'Risk and Capital Flight in Developing Countries', in *Determinants and Systematic Consequences of International Capital Flows*, Occasional Paper no. 77 (Washington, DC: International Monetary Fund), pp. 83–92.

Solberg, R. (1988) *Sovereign Rescheduling: Risk and Portfolio Management* (London: Unwin & Hyman).

Swiderski, K. (ed.) (1992) *Financial Programming and Policy: The Case of Hungary* (Washington, DC: IMF Institute).

World Bank (1988) *World Debt Tables* (Washington, DC: World Bank), volumes 1 and 2.

World Bank (1990) *Debt Management Systems* (Washington, DC: World Bank).

9 Adjustment and Rural Poverty: Monitoring ESRP

Rolf Kappel

Although the theoretical and empirical knowledge about structural adjustment in developing countries is continuing to grow, it is not yet well understood how structural adjustment policies affect the poor and why they may not be able to take full advantage of the improved economic environment. However, any countries undergoing structural adjustment need measures that alleviate the possible adjustment burden of the poor and supplement the incentives created by the structural adjustment policy. In short, the knowledge about relevant preconditions and consequences of structural adjustment should be augmented, and quick measures should be taken to prevent or minimise an additional incidence of and an exacerbation of poverty.

It is commonly agreed that structural adjustment policies simultaneously involve three levels of the economy:

1. The macroeconomic level, where major policy reforms are implemented.
2. The mesoeconomic level, with markets and infrastructure as *transmitters* or *transformers* (in both directions between the macro and micro level.
3. The microeconomic level, where individual economic actors feel the impact of structural adjustment measures and respond to the incentives and constraints created by the adjustment policy.

An assessment of the impact of structural adjustment programmes on economic actors in general, or on any subgroup of the population, must reflect all levels of the economy.

THE MACRO LEVEL: EXPENDITURE CONTRACTION AND SWITCHING

A straightforward way of analysing structural adjustment on the macrolevel is to study the changes of the components of GDP. This analysis allows a check on whether expenditure contraction or expenditure switching is dominating the adjustment process and which aggregates are affected by these processes. (Of course the absolute changes can easily be transformed into change rates.) In addition, the changes in the aggregates of GDP can be related to the policy measures of structural adjustment, that is, measures of stabilisation, liberalisation, private and public sector reforms and privatisation.

The equation for the changes of GDP components follows from the GDP identity and reads as follows:

$$\Delta X - \Delta M = \Delta Y - \Delta C_p - \Delta C_g - \Delta I_p - \Delta I_g \qquad (9.1)$$

where Δ = change in absolute values, X = exports, M = imports, Y = gross domestic product, C_p = private consumption, C_g = government consumption, I_p = private investment and I_g = government investment.

The changes in GDP show whether the adjustment process is (still) dominated by a contraction of the economy, which is normally to be expected during the stabilisation phase, or whether the general target of establishing growth has already been achieved. Changes of exports and imports, of private and public consumption as well as of investment explain how the overall process of adjustment has been generated.

The changes in the economic aggregates may serve as a reference to the analysis on the meso and micro levels of the impact of adjustment on the rural poor. Total income, private consumption and private investment can be compared with respective data for this population group. The comparison demonstrates whether the rural poor have done better or worse than the economic actors in general.

The analysis of public consumption and investment also provides a general reference for a more detailed analysis of the budgetary impact of adjustment. Particularly the expenditures for social services, such as health and education, can be compared with the changes of total public expenditure. Again these data may serve as comparative variables when social services for the rural poor are analysed on the meso and micro levels.

The data on changes of the trade balance are interesting for evaluating the switching processes initiated by the policies related to exchange rate, trade liberalisation and other measures. In many developing countries the rural poor contribute significantly to the production of tradables, particularly the production of agricultural commodities. Again the macro-analysis may serve as a reference to evaluate the relative performance – and to some degree the benefits – of the rural poor in that respect.

THE MESOLEVEL

Markets, Prices and Transaction Costs

In virtually all developing countries markets have been heavily regulated and prices have been administered over many years. Misallocations, severe instabilities and economic decline have been the result. Hence packages of liberalisation and deregulation represent an important part of adjustment programmes.

In particular the rural population has been heavily discriminated against through the administration of exchange rates and domestic agricultural prices. Overvalued exchange rates, high inflation rates, low food prices and high trade margins of public marketing boards in the agricultural sector have caused low and decreasing producer prices. As a consequence, growth of agricultural production was very low or even non-existent.

It is generally expected that the liberalisation of prices and markets, as well as changes of exchange rate regime, will improve the terms of trade for farmers, and thus create incentives to increase agricultural production. In the same way it is expected that a liberalised and deregulated commercial system provides a regular supply of consumer goods in rural regions, where the shelves of the shops have been rather empty for many years. In that sense adjustment programmes are expected to contribute to the alleviation of rural poverty.

The role of transaction costs is, *inter alia*, well known in trade theory. Apart from domestic prices, world market prices and the nominal exchange rate, transaction costs determine whether commodities and services are tradable or non-tradable. In this context, transaction costs include transportation, trade financing and insurance costs, trade-related taxes and fees, and the costs related to finding trading partners. The definition of tradables and non-tradables is given by the following equation:

$$P_x <= P^*E/(1 + c_{tr}) < P_n < P^*E\,(1 + c_{tr}) <= P_m \qquad (9.2)$$

where P_x = price of exportables, P^* = world market price, E = nominal exchange rate, c_{tr} = mark-up for transaction costs, P_n = price of non-tradables and P_m = price of importables.

The equation shows that tradables and non-tradables are simultaneously determined by world market prices, the exchange rate, domestic prices and transaction costs. The higher the transaction costs, the greater the price band and the production of non-tradables. In other words: high transaction costs impede trade and the international division of labour.

The concept of transaction costs is not only of interest for the analysis of national production and international trade but also for the analysis of local production, domestic trade and the division of labour. The concept of a price band, which simultaneously defines exportables, importables and non-tradables, can also be used to define commodities that a (rural) household will sell, buy or produce for self-consumption. As in the case of international trade, transaction costs play an important role.

Regarding production and trade in rural areas, the hypothesis is put forward that transaction costs are relatively high. As a consequence rural households tend to concentrate on the production of commodities and services for self-consumption. Under these circumstances, the division of labour and trade activities remain low. The major reason for high transaction costs is assumed to result from the limited capacity and bad accessibility of rural infrastructure and trade-related services.

Using the same notation as before, the following equation holds for this relationship:

$$P_s < = P/(1 + c_{tr}) < P_n < = P\ (1 + c_{tr}) < = P_p \tag{9.3}$$

where P_s = price of commodities sold, P = market price, c_{tr} = markup for transaction costs, P_n = price of non-tradables and P_p = price of commodities purchased.

The message of the equation is simple. The lower the market price of a commodity and the higher the transaction costs of buying and selling, the higher the household's propensity to produce commodities for self-consumption. In other words: low market prices – compared with the household's shadow prices – and high transaction costs impede the production of surpluses and cash crops, and impede the advance of the division of labour. Hence, even if adjustment policy is successful in creating price incentives to increase agricultural production, high transaction costs may impeded growth responses.

Social Infrastructure and Services

As mentioned before, adjustment programmes require a consolidation of public budgets, which may result in a decline in expenditure and/or the introduction of special fees for social services. However budgets are input variables, and the real impact of a budget cut, or the introduction of a fee, can only be observed on the meso and micro levels. Hence the monitoring of social services on the meso and micro levels

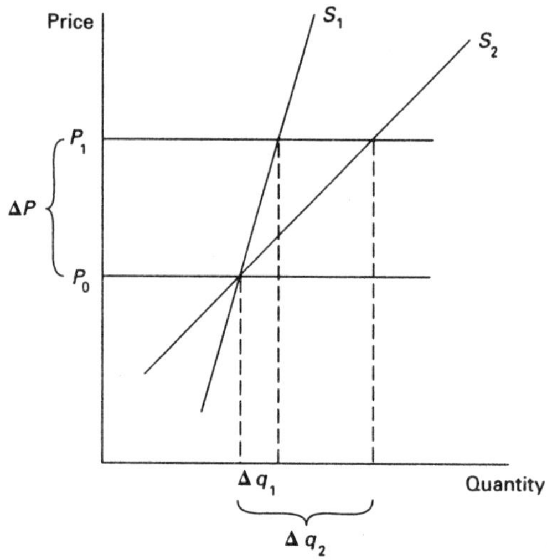

Source: Kappel (1991b).

Figure 9.1 Price incentives and supply responses

is a precondition for drawing any conclusions about the real burden of adjustment in these areas of social policy.

THE MICRO LEVEL: TOTAL FACTOR PRODUCTIVITY AND SUPPLY ELASTICITIES

Rural poverty is inseparably linked to the low total-factor-productivity of the smallholder sector. The often archaic agricultural technologies of smallholders are characterised by labour- and land-extensive production; and a substantial increase of production and income would require (among other things) a significant modernisation of production technologies. However experience shows that the technical modernisation of the smallholder sector is a rather slow process. As a consequence the potential for an increase of agricultural production in the short and medium run is limited. If the terms of trade for the rural population improve and if the supply of incentive goods increases, it is the low price elasticity of supply that may impede the growth of output (Figure 9.1).

Table 9.1 Stratification of adjustment policy and monitoring concerns

Level	*Monitoring concerns*	*Policy measures*
Macro level	Expenditure switching Expenditure contraction	Macroeconomic reforms
Meso level	Functioning of markets Development of prices Economic and social infrastructure/services	Market reforms Price/wage reforms Improve capacity and accessibility
Micro level	Impact of adjustment Adjustment capacity	Supplementary and complementary measures

Source: Kappel (1991b).

Of course the supply elasticity is not exclusively determined by the technical and organisational ability of individual farmers to respond to price incentives and/or the supply of incentive goods. The individual ability to adjust is, *inter alia*, heavily influenced by the accessibility and the capacity of the economic infrastructure (transaction costs) and – at least in the medium and long run – by the accessibility and capacity of social infrastructure. Access to functioning markets of factors of production and consumer goods, and to public services such as health, education and extension services, plays an important role. Hence the supply elasticity of the smallholders – in other words their ability to adjust – is determined by structural elements on both the meso and the micro levels.

Concept and Scope of the Swiss Monitoring Programme

Based on that very brief discussion of analytical issues, the focal points of a regional monitoring programme can be outlined, as illustrated in Table 9.1.

Following this outline, the concept of the Swiss Monitoring Programme (SMP) represents a mix or synthesis of statistical and narrative methods for gathering and analysing data. It can be divided into four overlapping modules, which comprise the macro, the meso and the micro levels (but with a strong emphasis on the latter two). Table 9.2 provides an outline of the major elements of the programme, and its four modules can be summarised as follows.

Table 9.2 Outline of the monitoring concept

Variables	*Level*	*Data collection*	*Data analysis*	*Data sources*	*Frequency*
Macroeconomic module:					
Expenditure switching and contraction	Macro		Statistical	National statistics	Annually
Price module:					
Consumer prices	Meso	Data sheet	Statistical	Shops/markets	Quarterly
Producer prices	Meso	Data sheet	Statistical	Traders/trade agency	Quarterly
Availability of cons. goods	Meso	Data sheet	Statistical	Shops/markets	Quarterly
Factor prices	Meso	Interview	Statistical	Traders/trade agency	Annually
Household module:					
Total production and income	Micro	Questionnaire	Statistical	Households	Annually
Nutrition	Micro	Questionnaire	Statistical	Households	Annually
Community module:					
Marketed production	Meso	Interview	Text	Traders/trade agency	Annually
Tariffs of social services	Meso	Interview	Text	Teachers/physicians/health workers/administration	Annually
Transport	Meso	Interview	Text	Agents/traders/trade agency	Annually
Storage	Meso	Interview	Text	Traders/trade agency	Annually
Communication	Meso	Interview	Text	Traders/trade agency/administration	Annually
Finance	Meso	Interview	Text	Traders/trade agency/ banks/administration	Annually
Extension services	Meso	Interview	Text	Households/administration	Annually
Water/energy supply	Meso	Interview	Text	Households/administration	Annually
Housing conditions	Meso	Interview	Text	Households	Annually
Health services	Meso	Interview	Text	Physicians/administration/ health workers	Annually
Education	Meso	Interview	Text	Teachers/administration	Annually

Source: Kappel (1991a).

First, the macroeconomic module concentrates on providing information about the adjustment process on the national level. The national account and balance of payments statistics as well as the monetary survey serve as a major data base. By analysing relevant economic aggregates, the macroeconomic analysis will reveal to what extent a sustainable development process is regained, and how expenditure switching and contraction contribute to the adjustment process.

Second, while the macroeconomic module covers national aggregates, the price, community and household modules refer only to the region where the programme is implemented. Simple data sheets are used to collect consumer and producer prices and to gather information about the variety and regular availability of important consumer goods. The price data are used to estimate the terms of trade development for rural smallholders, and the availability or non-availability of certain consumer goods indicates whether the region is sufficiently supplied with basic consumer/incentive goods.

Third, the community module primarily intends to cover meso-level information about the functioning and the structures of commodity and factor markets and about the capacity and accessibility of economic and social infrastructure and services. As mentioned above, the impact of adjustment and the capacity to adjust are codetermined by structures and processes on this level. The information is obtained through semi-structured interviews with selected key persons and is evaluated by text analysis.

Finally, the household module primarily serves to collect information about production, income and the general well-being of the rural population. The impact of adjustment on individuals, as well as their capacity or incapacity to adjust, are recorded with this survey. The data are obtained from formal household questionaires and are evaluated by statistical analysis.

Mozambique's Economic and Social Rehabilitation Programme (ESRP)

The aim of the ESRP, implemented in 1987, is to reverse the country's economic decline caused by the civil war and a ruinous economic policy that was followed for many years. As the agricultural sector provides about 60 per cent of the country's GDP and employs more than 80 per cent of the labour force, this sector plays a key role in the ESRP. Contrary to previous policy priorities, where large state farms and systems of collective production were strongly supported, the new policy focuses primarily on increasing the private production of the many smallholders in the rural sector.

Despite country-specific development targets, the ESRP more or less follows the standard stabilisation and structural adjustment scheme applied in many African countries. After several devaluations of the metical (Mt) and the attempt to follow a tight monetary and fiscal policy, the international trade system was liberalised, the exchange rate was managed more flexibly, the allocation of foreign exchange followed market oriented procedures and the tariff structure as well as the external debt and reserve management were reformed.

Simultaneously, the domestic price system was liberalised and administered prices (often minimum prices) were managed more flexibly. The fiscal system was reformed with an explicit emphasis on strengthening government revenues, reducing subsidies and increasing the allocation efficiency of public investment. The financial sector was liberalised to increase the effiiciency of private capital allocation, and many state-owned enterprises were privatised. Rehabilitation concentrated mainly on the transport and communication infrastructure and the agricultural sector. Finally, special emphasis was put on social policy to reduce the adjustment burden of the poor.

The Purpose of the Swiss Monitoring Programme (SMP)

The targeted monitoring of adjustment programmes can be seen as a necessary step towards a better understanding of the links between adjustment and poverty. This is the major goal of the Swiss Monitoring Programme (SMP), implemented in the Province of Cabo Delgado in northern Mozambique in 1990. This regional monitoring programme, which focuses exclusively on the links between adjustment and rural poverty, is intended to complement the nation-wide monitoring of adjustment stipulated by the World Bank within its Social Dimensions of Adjustment (SDA) initiative. The SMP is funded by and carried out on behalf of the Swiss Development Cooperation (SDC). The SMP is designed to answer three key questions.

The first relates to the reform of the exchange rate regime, of the price policy and of the commercial system. It is well known that price incentives and a regular supply of consumer ('incentive') goods through a liberalised commercial system represent key elements of orthodox adjustment programmes. Hence, does price and trade liberalisation improve the terms of trade of the rural poor and create incentives to increase production?

The second question relates to the hypothesis that the ability of the rural poor to adjust may be limited by high transaction costs, by traditional production technologies with low levels of total-factor productivity and inelastic supply behaviour. Even if price and market reforms are successful in creating incentives to increase production, these structural bottlenecks could impede growth and adjustment. Hence, are growth and adjustment impeded by archaic production technologies and low investment, limited capacities of production- and trade-related infrastructure and services (transport, storage, water, communication, trade and financial services, and so on?

The third question relates to the much debated hypothesis that adjustment programmes may have a negative impact on the living conditions of the poor. As a consequence of tight fiscal and monetary policy, public investment and the financing of recurrent costs of infrastructure, health services, education and rural extension services may be curtailed. On the one hand this may impede the advance of basic needs satisfaction (or even worsen the deplorably low levels); on the other hand constrained or reduced public expenditures may stand in the way of successful adjustment. Hence, do the rural poor feel a significant adjustment burden resulting from the ESRP?

The Project Region and the Survey Samples

The surveys and interviews were carried out in four districts of the Province of Cabo Delgado in northern Mozambique. In each district, the surveys and interviews were conducted in a *bairro* of the district centre (a small town) and in two villages (one village with good access to the district center and one rather remote village). In each *bairro* and village, 20 families were selected at random for the household interviews. The total sample size of 240 households was sufficient for trend estimates with acceptable error margins. With an average household size of six (three adults and three children) the selected households covered a sample population of some 1400.

The four districts were chosen to cover a broad spectrum of ethnic variety as well as agricultural and other economic activities. Agriculture was the most important source of income in all districts, but other economic activities played an important role as well. Mocimboa da Praia is a coastal district and fish are a considerable source of income. Farmers in Macomia are traditional producers of cashew nuts, a commodity with rather favourable prices on domestic and world markets. Mueda is an important regional centre on the *plan alto*, an area with

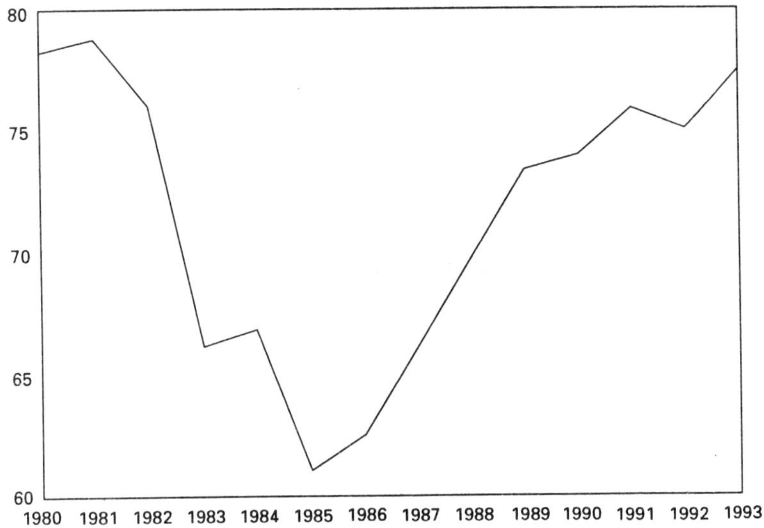

Source: Kappel (1991b).

Figure 9.2 Gross domestic product (Mt billions, 1980 prices)

large agricultural surplus production and very lively tade activities. In addition, the high plateau has a climate significantly different from the plains and coastal areas. Nangade is the most northern distinct, a very remote area with difficult access to other district centres.

Summary of Major Results and Conclusions

Because of space limitations it is not possible to present in detail the results of the monitoring programme carried out in Mozambique since 1990, therefore just a few major results and conclusions will be summarised.

Changes of gross domestic product and its components

Figure 9.2 shows the development of GDP between 1980 and 1993. It is obvious that the implementation of the ESRP in 1987 (after a first phase of some liberalisation in 1986) reversed the downward trend in economic development. Without going into the details of the national accounts, the evolution of major aggregates can be described as follows:

First, the decrease of GDP throughout the 1980s was stopped and turned into respectable growth rates between 1987 and 1989. Afterwards growth was sluggish, particularly in industry and commerce. Much of this relative setback must be attributed to increasing insecurity caused by the ongoing civil war. In 1992 the country was severely affected by one of the worst droughts in its history, with a dramatic decline in agricultural production. Since the signing of the peace accord in autumn 1992 the economy has recovered slowly. The economic growth rate of 3 per cent recorded for 1993 represents a per capita growth rate of about 0.4 per cent.

Second, while per capita consumption showed growth of 2–4 per cent between 1987 and 1989, average consumption levels declined between 1990 and 1992, and reversed again in 1993 with a growth rate of about 2.7 per cent. Despite these moderate improvements, the food security situation of the majority of the people is still very critical. Around 90 per cent of commercial food is provided through food aid.

Third, the ongoing process of liberalisation, deregulation and privatisation has had a visible positive impact on the development of the private economy, even if sectoral growth rates vary considerably from year to year. However, as in many other adjusting countries, private investment is growing rather slowly. Apart from structural bottlenecks that impede private investment, it will take time to reestablish the trust of the private sector in the country's peaceful and stable future.

Fourth, public expenditure has grown continuously since 1987, while revenues have lagged behind quite drastically. The increasing deficit of around 30 per cent of GDP between 1990 and 1993 was financed through grants – in other words, the government was still far from capable of managing sustainable budgets. However considerable shifts in public expenditure have taken place in the course of the public sector reform. Most noteworthy is the growing share of expenditure on health and education. The levels of recurrent expenditure have grown by more than 30 per cent since 1987 and the levels of investment have more than tripled.

Fifth, fiscal and monetary policies have not yet succeeded in bringing down inflation to acceptable levels. With the exception of 1991, when inflation was estimated at 33 per cent, average price increases have been between 40 per cent and 50 per cent per annum over the last six years. To some extent the country is caught in an inflation-devaluation spiral. Fiscal consolidation, a more disciplined monetary policy and a further deindexation of the economy seem to be inevitable steps that must be taken to overcome this dilemma.

Finally, the exchange rate policy and a nonadministrative system of foreign exchange allocation have resulted in a noteable improvement of the trade balance. Export shares of GDP have doubled over the last six years, while import shares have grown by 50 per cent. Nevertheless, with a current account deficit of around 60 per cent of GDP, for the foreseeable future the country will be dependent on foreign capital supply and measures of debt alleviation.

Smallholders' economic activities and incomes

The major economic activities of the population in the region of Cabo Delgado show the typical pattern of rural life. Virtually all the households in the survey sample produce subsistence and cash crops (mainly cassava, maize, sorghum and rice), 24 per cent are engaged in animal husbandry, 18 per cent harvest cashew nuts, 15 per cent catch fish and 3 per cent grow vegetables. Most of the households have some cash income from economic activities other than traditional crop production.

Crop production is still to a large degree subsistence production. On average only about 20 per cent of the harvest is for commercial purposes the rest is for self-consumption or is kept as seed. About 60 per cent of the average household cash income comes from crop production. The remaining 40 per cent comes from a large range of farming, fishing and nonfarm activities.

The majority of the people in the region are extremely poor. The average annual per capita cash income (Figures 9.3 and 9.4) of Mt 16 000 and Mt 25 000 in 1990 and 1991, respectively, correspond to an equivalent of US$17 at the official exchange rates for the years 1990 and 1991. The value of the average total annual income per capita (including income in kind), shown in Figure 9.5, corresponds to US$47.

As income figures based on exchange rates are of very limited use under such circumstances, a simple survey indicator on nutrition may illustrate the situation. Every year only 35–40 per cent of the households were certain that their food stocks would be sufficient to feed the members of the household until the next harvest began. And indeed 35–40 per cent of the households reported that they encountered serious difficulties in this respect at the end of every year. The main reasons for this are bad weather conditions; large preharvest losses caused by plant diseases, animals, weeds, floods and fires; too much commercial food production; robbery; costly national ceremonies and the consequences of the war. The inability to overcome these problems is perhaps another good indicator of the extreme poverty of the people.

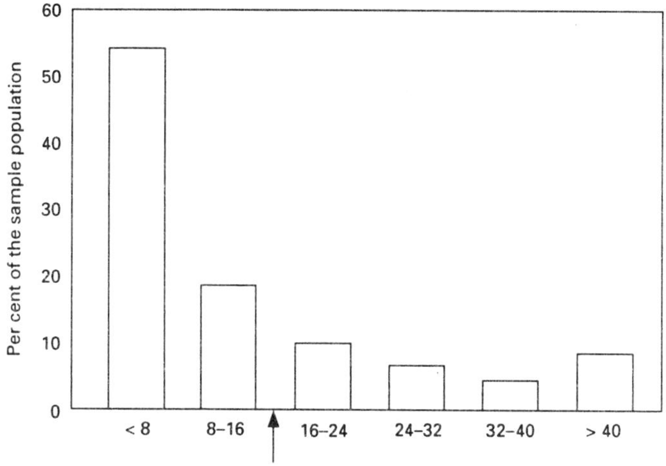

Source: Kappel (1991b).

Figure 9.3 Average annual per capita cash income, 1990 (Mt 1000), showing a mean value of 16

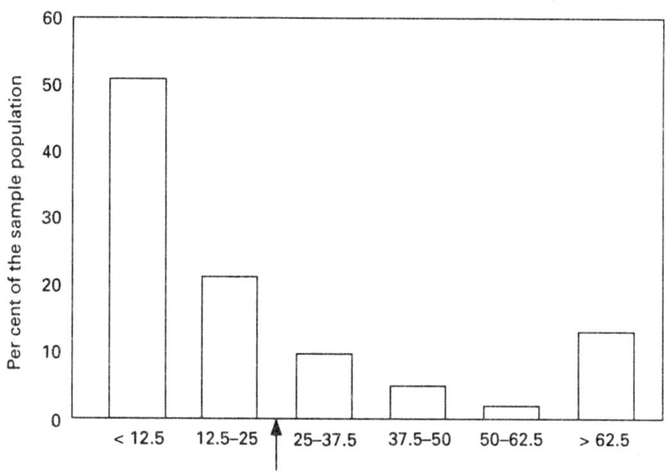

Source: Kappel (1991b).

Figure 9.4 Average annual per capita cash income, 1991 (Mt 1000), showing a mean value of 25

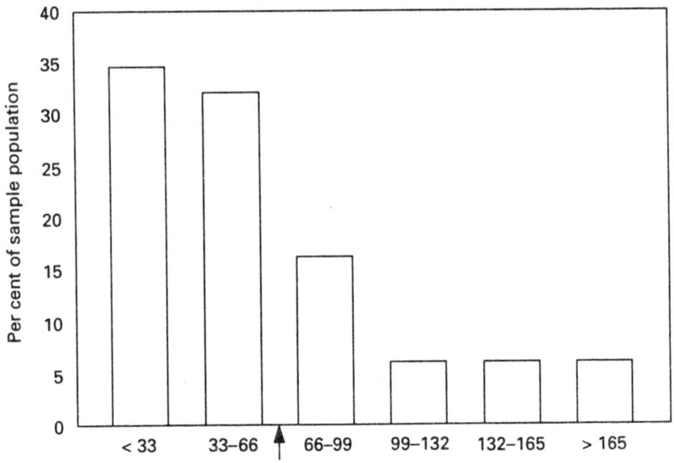

Source: Kappel (1991b).

Figure 9.5 Total income in Mozambique, 1991 (Mt 1000), showing a mean value of 66

As is to be expected, agricultural production is characterised by archaic technologies.

Eighty per cent of households use their own seeds, and no fertilisers (natural or chemical) are applied. Workers in the fields use only very simple tools such as hoes, scythes, hatchets and rasps. On average about 30 per cent of households invest in new agricultural tools every year, the sum invested being about US$7. Less than 5 per cent of the farmers receive extension services, and even that small amount of support is not considered to be of any help.

In general, there was no indication of a scarcity of arable land in the region. What was reported was that the larger the population of a village or town becomes the longer the journey to the fields. On average it takes between one and two hours to get to the fields, but for some the journey takes four hours or more. In addition it was claimed that the fertility of newly acquired land is often significantly lower than the fertility of land already cultivated.

There exists a rudimentary farm-labour market in the region: about 15 per cent of the households reported that they hire workers during labour-intensive times of the year. About 7 per cent of the households reported that they ask neighbours for support. Most of the people hired are paid in cash, although remuneration in kind still occurs.

This brief summary is sufficient to confirm the low supply elasticities among smallholders in the region. If they want to respond to incentives arising from an improved economic environment, the only choices they have are to increase their holding of arable land and hire additional farm labour; but even the expansion of labour is rather limited. The traditional division of labour means that an enormous share of farm and household work is shouldered by women, and it is inconceivable that they would be able to increase their work load. Progress in agricultural and household technologies, which would improve factor productivity, are currently out of their reach.

Given the important role of agricultural production as a source of income, real annual incomes vary considerably, depending on variations in rainfall and other environmental conditions. As mentioned above, more than 60 per cent of the farmers claimed that they suffer from significant preharvest losses as a result of plant diseases, crops being destroyed by animals and weeds impeding seed germination. Hence it is not possible to present reliable quantitative estimates of the development trend of real incomes.

However the surveys documented that no significant changes in personal income distribution have taken place. For example, Figures 9.3, and 9.4 show that there was a very similar pattern of income distribution in 1990 and 1991. As can be seen, the range of cash incomes is rather large and covers income differences of a factor higher than five. Not surprisingly, the inequality of incomes reduces if one takes into consideration subsistence income in kind (Figure 9.5). However, it must be emphasised that the large majority of the households represented in the sample belong to the poorest stratum of the population in Mozambique. Hence it may not be concluded from these data that adjustment does not affect personal income distribution in general. The new wealth of the traders, correctly perceived by the population and mentioned below, is only one example to indicate that the ESRP has had an impact on the distribution of income and wealth.

Terms of trade of the farmers

As mentioned above, one of the main targets of the ESRP is to create price incentives to increase agricultural production. Table 9.3 shows that increase in producer prices (after 1990 minimum prices) were very high for the most important agricultural commodities in the region. Nevertheless the nominal price increases were not sufficient to cover the price increases of consumer goods.

Table 9.3 Producer prices of farmers, 1986–93
(fixed or minimum prices, Mt per kg)

Commodity	*1986*	*1988*	*1990*	*1991*	*1993*
Maize	13.0	65	126	190	425
Rice	16.0	75	167	260	508
Sorghum	12.0	65	109*	150*	300*
Mafurra	8.0	35	70	120	240
Mandioca (dry)	4.5	40	59*	80*	140*
Beans (top quality)	23.5	150	295	400	1050
Beans (second quality)	15	105	184	270	710
Groundnuts	20	150	295	440	990
Cashew nuts	10.0	165	380	500	1100
Sunflower	15.0	75	150	200	540

* Free prices

Source: Kappel (1991b).

Table 9.4 shows that the bivariate terms of trade of the farmers (based on an unweighted producer price index calculated from Table 9.3) fell dramatically for some of the most important consumer items and, at least until December 1993, never really recovered. Exceptions from this drop in terms of trade fall into two categories: on the one hand the prices of some consumer goods are still administered and consumers are rationed (for example, salt and cooking oil which are often not available in markets); on the other hand the terms of trade improvements for clothes refer only to second-hand goods supplied through aid programmes.

There can be no doubt that the majority of prices of consumer goods have increased more than the fixed or minimum producer prices. This is a strong indication that the terms of trade of the farmers deteriorated after implementation of the ESRP, but this conclusion must be treated with care.

Before 1987 the prices of most consumer goods were very low in real terms, but the goods were rarely available in the shops. Low prices and the widespread rationing system had dried out the formal supply routes. Commerce flourished only on the black market and at much higher prices than in the formal economy. However information is very limited about absolute and relative prices of the shadow economy at that time. According to scarce information about black market operations, it may be concluded that the terms of trade losses are not as large as indicated by the above comparison of current prices in a largely

Table 9.4 Terms of trade of farmers*; selected consumer goods, December 1986 to December 1993

	Dec. 1986	*Sept. 1988*	*Dec. 1990*	*Dec. 1991*	*Dec. 1993*
Sugar	100	48	35	20	22
Salt	100	462	143	168	130
Cooking oil	100	162	83	108	107
Milk powder	100	45	63	33	19
Cookies	100	62	39	47	38
Soap	100	79	50	34	35
Matches	100	28	19	15	24
Batteries	100	26	13	17	37
Capulanas	100	52	67	65	72
Shirts (second-hand)	100	262	143	200	217
Trousers (second-hand)	100	336	250	307	342
Blouses (second-hand)	100	127	200	180	217
Shoes (new)	100	163	16	7	7
Plates	100	155	84	97	98
Cups	100	161	125	141	138
Radios	100	204	111	55	57
Petrol	100	57	14	8	6

* Terms of trade of the farmers = producer price index/ price index consumer good

Source: Kappel (1991b).

liberalised system with former prices in a rationing system. However it is safe to conclude that the terms of trade for the farmers did not improve after the implementation of the ESRP and that this policy goal has not yet been achieved.

Virtually all the farmers acknowledged that the supply of consumer goods has significantly improved and become much more reliable. This is considered a positive result of the liberalisation package. On the other side of the coin are higher prices for these commodities, and this ambiguity is reflected in the overall perception of the ESRP. Taking both aspects into consideration, 53 per cent of the farmers felt that their economic situation improved after the implementation of the ESRP, 23 per cent felt that their situation had not improved, and 24 per cent thought that their economic situation had not changed at all. There was unanimous consensus among the farmers that the traders and the political class were the big winners of the reform.

Certainly the ESRP liberalisation package and some of the food aid operations carried out by international donors have boosted the commercial activities of the traders. Growing truck fleets, renovated shops, new warehouses and increasing personal wealth indicate good business and growing profits. In addition it must be taken into account that the rural traders operate in regional quasi-monopolies with virtually no competition, in other words, prices in the region are not competitive but monopolistic. In practically all villages there is only one shop, and even if there are two or more shops in a village or town, there is little competition between them. Most of the traders belong to the same ethnic group and their solidarity, family links and professional superiority causes them to behave like price setters in a cartel. Bearing in mind that the traders also hold a monopsonistic position when it comes to buying the harvest from the farmers, it becomes obvious that without initiating increased competition, politicians may find it very difficult to enforce an improvement of the farmers' terms of trade.

Markets, economic infrastructure and commercialisation

While the liberalisation package has undoubtedly increased (formal) market transactions, the smallholders' access to markets is still hampered by a very deficient economic infrastructure. This is particularly true of remote villages where bad roads impede economic activities in virtually every aspect. The opportunities for selling agricultural or other commodities, and for purchasing agricultural tools, intermediate products and consumer goods are still very limited. After four years of observation, the differences were striking between these remote places and the district centres and well-connected villages, where the economy has become very lively.

Despite the improvements in the regional centres of economic life, the generally bad road system, which was barely maintained during the civil war, is a considerable barrier to increased economic activity. Transportation and information costs are high and have a significant impact on markets for agricultural commodities, for intermediate, investment and consumer goods, and for capital and labour. Rehabilitation of the road system would certainly reduce transportation costs and would allow producers and traders to expand in response to the liberalised environment.

A rather limited transport and storage capacity for agricultural commodities is another meso-level bottleneck in the region. During the four years to December 1993, two bumper harvests were to a certain extent wasted because, *inter alia*, the transport and storage capacities of private traders and the public marketing organisation AGRICOM were inadequate. In some villages post-harvest losses were considerable because the harvest had to be stored under completely inappropriate conditions for too long a time.

Delay in marketing the produce has also been caused by severe liquidity shortages, particularly in the years with exceptionally good harvests. The credit supply of the (then still very active) public marketing organisation, AGRICOM, was insufficient in those years and AGRICOM was unable to pay on time for the inflow of commodities. As a consequence the traders experienced liquidity problems and delayed their purchases from the farmers. The problem resulted not only from policy errors in credit allocation on the macro level, but also from the very substandard finance sector in general. Only bank branches in the capital of the province were able to handle trade credit, and even they had to operate on the basis of extremely weak credit and bankruptcy regulations.

Existing and applied economic regulations do not promote the development of small and medium enterprises, but represent a major obstacle to starting or extending activities of this sort. Many farmers have long understood that commerce and trade craft offer interesting business opportunities, but economic regulations often inhibit any efforts in that direction. Apart from the virtually nonexistent access to formal credit, there are administrative barriers such as the dozens of forms that have to be filled in, the advance payment of fees and taxes and the completely arbitrary and harassing regulations of local authorities that impede entrepreneurship at all levels. Economic activities are suppressed or forced into the black economy, which exposes entrepreneurs operating under these circumstances to the risk of blackmail. Deregulation, a catchword that is often quoted without specifying exactly what it means and what is expected from it, would promote the development of small and medium-sized enterprises in the region.

Health and education

Health service institutions in the Cabo Delgado region consist of primary-health-care facilities called health centres and health posts. Health centres are small hospitals located in district centres. The staff carry out diagnostic and curative work on a large number of illnesses and even perform small surgical operations. The health posts are (at best) staffed with three to five people, typically two or three nurses and a midwife. However in many cases only a health worker is available, who has received only very basic training. In addition to treating a few types of disease, the nurses and health workers have to decide whether a patient should be transferred to a nearby health centre.

A major problem for both the health centres and the health posts is the supply of medicines, medical material, and equipment. Most institutions suffer from an irregular supply, and practically all staff members interviewed claimed that regular vaccination campaigns are not possible. In addition, payment of the medical staff is often delayed for up to three months. (A special case are the health workers, who are not on the payroll of the Ministry of Health but receive payment from patients on a voluntary basis.)

A much debated measure of the ESRP was the introduction of consultation fees and other charges. Previously the Mozambiquan health system had been, with a few exceptions, entirely free of charge. The question arose as to whether the new measure reduced the accessibility of health services to the poor. Without being able to provide a definite answer (and a tentative answer only for the four districts in Cabo Delgado), there were some indications that consultation fees and other charges were not the major problem when it came to adequate health services for the poor.

The fees changed varied between Mt 100 and Mt 500 per consultation, a rather small amount equivalent to about 1–3 kg of the staple food, cassava. The costs for a hospital bed varied between Mt 50 and Mt 500 per day. However there was obviously leeway to adjust the charges to the patient's ability to pay, and payments in kind were also accepted. Moreover, it must be concluded from several interviews that patients who were seriously ill and unable to pay for consultations, hospital beds or necessary medicine were not rejected and received the treatment free of charge.

Given the low fees and charges, and hence their small or negligible contribution to cost recovery, why charge at all. The main purpose of introducing fees was their screening function, in other words the measure prevents over-utilisation of very scarce resources in cases where consultation is not absolutely necessary. Economists are familiar with the fragile and questionable supply of free goods, and there is ample evidence that public systems where goods and services are supplied free of charge will be overutilised and danger of collapsing.

The hypothesis that the fees do not prevent the poor from gaining access to health service is, *inter alia*, supported by two findings: the expensive consultation fees charged by traditional healers and the high cost of medicine on the black market. Depending on the seriousness of the illness, the cost of treatment by traditional healers varies between Mt 500 and Mt 20 000 and may well exceed that upper limit. This indicates a rather high willingness and ability to pay, confirmed by frequent consultations with traditional healers.

People's willingness and ability to pay for medicine seems to be quite high. In every town or village it was confirmed that medicines such as antibiotics are often bought on the black market. Given the chronic supply difficulties of the official health system, it is not surprising that black markets flourish. Apart from the positive aspect of that supply channel, there is of course the negative aspect of inappropriate or even dangerous self-medication. There are strong indications that many people ask for fashionable medicine – where possible, injections rather than pills – even when their ailments are harmless.

It is obvious that extension of the technical capacities of the primary health care system, improved staffing levels and an orderly supply of medicine and medical materials would be decisive in improving the health situation in rural areas. However, despite the abovementioned increases in public expenditure in health, the availability of health services and drugs is tending to deteriorate in the region. This indicates a fundamental problem of priorities in the national health policy and has nothing to do with the adjustment programme and its implications. Compared with this fundamental problem, the 'screening' fees charged in the official health care system are of minor importance.

The level of education in the Cabo Delgado region is very low. Only 30 per cent of adults have ever attended school, and on average these did not progress further than second year. Programmes to teach the alphabet were in place in about half of the villages and towns studied in the sample; but fewer than 1 per cent of adults were enrolled in these programmes, and in many villages programmes had been discarded.

The educational situation for children is a little more favourable. At the time of the study about 60 per cent of children aged 7–15 were attending school or were currently enrolled – the actual enrolment rate was around 40 per cent but the drop-out rate was high. The school statistics give clear message: on average, between the first and the second years the number of students declines by about 40–50 per cent and from the second to the fifth year it declines by 40–50 per cent. Hence only 25–30 per cent of students continue their education for five years.

The teachers consulted in the study gave the following reasons for the high drop-out rates (frequency in descending order):

1. Parents' lack of money or the increasing cost of school materials.
2. Parents' lack of awareness of the value of and the need for education.
3. Older children are needed to work in the fields or in businesses, for part of the year, younger children often accompany their parents to work because of the lack of childcare facilities in the villages.
4. School buildings are unattractive and in a poor state of repair.
5. Enrolment of students for the first year of school is limited by maximum class size.
6. Religious and traditional rites impede regular school attendance, particularly of the older students, who are considered to be adults once they have gone through certain initiation rites.

As in the case of health service, the low school enrolment rates and the deficiencies of the education system are fundamental to underdeveloped countries. The one negative effect of the ESRP that may be of some importance is the increased cost of school materials, although many students reported that they had gone to school without schoolbooks, notebooks and pencils before implementation of the ESRP. The irregular supply of schoolbooks to shops in the small towns and villages seems to be an old problem of policy priorities and logistics.

CONCLUSIONS

Only a small fraction of the results of the monitoring programme has been summarised in this chapter, and nothing has been said about the conclusions drawn and recommendations given to the national and the regional administration. Nevertheless at least two of the findings from the study are clear.

First, the adjustment programme implemented in Mozambique has contributed to an improved economic environment for rural smallholders, even though progress is limited. Much remains to be done in order to achieve the main goals of stabilisation and structural adjustment, and in this sense the results summarised here can only be interpreted as an intermediate assessment. At the same time it is obvious that the smallholders' ability to utilise fully the improved economic environment is rather limited. Without national support and/or technical assistance through development aid, the effects of adjustment and the alleviation of rural poverty will remain small. Financial aid and programmes and technical assistance must be targeted and coordinated within a single conceptual framework.

Second, it seems worthwhile to set up regional monitoring programmes in order to understand the interaction between the macroeconomic, the mesoeconomic and the microeconomic levels. Although regional programmes cannot substitute for national survey, they have the advantage of producing quick and up-to-date results compared with cumbersome national surveys, which can be conducted only every five or so years at best. From a policy point of view, regional monitoring programmes seem an interesting and efficient complement to the costly and time-consuming nationwide monitoring programmes.

References

Corbo, Vittorio, Stanley Fischer and Steven B. Webb (eds) (1992) *Adjustment Lending Revisited* (Washington, DC: IMF).

Cornia, Giovanni Andrea *et al.* (1987) *Adjustment with a Human Face* (Oxford: Clarendon Press).

Ferroni, Marco and Ravi Kanbur (1990) *Poverty Conscious Restructuring of Public Expenditures* (Washington, DC: IMF).

Government of Mozambique, Ministry of Health (1988) *Prospects for Developing Health Care* (Maputo, Mozambique).

Government of Mozambique, (1992) *Strategy and Program for Economic Rehabilitation 1989/92*, report prepared for the Consultative Group for Mozambique (Paris, France).

Government of Mozambique (1992) *Strategy and Program for Managing the Transition to National Reconstruction*, report prepared for the Consultative Group for Mozambique (Paris, France).

Grootaert, Christiaan and Timothy Marchant (1991) *The Social Dimensions of Adjustment Priority Survey*, Working Paper No. 12 (Washington, DC: IMF).

Kappel, Rolf (1990a) *Mozambique: Restoring Rural Production and Trade*, Vol. I: Main Report (Washington, DC: World Bank).

Kappel, Rolf (1990b) *Mozambique: Restoring Rural Production and Trade*, Vol. II: Statistical Appendices (Washington, DC: World Bank).

Kappel, Rolf (1990c) *Making Adjustment Work for the Poor: A Framework for Policy Reform in Africa* (Washington, DC: World Bank).

Kappel, Rolf (1991a) *Monitoring Adjustment and Poverty in Rural Africa*, study conducted on behalf of the Swiss Development Corporation (Zurich, Switzerland).

Kappel, Rolf (1991b) *Adjustment and Rural Poverty in Mozambique: First Results of the Swiss Monitoring Project in Cabo Delgado* (Zurich, Switzerland).

Kappel, Rolf (1992) *Anpassung und landliche Armut; Monitoringbericht zuhanden der DEH* (Zurich, Switzerland).

Kappel, Rolf (1994) *Adjustment in Africa. Reforms, Results and the Road Ahead* (Washington, DC: World Bank).

10 How to Stop Inflation?

Karl Socher and Theresia Theurl

INFLATION IN THE TWENTIETH CENTURY

> Inflation is a process of continuously rising prices, or equivalently, of a continuously falling value of money. . . . A continuously falling value of pins, or of refrigerators, or of potatoes would not be regarded as a major social problem, important though it might be for the people directly engaged in the production and sale of those goods. The case of money is different precisely because the role that it plays in co-ordinating economic activity ensures that changes in its value over time impinge upon the well-being of everyone.[1]

History is replete with many and long periods of inflation, whose features have been manifold. A number of adjectives have been used to describe different types of inflation in greater detail and to distinguish them from each other: mild, moderate, creeping, rapid, acute, severe, extreme, high, persistent, chronic, trotting, galloping, hyper, open, supressed, anticipated, unanticipated, and many more. These characterisations focus on scale, duration, causes, dynamics, expectations, repercussions and the urgency of stabilisation. However they are neither defined in an exact manner nor used in a uniform way.

> High inflation means different things to different people. In Germany, it means 3 percent or more per year; in Mexico, 20 per cent per year; in Brazil, 15 percent per month; and in Argentina, 6 percent per week.[2]

More important than exact quantitative definitions and resulting denominations, however, is the fact that different types of inflation are characterised by:

- the causes of their emergence;
- how they are nourished (persistence, dynamics);
- their repercussions;
- the way they are to be stopped;
- the costs involved in their termination.

Inflationary experiences differ from each other, but an external shock can often be clearly identified as the origin of inflation. Wars, civil disorder, political revolution or serious social unrest are the classical causes of extraordinarily high budget deficits and monetary expansion. In most cases high rates of inflation rely on direct financing of the budget with the help of the Central Bank. The inflationary effects of the American War of Independence and the French Revolution financed by the issuance of assignats provide early examples of this.[3] Hyperinflation in Austria, Hungary, Poland, Germany and Russia followed the First World War. Equally, after the Second World War suppressed inflation in many European national economies turned into open inflation, which was contained only years later. In Germany stabilisation was achieved in 1948 by means of a comprehensive monetary reform; in Austria, however, it was not achieved until 1951/52 after two earlier and not very effective attempts of stabilisation. Greece, Hungary and China experienced hyperinflation after 1945.

The origins of inflation are complex, but four general features have been identified. Some countries, predominantly in Latin America, have suffered from high inflation. Among these, cases of hyperinflation (for example in Bolivia in 1984/85) are to be distinguished from chronic high inflation[4] (for example in Argentina, Brazil and Uruguay in the 1960s, Argentina, Chile and Uruguay in the 1970s, Israel in the early 1980s and Argentina, Brazil, Peru and Mexico at the end of the 1980s and the beginning of the 1990s). In 1988 and 1989 no less than 35 countries suffered from annual inflation rates exceeding 20 per cent. Out of these, nine economies experienced annual inflation rates of more than 100 per cent and five experienced more than 1000 per cent.[5]

In the cases cited above the causes can be found in the debt crisis of the developing world, in trade shocks or in political disturbances. Despite these pecularities the inflation-nourishing environment – budget deficits, inadequate monetary expansion, devaluation of the domestic currency – is comparable with the circumstances of the abovementioned war and postwar inflations. These examples of high inflation and the postwar inflationary experiences are analysed in an extensive literature.[6] Programmes aimed at stopping high rates of inflation have been monetary reforms, that is, the establishment of new monetary regimes. Apart from these high rates of inflation, single-or double-digit (annual) levels of inflation accompanied by stubbornness are important phenomena of the postwar period. In the 1960s the emergence of creeping inflation was deplored; this term refers to annual inflation rates that hardly exceeded 5 per cent.[7]

At the end of the 1960s a change occurred that resulted in a sharp acceleration in the rate of inflation. At the beginning of the 1970s there was the collapse of the international monetary system of Bretton Woods, followed by the oil price shock. At the centre of academic and political discussion at that time were the following factors: a long-run tendency towards inflation in the industrialised world; the international dimension of inflation, its simultaneous emergence with decreasing rates of economic growth and its persistence; the emphasis on cost factors, on distributional aspects and on market imperfections as the causes of the emergence and persistence of inflation; the consideration of expectations in explaining inflation; and the experiments with new stabilisation instruments such as incomes policies.[8] The cures for inflation employed during 1972/73 and 1979/80 were stabilisation measures (monetary, fiscal, and incomes policies).

In 1979 the foundation of the European Monetary System – EMS, a system of fixed but adjustable exchange rates – contributed to a better reconciliation of the objectives of greater stability at home and abroad. The EMS economies succeeded in reducing their inflation rates in the course of the 1980s, and inflation rates declined internationally.

In addition to extreme inflation (hyperinflation and high inflation) and low inflation with annual rates of less than 15 per cent, the post-war period also witnessed moderate rates of inflation.[9] After the containment of high inflation, phases of moderate inflation characterise an improvement in economic performance. These phases may also constitute the stage before high inflation rates occur, or they may develop out of a low inflationary period. Moderate inflation can ultimately be reduced to low inflation. Such a process of stabilisation usually involves substantial costs in terms of output reduction and unemployment. Commitment to a credible deflationary policy, tight fiscal and monetary policies and the removal of backward-looking fixing of prices and wages (indexation) are necessary aspects that must be included in a stabilisation programme for moderate rates of inflation.

A NEW TYPE OF INFLATION

In the 1990s a new type of inflation has emerged and the question of how to stop inflation has become a major issue once again. This specific form of inflation characterises the transformation process of the centrally planned economies into free-market economies (see Table 10.1) and will be discussed in this section.

Table 10.1 Eastern Europe and CIS consumer price index (percentage change against previous year)

	1992	*1993*	*1994**
Czech Republic	11	21	11
Slovakia	10	23	18
Hungary	23	23	25
Poland	43	37	30
Slovenia	93	23	20
Bulgaria	91	75	55
Romania	210	250	200
Croatia	666	1600	...
Russia	1100	900	500
Belarus	1000	1600	...
Ukraine	1600	3700	...
Kazakhstan	885	1350	...
Armenia	...	1800	...
Azerbaijan	...	1000	...
Kirgizia	...	1200	...
Moldova	...	1200	...
Tadzhikistan	...	2100	...
Turkmenistan	...	1900	...
Uzbekistan	...	1100	...

* Forecast

Source: WIIW forecasts, Austrian National Bank.

The new type of inflation can be classified as one of high rates with the danger of persistent high levels (for example in Poland) and a transition to hyperinflation (for example in the states of former Yugoslavia and several states of the former Soviet Union). There have been successful stabilisation and transformation programmes that, despite the costs incurred, have enabled several reform countries such as the Czech Republic, Hungary, Slovenia and the Baltic States to master the transition to moderate and even low inflation. Hence, stopping the new type of inflation implies implementation of either a restrictive monetary policy or a comprehensive monetary reform. The application of the instruments of stabilisation policy in the conventional monetary system of centrally planned economies is not effective.

Specific Challenges for Macroeconomic Management

An essential feature of the new type of inflation is the difficulty of containing it, which is much more complex and demanding than the termination of all historical episodes of inflation. Money has to be brought into position so as to fulfil free-market economic functions of coordination and control. For this reason an indispensable element of any transformation process is the creation of a monetary order that is in harmony with the principles of a market economy and guarantees a stable currency. The implementation of credible and consistent stabilisation and transformation programmes requires effective macroeconomic management. It has to incorporate the best possible reform structure and implementation patterns that take into account the respective monetary orders (the old, the interim and the desired one) and their overall economic implications. The timing and sequencing of the subsequent sets of tasks need to be decided, as set out below:

- Elimination of systemic monetary disequilibria.
- Creation of free-market decision-making and coordination mechanisms.
- Institutionalisation of financial markets.
- Ensure monetary control in line with market principles.
- Integration with the international monetary system.
- Political demarcation of the currency area (escape from inflation-nurturing monetary unions).

In fact all the reforming countries have attempted to fulfil these requirements: by reducing the monetary overhangs they accumulated under the old system, by breaking down the single-tier banking system and by setting up independent Central Banks. Yet in no case was it possible to avoid high inflation in the process of transition. Several reasons can be given as an explanation of this phenomenon. While devising the stabilisation programmes in transitional economies one must take into account information and statistics that are defective and obsolete. Further lack of experience with systems transformation aggravates the situation and ultimately leads to the conclusion that the means of stabilisation applied to economies in transition show different effects those shown by market economies. Even without this information and the effectivity problems, politicians and economists of the respective economies are overstreched with the conception and implementation of reform programmes.

Macroeconomic management faces multiple problems in a situation where the planning and administrative organisation of a socialist economy has already been destroyed, while the construction of coordinating institutions that are suitable for a market economy requires a substantial period of time. The problem concerning the optimal path of liberalisation lies in the need for very sophisticated planning of the different steps towards a market economy. Macroeconomic management in transition economies will also have to rely on the support of international organisations such as the International Monetary Fund. Also important is the international organisations' conceptional contribution by means of which the fine-tuning of the essential elements of stabilisation and restructuring programmes takes place. The reform countries are entitled to technical support for the establishment of institutions based on free-enterprise economic principles, such as foreign exchange markets and Central Banks. Moreover the significance of the international organisations' support for economies in transition lies in indirect effects. These are predominantly symbols of the will and the capacity to undertake reforms *vis-à-vis* foreign creditors, potential investors and the population concerned.

Macroeconomic management faces another grave problem. In many cases the fragile political framework of economies in transition was, and is, designed in a way that does not allow for an optimal sequencing of reforms. A recent and very impressive example is the former Soviet Union.

Transferability of Successful Stabilisation Concepts

The special features of the task of stabilisation raise the question of whether experiences can be applied that have been derived from post-war stabilisations and IMF-supported stabilisation programmes in high-inflation countries. According to our assessment, there are apparent similarities concerning the persistence and dynamics of inflation that can be used in the design and implementation of stabilisation programme. These similarities include:

- Stylised facts about the process of inflation.
- Budget disequilibrium–monetary alimentation–inflation–devaluation.
- The behaviour of governments and interest groups.[10]
- Protection and escape mechanisms of inflation-sensitive agents.
- The temporary abolition of wartime market mechanism.
- Costs of inflation and stabilisation.
- The significance of a stabilisation – facilitating monetary order for the functioning of a market economy.

A new challenge arises in that the current stabilisation attempts have to take place in an environment of a basic monetary transformation where monetary markets largely do not exist. Before reforms take place, economies in transition show unique features such as the pronounced uncertainty of economic agents, the distortion of prices and structure of production, excessive liquid funds combined with bottlenecks in the supply of goods, economic insulation, and non-convertible currencies. Yet the most aggravating problem in the early stage of transformation arises from the combination of institutions and patterns of behaviour from the old system (which are resistent to change) with the only rudimentary incentive structures of the free enterprise economies. These peculiarities have a twofold impact: On the one hand they affect the choice of a new monetary regime; on the other hand they nourish expectations of deviating effects, or have already caused them. These peculiarities have made the programmes inconsistent and ineffective, a fact that has impaired the programmes' credibility and led to output decline and persistent inflation.

The subsequent discussion will cover general elements derived from past stabilisation programmes and from results gained from systems transformed thus far. It is necessary, however, to investigate each case of stabilisation with its individualities in order to identify the elements of a stabilisation programme that can be transferred.

Stylised Facts of the New Type of High Inflation

There is general agreement among economists about the basic facts of the development and acceleration of inflation. These facts have been frequently observed in transition economies:[11]

1. High inflation is only one dimension of monetary disorder.
2. High inflation is always accompanied by an increase in the volume of money.
3. The increased volume of money is connected to persistent current-account financing of enormous budget deficits, followed by contributions to the budget.
4. At the beginning of a period of increased money supply, if this is greater than the increase in price levels in the long run the real stock of money grows. The velocity of circulation falls below its long-run value because economic agents with no experience with inflation need time to comprehend the gravity of new situation and to adjust.
5. When inflation accelerates and the rate increases faster than the volume of money, the real stock of money begins to decline. As

one velocity of inflation increases, people spend faster as they become aware of devaluation.

6. The consequence of this pattern is an augmented erosion of the monetary system. Money cannot fulfil its tasks: its value erodes first as a store, then as a unit of account and finally as a means of transaction. A substitution takes place from the domestic currency to a stable foreign one.
7. There follows a persistent and/or accelerating inflation (perhaps turning into hyperinflation), long-term nominal contracts disappear and are substituted by short-term, indexed contracts. Backward-looking pricing begins, and endogenous changes in pricing patterns occur.
8. An increasing dynamics of inflation leads to a rise in the real budget deficit as a percentage of real expenditure. At the end of a hyperinflation period real expenditure cannot increase any more, and the real stock of money becomes almost nil.
9. When there are flexible rates, the exchange rate also follows a typical sequence. At the beginning of an inflationary period, the exchange rate is almost stable, then it falls roughly in accordance with the inflation rate. During hyperinflation the exchange rate declines more rapidly than the inflation rate.[12] In the last stage the exchange rate may rise proportionately less than the price level because it takes some time to exchange the receipts of money into foreign currency, which is increasingly done by economic agents, so that a transaction made at the actual exchange rate would produce a loss.
10. The balance of payments may show a deficit in its capital accounts because of the flight of capital and the importation of foreign bank notes. The current account usually has a surplus because the depreciated exchange rate makes foreign purchases from the inflationary country cheap.
11. In most cases the interest rate is low, and real rates are negative over a long period of time. In such a situation it is an advantage to borrow money by order to purchase goods or foreign exchange (as long as the exchange rate is depreciating faster than purchasing power). Banks profit even during a period of negative interest rates as long as the difference between interest paid on deposits and loans remains large and positive. These factors help to expand the volume of credit and constitute a further contribution to the monetary feeding of inflation.

WHEN TO STOP INFLATION?

The importance of macroeconomic management

The effectiveness and cost of monetary reforms are influenced not only by their content but also by the process of preparation and implementation. Past reforms that were precisely prepared were initiated without being anticipated by the public, were conducted rigorously and in one step, and resulted in a low cost of preparation and implementation. In this context it is especially fruitful to compare the monetary reforms carried out in Austria and Western Germany after the Second World War.

> One monetary reform [step] may not give rise to a flight from money, but it is extremely doubtful that most individuals will remain calm after a second or third programme. . . . It is probably true that monetary reforms are also subject to diminishing returns.[13]

It is essential to involve the intervention of a regulating institution in far-reaching monetary reforms rather than to allow evolutionary processes to occur. There is a trade-off between the speedy implementation of the reform, which has to take place in a situation of high uncertainty and must avoid a perpetuation and deterioration of negative monetary preconditions, and delaying the reform until a time when its need can be calculated more exactly and the future environment can more easily be taken into consideration. The risks involved in the first strategy lie in the post-reform phase, that of the second in the pre-reform phase.

The Calculation of Optimum Timing

> 'There are basically two answers to the question of why there is inflation. One is that inflation is an integral part of a country's public finances. The other is that inflation continues because it is too hard or too costly to stop.'[14]

As a rule, economies in transition cannot rely on a well-functioning tax system; thus seigniorage constitutes an important source of revenue. However Dornbusch and Fischer point out that 'seigniorage is rarely an explicit reason for a government to pursue inflationary policies'.[15]

With respect to economic calculations aimed at stopping inflation, the costs and gains of inflation as well as the advantages of a stable currency and the burden of reducing the rate of inflation – the so-called stabilisation crisis – should be weighed carefully. Generally this calculation is strongly determined by the anticipated dynamics of inflation. The forecast of the latter is much more unfavourable in economies in transition than in market economies because the market mechanism is not yet functioning. In addition to economic considerations, political reasoning influences the timing of stabilisation.

Only under certain circumstances can the optimum time for stabilisation be laid down exactly. If agents have rational expectations, if inflation is correctly foreseen and everyone adapts their transactions accordingly, only unexpected policy measures or external shocks will create real effects.

Hyperinflation is linked to complete erosion of the monetary system and adoption of the functions of money by other media. Hence hyperinflation can be stopped almost overnight with minor output costs. Yet it is often overlooked that hyperinflation incurs high costs by causing massive allocative distortions. Also, 'the move to hyperinflation brings about a loss of governability and an arbitrary redistribution of income and wealth[16] resulting in undersirable economic, social and political developments.

The Benefits of a Stable Currency

A stable currency is one of the indispensable preconditions of a well-functioning market economy. This is true if, in the short run, the costs of stopping inflation are higher than the benefits of a stable currency. Two benefits that occur shortly after stabilisation are frequently not fully appreciated: capital flight comes to an end and is usually reversed; and gains from seigniorage are then reaped by the domestic economy.

The Benefits of Inflation

The benefits of inflation accrue to those sectors that receive the newly printed or issued notes and coins and to those that can adopt their prices, wages, rents, interest rates and so on faster than other sectors. In most cases it is the government that benefits most from inflation. Adapting to rising prices is more difficult in the household sector (wages, interests, rents, pensions), whereas the business sector tends to win. As a consequence the capital stock may increase. The distortion of relative prices, however, makes investment inefficient. If the additional money is directed to consumers – for instance by means of transfers or subsidies for consumer goods – inflation could favour consumption rather than investment. With respect to inflation in the CIS states, it is notable that budget deficits are partly the result of losses experienced by government-owned firms, of high wages and price controls. In these states there has been no stimulation of investment.

The Costs of Inflation

The costs of inflation are the consequence of a redistribution of income and wealth. Only when complete indexation is possible will the costs and benefits for agents receiving income and those owning wealth disappear. The remaining net costs in comparison with a stable currency will then be the costs of printing money, minting coins and calculating the indexation of all transactions.

Other costs resulting from distortions in allocation are as follows:

- Distortion of the price structure leads to market inefficiencies. Calculation is disturbed and costly. Goods, capital and land are bought when the real rate of return is negative because a loan bears a larger negative interest rate. Distortion is also caused by unforeseeable and accelerating inflation and a lack of immediate adaptation of nominal contracts.
- Capital flight causes the exchange rate to deteriorate and therefore makes foreign purchases (of goods and services, capital and land) too inexpensive.
- The use of foreign currencies (for example dollarisation) means that seigniorage accrues to the foreign Central Bank; and by forgetting the nominal values of foreign exchange in the form of bank notes, coins and deposits, the real resources of the inflationary country have to be used.

The Costs of Stopping Inflation

The costs of stopping inflation are loss of output and employment and distributional effects. The more pronounced expectations of inflation are, the more widespread backward-oriented pricing is and the more long-term contracts are made. The lower the credibility of the stabilisation programme and the more heterodox the contents of the programme, the higher the costs and the longer the duration of the process of adaptation.

Empirical evidence shows[17] that output and employment losses are particularly pronounced if nonaccelerating (moderate or high) inflation levels are sustained for a longer period of time. When economic agents and policy makers learn to live with inflation, stabilisation programmes often fail. Output and employment have declined in transition economies, reinforced and aggravated by the comprehensive restructuring of their economies.

In the cases of countries where attempts have been made to control hyperinflation (for example in Austria in 1922), output recovered but unemployment rose. These effects can be explained by the low productivity of labour, the hoarding of labour in phases of high or hyperinflation and by the more efficient calculations of the stablised currency.

THE POLITICAL ECONOMY OF STOPPING INFLATION

Monetary reforms result in economic costs for agents. The distribution of these costs to the different groups of a society can be quite uneven and differing safety and escape mechanisms exist for individual groups, the interests of some of which can be dominant. The new political economy demonstrates that the self-interests of politicians and bureaucrats may differ from the preferences of the majority of the voters. In addition, under certain circumstances the preferences of a minority of the voters can dominate economic policy. In both cases inflation will only be stopped if the economic cost–benefit indicators show that the ruling politicians will benefit as a result.

The most important distortion of economic cost–benefit analysis occurs when the future advantages of a stable currency are not included and the focus is on the immediate net benefits of stabilisation.

Macroeconomic management has to work against shortsighted group interests. If inflation is to be stopped before reaching the level of hyperinflation, credibility becomes a most important objective, so that inflationary expectations are reversed and confidence in the currency and the monetary system is restored. Credibility management should always be taken into account when stabilisation programmes are drafted for economies in transition.[18]

Monetary reform usually takes place in an atmosphere of conflict between the need to ensure the effectiveness of the reform and adherence to the basic rules of the democratic process. Past reforms that have stressed the necessity of maintaining democratic rules have led to the following:

- a delay in the realisation of reform targets;
- the necessity for additional reform steps;
- extension of the duration of reform;
- the increased influence of pressure groups;
- the postponement of vital steps, resulting in an increased burden on economic agents.

In nations where the problem-solving capacity of the parliamentary system is low and expectations of (internal and external) economic agents are dominated by this fact, a continuation of monetary disorder could destroy the political system. This danger is greatest in young democratic systems where attempts at economic reform have failed. Under such circumstances a credible and effective reform cannot be undertaken by incumbent politicians and external support may be required, as was the case in Austria after the First World War when a large foreign loan was organised by the League of Nations. Confidence was immediately restored, even without an announced plan to reduce the budget deficit. Representatives of creditors had seats in both the government and the Central Bank so as to monitor the stabilisation measures, which did much to foster credibility. In addition parliament delegated emergency powers to the government so that it might conduct the consolidation programme for the next two years.[19]

Another way of restoring confidence was tried by Estonia, which pegged its currency to the Deutsche Mark and committed itself to finding an adequate monetary policy by introducing a currency board.[20]

Likewise, a country may be able to restore confidence by pegging its exchange rate to a foreign currency or a basket of currencies, as Poland and the former Czechoslovakia did in the early 1990s. This strategy imposes considerable demands on economic policy, which has to be subordinated to the exchange rate target – the credibility of such programmes depends entirely on this requirement being met. Czechoslovakia's stabilisation programme was pursued consistently, but at times the Polish authorities tried to combine a strict exchange rate regime with accommodating monetary policy and a soft wage policy. As a result they failed to halt inflation and had to soften the exchange rate peg.

For economies in transition the most general precondition for the credibility of stabilisation programmes is their embodiment in consistent, comprehensive reforms that include the creation of an independent Central Bank, the targeting of monetary stability, a prohibition on the printing of money, and possibly the introduction of a new currency as well as fiscal reforms. Macroeconomic programmes should be brought in to line with both structural reforms and *ordnungspolitische* reforms (that is, reforms of the economic order). Consistency, which is tantamount to strictness, is the precondition for a stabilisation programme's effectiveness.

For some, a consistent programme might entail high adjustment costs. Whether these costs are accepted depends on their size, distribution and duration on whether a basic political consensus exists and on whether there is adequate information about the contents and aims of the programme. The degree of acceptance is also contingent on how successfully the strict interdependence between monetary stabilisation and the new economic system is taken into consideration. The issue of consistency and credibility is central to success. It is important for the monetary reform to mark the beginning of a period of prosperity for all groups.

THE MANAGEMENT OF STABILISATION

Fiscal Reforms

Budget deficits are usually the main source of inflationary money creation. Balancing the budget is a necessary precondition of stabilisation and a number of tools can be employed to increase revenues or cut expenditure. With inflation tax, receipts in real terms diminish, but after stabilisation the government will gain from the reduction in real tax losses.[21] Further relief is derived from the devaluation of government debt accumulated during inflation.

However stabilisation of the budget is not sufficient in itself – overall fiscal reforms are necessary: 'Thorough-going fiscal reform, both with respect to the tax base and tax administration, is important because it protects against shocks. With a broad tax base and an indexed tax system, shocks to the budget can be met by small changes in marginal taxes. Without those safeguards, inflationary finance is the automatic response.'[22]

Economies in transition have inefficient tax systems, and deficits that must be relieved by public spending. The main problem regarding public spending (especially in Russia and other CIS states) is the financing of state enterprise losses. However if governments halt this practice unemployment increases substantially, with heavy social and political consequences because of the lack of adequate unemployment benefit. Claassen[23] and others have proposed that unemployment benefit could be financed by means of foreign loans until work is available in the restructured industries. Claassen estimates that the funds required to do this in Russia would amount to US $3 billion per annum over an estimated period of reconstruction of about two years. This amount is comparatively low in relation to the aid and loans already disbursed to Russia or that promised by the IMF.

Reduction of Monetary Overhangs

At the beginning of the reform process the household sector tends to accumulate wealth that is worthless in real terms, while enterprises owe money to the state banks. This situation results from the practical application of decision making to coordinating mechanisms. The two main strategies for clearing up old monetary burdens are (1) currency reform, where existing claims and liabilities are devalued against capital assets on a discretionary basis, or (2) inflation as a means of adjustment, to take place of the beginning of the transformation process. Both options are aimed at ensuring that an official (perhaps new) currency succeeds in the monetarisation of the economy. However they represent only a first step and will contribute little to stabilising the economy unless they are followed by further action.

A successful break with the old currency system can make devaluation more transparent, increase the credilbility of the reform programme and create the prerequisites for a stable official currency. So far, none of the reforming countries have opted for this initial method. Instead the old monetary burdens have been reduced by means of inflation as a means of adjustment, an approach which requires more time to reach initial stabilisation and imposes higher demands on the stabilisation programme, which in turn is designed to keep adjustment inflation within limits. This corrective mechanism is rendered even more complicated by the fact that it has to be fine-tuned with the transformation of decision-making and coordination mechanisms.

The burdens of the previous monetary systems have differed among the individual reforming countries. Hungary, which began its reform process much earlier than the others, attempted to stabilise its economy without a clear-cut programme by continuing along the lines of gradual transformation, in the course of which the monetary overhang was reduced gradually. This implied a long period of slowly receding adjustment inflation. The majority of the other reforming countries are implementing (or planning) stabilisation programmes that are based, apart from restrictive monetary policy, on other pillars (budget, wages, exchange rates), and in each case these programmes have been drawn up and implemented in cooperation with the International Monetary Fund. Their common fundamental approach is to ensure macroeconomic stabilisation as the basis of all subsequent steps of systemic reform. Apart from specific national features, the approaches also differ in the way exchange rates are handled as an element of the stabilisation programme, in the formulation of incomes policy and in the degree of rigidity of application.

Incentive Structures for Enterprises, and Commercial and Central Banks

As a first step, the nonmonetary core of a market economy – that is, the legal system, market pricing, property privatisation, demonopolisation, competition rules, market-entry conditions and the defining of government competences – have to be institutionalised. In the reforming countries, even when it has been possible swiftly to pass the necessary regulations, they have not been fully implemented in the required time. Opposition by the parties involved, political and social concerns, and above all, the lack of human capital required to implement the regulations have slowed down privatisation, balance-sheet adjustment and the introduction of a bankruptcy code. The result is a hodge-podge of incentive structures that reduce the efficiency of the stabilisation programmes and entail continual adjustment as well as a persistently high inflationary base.

In the absence of financial markets and without requiring banks and manufacturing industries to aim at profitability and act in accordance with market principles and because losses were once covered by the state, stability-oriented economic-policy regulations could (and still can) be circumvented. Controls such as interest-rate adjustments and credit restrictions are bound to fail in such a set-up. On the contrary, adverse credit selection (also as regards to the supply of Central Bank money) as well as debt chains among enterprises place new and market-oriented enterprises at a disadvantage, with the result that they and the banks tend to abandon any change in their methods of operation. The undercapitalised commercial banks are no longer willing to restrict lending to unprofitable enterprises because many of these borrowers are simply too large to go bankrupt. As most of the commercial banks are still owned by the state, managers see no point in letting their major customers slip into insolvency. In the end the passive stance taken by the commercial banks has to be compensated for by the leniency of the

Central Bank, which knows that the continuation of a restrictive policy would jeopardise the functioning of the entire financial system.[24] Under the circumstances, the reaction of economic agents is rational and will not change until the balance sheets of enterprises and banks are tidied up and a clear ownership structure and a bankruptcy code have been established – in fact, not until responsibility and decision-making powers are united in a single body. The restructuring of the banking system, the establishment of a supervisory body and the safeguarding of the independence of a central bank are necessary preconditions for successful systems of transformation.

The Role of the Exchange–Rate System

Economies in transition that choose the exchange-rate system should be aware of the following factors:[25]

- The link to the international monetary system.
- The nominal anchor of the stabilisation programmes.
- Trade performance.
- The transfer of credibility to reform programme.

The centrally planned economies were based on domestic currencies while integration with the international division of labour requires the use of a convertible currency, which alone gives a country's monetary policy its required credibility. The availability of convertible currency makes it possible to attract foreign capital, to adopt world-market price relations and to direct foreign trade flows towards the West. The choice of an adequate exchange-rate system becomes a central decision.

Transition economies are gradually introducing convertibility (capital and trade, internal and external). The decision regarding an economy's exchange-rate regime ultimately depends on whether it is to serve as an instrument for stabilising expectations and price levels or as an economic adjustment instrument (including export promotion). The long-term strategy for paving the way for money to assume its new function suggests the advantage of the first option. In a globally changing environment this strategy requires a great deal of information where the extent of internal and external adjustment is difficult to estimate. An adequate exchange rate and the extent of the initial devaluation have to be determined, taking into account the expected rate of inflation and avoiding subsequent corrective adjustments.

The great risk of the strategy based on the exchange rate lies in the development of progressive overvaluation and expectations of devaluation, if disinflation fails, because the strict consistency condition for the entire programme has not been taken into account. The credibility of programmes suffers substantially (as in the case in Poland) if the exchange-rate target is abandoned and a currency with a more flexible exchange rate is adopted. A possible solution for finding the proper exchange rate is the use of a crawling peg from the very beginning of the reform process. This combines the advantages of a fixed rate with the necessary flexibility in the transition process. This instrument was used in Poland.

Cushioning Stabilisation with an Incomes Policy

In order to correct overall distortions in the context of monetary reform in situations of chronic inflation, police makers must reckon with a considerable decline in output and employment, whereby the individual economic burden is high and is distributed asymmetrically. Heterodox stabilisation programmes were applied with varying degrees of success in the 1980s in Latin American countries. The orthodox elements of a restrictive monetary and fiscal policy were combined with measures of incomes policy (temporary wage-price agreements and freezes). They focused on the avoidance of unemployment and recession by breaking inflation inertia (backward-oriented pricing, indexation) and facilitating the adjustment of price structures. Stabilisation can be thought of as an operation. The essential need is surgery; anesthetics may or may not be used. In this analogy, the change in the monetary-fiscal regime represents the surgery and incomes policy the anesthetic.[26] It is well known, however, that price controls that do not cure the causes of inflation cannot work permanently.

Austria's 'second round' in the postwar stabilisation programme was a heterodox stabilisation programme reinforced by a cooperative incomes policy. Between August 1947 and July 1951 five wage-price agreements were negotiated by the representatives of employers and employees. The negotiations were coordinated by the relevant ministries and sanctioned by Parliament and government. Regulated prices, tariffs in the public sector, transfers, subsidies, wages and tax rates were the central elements of the arrangements. Each new agreement was preceded by an estimation of the cost of living, which included increases in wages and transfers. The augmenting costs of this agreement led to a rise in the prices of goods. Each agreement interrupted the wage-price spiral for increasingly shorter periods. This was the main feature of an administrative search for the true set of relative prices. Each agreement solved pressing problems only in the short run, and a permanent stabilisation was impossible. In 1951 the controlled prices were increased by more than they had been in the past because the government and the social partners wanted a longer duration of new price level; but demand had not risen enough and was not able to support the higher prices. For the first time since the war some prices began to fall below their controlled level. This unexpected fall created the necessary confidence to launch a successful stabilisation programme, although measures taken, would not have been sufficient to stabilise the Austrian schilling.[27]

A basic problem for economies in transition lies in the scale and complexity of their need for reform, which seldom allows for the mitigating effects of orthodox programme. It is this aspect that considerably endanger the completion of reforms. Hence, wise and effective external and international support is necessary.

Monetary Management in the Post-reform Phase

High inflation means demonetisation of the economy. The higher the rate of inflation, the smaller the real stock of money at the moment of stabilisation, and the higher the possible expansion of the volume of money relative to the real stock of money that existed before inflation started. Remonetisation of the economy is necessary in that 'any policy package that makes a fetish out of limits on money growth to secure credibility is heading for trouble. The trouble shows up in high real interest rates . . . that are prolonged to the point where either serious recession or a violation of the money growth limits result.'[28]

For economies in transition specific requirements are imposed on macroeconomic management because information about the amount of money required in the new economic order cannot be derived from the past. In a market economy more money is demanded than in a planned economy, because more transactions have to be financed.

Political and Monetary Separation

Both in the past and nowadays the break-up of a political union is followed by the disintegration of its monetary union. The uncoordinated separation of the crown currency after the First World War is one example. The flight out of the inflationary crown of Austria led to competition in making the banknotes of the former monetary union of the different parts of the Habsburg Empire with the stamps of the new states, a practice that led to negative external effects by flow of unstamped notes to the remaining parts of Austria.

Following the political disintegration of Yugoslavia, Czechoslovakia and the Soviet Union, the former currency areas disappeared and the new states introduced new currencies. The Czech Republic and Slovakia dissolved their currency union in a jointly defined orderly manner. The political dissolution of Yugoslavia was preceded by the economic disintegration of the previously highly integrated Yugoslav market. The introduction of separate currencies in four former Yugoslav republics marked the flight from runaway inflation in the rest of Yugoslavia and the decision of these republics to seek their own brand of economic transformation and stabilisation. Only in Slovenia were the reform efforts crowned with success.

The former Soviet Union presents the most conspicuous example of monetary disintegration in an extremely inflationary environment in which systemic reform has barely got going. To remain in the rouble zone, which is dominated by the Russian Federation, means to follow a common path towards monetary stabilisation and to renounce an independent course of economic policy. Up to now, numerous attempts to coordinate these two goals have failed. Several members of the former rouble zone – beginning with the Baltic States – have meanwhile introduced their own currencies. It is imperative that each of the members reaches a decision regarding its future currency area in due course. This decision will have to take into consideration both the intended trade orientation and an assessment of Russia's chances of monetary stabilisation compared with those of the respective country. In the present situation the Russian rouble thoroughly fails to come up to the requirements of a common currency. A separation of the currency area should be based on a common reform programme. If this strategy is not feasible because of political or other reasons, it is in the interests of the individual states to undertake a separation at the earliest opportunity.

The Creation of a New Currency

In most situations where attempts have been made to curb high inflation, confidence has been restored by the creation of a new currency, either a parallel currency (Germany after the First World War) or a change in the name of the currency (Germany after the Second World War from Reichsmark to Deutsche Mark). For economies in transition the creation of a new currency symbolises the creation or a new state and/ or successful stabilisation. Apart from the symbolic aspect of a change of name, non-uniform conversion rates for various categories of liabilities and assets can eliminate a perceived monetary overhang and force redistribution of wealth. 'Given these considerations, the introduction of a new currency is likely to exert a variety of real and financial effects on the economy depending, in particular, on the state of expectations.'[29]

The Creation of a Parallel Currency

A parallel currency could be either private money (or monies) or government-created money, for instance by currency boards. The introduction of private money would be an alternative to the use of foreign money and would leave seigniorage intact. But in most cases where private money has developed it has been forbidden by the government or the Central Bank, so we cannot say whether private money is effective. It would probably function well only in small countries such as Slovenia (where its use was tried). In large countries such as Russia the dollar is already widely used so private money would be unable to serve the whole country and, above all, would be unlikely to attract the required confidence. During the period of transition banking supervision is not efficient enough to underpin the credibility of private banks.

CONCLUSIONS

Inflation is endangering the process of transition, which can be successful only with privatisation and the creation of markets. There is also the problem of the vicious circle of privatisation being difficult because the value of enterprises cannot be estimated due to the lack of market prices, which can only be established private enterprise. Inflation makes this vicious circle even more dangerous, because both privatisation and the creation of market prices becomes more difficult.

This may explain why friction is caused by the gradual realisation of monetary stabilisation, which is the only possible option in the given political and social environment. Economic costs are involved in the continuous decline of output and diminishing employment rates, as well as in the sluggish reduction of inflation. The speed and quality of the economic adjustment process depend on how the concomitant monetary problems are solved – the sooner a stable currency can be created, the greater the benefits for the economy.

When a government promises stable purchasing power but this is not achieved, confidence in the state declines and political unrest may inhibit stabilisation through macroeconomic management. Finally, because a democratic government may not be able to devise a concise plan for stabilisation, inflation may destroy confidence in the market economy and democracy itself. This confirms the message of Vaclav Klaus: 'Political and social consensus is . . . a crucial precondition for creating a stable monetary order.'[30]

Notes

1. Laidler and Parkin (1975), p. 741.
2. Dornbusch, Sturzenegger and Wolf (1990), p. 2. These authors define inflation rates of 1000 percent and higher as hyperinflation. For Cagan, hyperinflation starts when the inflation rate exceeds 50 per cent per month. This would imply an annual rate of more than 12 000 per cent, (see Cagan, 1956). Dornbusch, Sturzenegger and Wolf define high inflation as a monthly inflation rate of 15–20 per cent (over a longer period of time. Moderate inflation occurs, according to Dornbusch and Fischer, with persistent annual inflation rates of 15–30 per cent. See Dornbusch and Fischer, 1993).
3. For a description and analysis of inflations of past centuries, see essays in Capie (1991), Bresciani-Turroni (1937), van Walré de Bordes (1924).
4. Chronic inflation exhibits the following key characteristics: it lasts for long periods of time; it has an intermediate intensity: it has no inherent propensity to accelerate; economic agents learn how to live with inflation. Hyperinflation has a high intensity; inflation rates accelerate exponentially. Hyperinflation shows the tendency to destroy itself. See Vegh (1992) for further definitions.
5. For further information, see Dornbusch, Sturzenegger and Wolf (1990).
6. See for example, Vegh (1992), Dornbusch and Fischer (1986).
7. With respect to the competing explanatory models as well as for the discussion of cost–push versus demand–pull inflation, see Johnson (1967).
8. See, for example Claassen (1978), Meiselman and Laffer (1975), Laidler and Parkin (1975), Haberler (1972), Haberler (1976), Frisch (1977).
9. For case studies of moderate inflation and their theoretical background, see Dornbusch and Fischer (1993).
10. See Dornbusch and Edwards (1991), Theurl (1994).
11. See Vegh (1992), Bernholz and Gersbach (1992), Gersbach and Nedwed (1990), Riese (1986), Dornbusch, Sturzenegger and Wolf (1990), Portes (1993).
12. See Haberler (1970).
13. Gurley (1953), p. 95.
14. Dornbusch and Fischer (1993), p. 3.
15. Dornbusch and Fischer (1993), p. 40. Yet Poland is the only economy in transition treated in the case studies from which this conclusion has been derived.
16. Dornbusch, Sturzenegger and Wolf (1990).

17. See Sargent (1982), Vegh (1992), Dornbusch and Fischer (1986), Wicker (1986), Dornbusch and Fischer (1993).
18. The following considerations correspond directly with the other reform elements listed in the section on management of stabilisation. Compare these with the emphasis on near-term credibility in Dornbusch, Sturzenegger and Wolf (1990).
19. See Theurl (1994).
20. A currency board proposed by J.M. Keynes was in place in Northern Russia between 1918 and 1919. Recently, the currency board solution has been proposed for the countries of the former Soviet Union and Eastern Europe by different authors. The creation of a currency board as substitute for an autonomous Central Bank has the advantage of possibly creating more confidence than a Central Bank as such, if the statutes are fixed and not changeable – the issuance of fiat money above its stock of reserves would then be completely ruled out. See Hanke and Schuler (1993). A similar proposal was made by Socher (1993).
21. See Tanzi (1977).
22. Dornbusch, Sturzenegger and Wolf (1990), p. 56.
23. See Claassen (1993).
24. See Bofinger (1993), Calvo and Coricelli (1991).
25. Empirical findings about the efficacy of exchange-rate-based stabilisation programmes are ambiguous. See Vegh (1992), Dornbusch and Fischer (1993), Aghevli and Khan and Montiel (1991).
26. Dornbusch, Sturzenegger and Wolf (1990), p. 51. For an evaluation of heterodox programmes, also see Vegh (1992).
27. See Weber and Socher (1960), Theurl (1994).
28. Dornbusch and Fischer (1986).
29. Agéor and Lennblad (1992), p. iii.
30. Klaus (1993), p. 527.

References

Agénor, P. and Lennblad, A. (1992) *Inflation and Monetary Reform*, IMF Working Paper, WP/92/60 (Washington, DC: International Monetary Fund).

Aghevli, B., M. Khan and P. Montiel (1991) *Exchange Rate Policy in Developing Countries: Some Analytical Issues*, Occasional Paper no. 78 (Washington, DC: International Monetary Fund).

Bernholz, P. and H. Gersbach (1992) 'The Present Monetary Theory of Advanced Inflation: A Failure', *Journal of Institutional and Theoretical Economics*, vol. 148, pp. 705–9.

Bofinger, P. (1993) 'Erfahrungen mit Geldpolitik bei Existenz starker mikroökonomischer Verzerrungen', in H. Herr and A. Westphal (eds), *Transformation in Mittel- und Osteuropa* (Frankfurt: Campus), pp. 83–108.

Bresciani-Turroni, C. (1937) *The Economics of Inflation* (London: George Allen & Unwin).

Cagan, P. (1956) 'The Monetary Dynamics of Hyperinflation', in M. Friedman (ed.), *Studies in the Quality Theory of Money* (Chicago, Ill.: University of Chicago Press), pp. 25–117.

Calvo, G. and F. Coricelli (1991) 'Stabilizing a Previously Centrally-Planned Economy', *Economic Policy*, no. 14, pp. 32–52.
Capie, F. (ed.) (1991) *Major Inflations in History* (Hants: Edward Elgar Publishing).
Claassen, E. (1978) *Weltinflation* (Munich: Verlag Franz Vahlen).
Claassen, E. (1993) 'Russland im montären Chaos', *Neue Zürcher Zeitung*, vol. 21.
Dornbusch, R. and S. Edwards (eds) (1991) *The Macroeconomics of Populism in Latin America* (Chicago, Ill.: University of Chicago Press).
Dornbusch, R. and S. Fischer (1986) 'Stopping Hyperinflations Past and Present', *Weltwirtschaftliches Archiv*, vol. 72, pp. 1–47.
Dornbusch, R. and S. Fischer (1993) 'Moderate Inflation', *World Bank Economic Review*, vol. 7, pp. 1–44.
Dornbusch, R., F. Sturzenegger and H. Wolf (1990) 'Extreme Inflation: Dynamics and Stabilization', *Brookings Papers on Economic Activity*, 1990/2, pp. 1–84.
Frisch, H. (1977) 'Inflation Theory 1963–1975: A "Second Generation" Survey', *Journal of Economic Literature*, vol. 15, pp. 1289–317.
Gersbach, H. and H. Nedwed (1990) 'Die Selbststabilisierung von Hyperinflationen: Eine überraschende monetäre Arithmetik', *Kredit und Kapital*, vol. 23, pp. 318–32.
Gurley, J. (1953) 'Excess Liquidity and European Monetary Reforms, 1944–1952', *American Economic Review*, vol. 43, pp. 76–100.
Haberler, G. (1970) *Der Internationale Handel*, 10th ed (Berlin: Springer).
Haberler, G. (1972) *Incomes Policy and Inflation* (Washington, DC: American Enterprise Institute).
Haberler, G. (1976) *Some Currently Suggested Explanations and Cures for Inflation* (Washington, DC: American Enterprise Institute).
Hanke, S. and K. Schuler (1993) 'Currency Boards and Currency Convertibility', *Cato Journal*, vol. 12, pp. 687–705.
Johnson, H. (1967) *Essays in Monetary Economics* (London: George Allen & Unwin).
Klaus, V. (1993) 'Creating a Stable Monetary Order', *Cato Journal*, vol. 12, pp. 527–31.
Laidler, D. and M. Parkin (1975) 'Inflations: A Survey', *The Economic Journal*, vol. 85, pp. 741–809.
Meiselman, D. and A. Laffer (eds) (1975) *The Phenomenon of Worldwide Inflation* (Washington, DC: American Enterprise Institute for Public Policy Research).
Portes, R. (ed.) (1993) *Economic Transformation in Central Europe* (London: Centre for Economic Policy Research).
Riese, H. (1986) *Theorie der Inflation* (Tübingen: J.C.B. Mohr).
Sargent, T. (1982) 'The Ends of Four Big Inflations', in R. Hall (ed), *Inflation: Causes and Effects* (Chicago, Ill.: University of Chicago Press) pp. 41–97.
Socher, K. (1993) 'Mögliche Wege aus der russichen Inflation', *Neue Zürcher Zeitung* (5.6).
Tanzi, V. (1977) 'Inflation, Lags in Collection and the Real Value of Tax Revenue', *IMF Staff Papers*, vol. 24, pp. 154–67.

Theurl, T. (1994) *Experiences with Monetary Reform in Western European Countries with different Levels of Development*, East European Series, No. 4 (Vienna: Institute for Advanced Studies).

van Walré de Bordes, J. (1924) *The Austrian Crown* (London: P.S. King & Son).

Vegh, C., (1992) 'Stopping High Inflation', *IMF Staff Papers*, vol. 39, pp. 626–95.

Weber, W. and K. Socher (1960) 'Inflation und Inflationsbekäpfung in Österreich seit 1945', in G. Bombach (ed.) *Stabile Preise in wachsender Wirtschaft* (Tübingen: J.C.B. Mohr), pp. 51–74.

Wicker, E. (1986) 'Terminating Hyperinflation in the Dismembered Habsburg Monarchy', *American Economic Review*, vol. 76, pp. 350–64.

11 Managing Foreign Trade Policy in a Small Economy

Tomislav Presečan

Work on the economics of transition seems to have flourished during recent years. However, it looks as if there are no general solutions regarding the appropriate course of change in foreign trade policy for economies in transition, or whether radical change is needed. This chapter presents the case for liberalisation in a small transitional economy.

ON THE THEORY OF FOREIGN TRADE POLICY

Textbook case studies, models of small-economy trade policy and the experiences of this century suggest that free trade is the best solution; that is, hardly any attempt to influence international prices will work to the benefit of a small economy. This is consistent with the factor proportions theory of foreign trade, that is minimum or practically no limitation on trade flow leads to maximisation of the welfare of all the partners in trade. The new trade theories, based on economies of scale, imperfect competition and product differentiation, recognise many more cases where policy intervention is necessary. Still, as Helpman and Krugman (1989) put it, '. . . free trade is still a useful rule of thumb. . .'[1]

Since the late 1980s economies in transition have started from entirely different positions. Trade policies pursued by their governments have caused highly distorted price structures. So far, the policies have been inward oriented, resulting into disastrous consequences for their development. Now, a radical change in their development strategies is providing room to correct some of these accumulated distortions simply by reforming their trade policies. In small economies this necessarily means trade liberalisation. Small economies generally find it difficult to influence their own terms of trade and have to accept the existing world market price levels. Any move towards trade restrictions would mean lower GNP (measured in terms of international market prices), reduced consumption, less variety of goods on domestic markets and probably an increase in the quasi-monopolistic power of domestic producers, implying a lower level of domestic welfare. Protecting in selected sectors in small economies usually means the loss of jobs in other sectors.

In fact most of the transitional economies that emerged with the break-up of federal socialist states (the former Soviet Union and former Yugoslavia) are characteristic small economies. Their foreign trade policy heritage is impeding their adjustment process as they are reluctant to move towards more liberal foreign trade policies, which are needed for the overall transformation of their economic systems. Such reforms, in the opinion of many, work best if they are implemented gradually, for there are many factors that prevent sweeping changes. Foreign trade policy that might hasten the changes should therefore be avoided.

One of the main sectors that calls for restraint in foreign trade policy in a typical small transitional economy is the capital goods production sector, which was chosen as the founding sector of the socialised economy. Naturally it enjoyed the highest level of protection. The more important this sector is to the domestic economy in terms of employment and regional importance, the higher its influence over trade policy reforms.

The durable consumer goods sector has a similar influence, but with some differences. Such production was originally developed for purposes of import substitution but it failed to reach a sufficiently high level of efficiency to compete in the domestic market, let alone the international market. However, given the high level of subsidies provided, some products are now exportable and the sector is pushing for the liberalisation of essential imports of raw materials and intermediary products.

THE CROATIAN CASE STUDY

The fall of the Berlin Wall heralded the break-up of the Russian empire into small national economies. The dissolution of Yugoslavia has resulted in war and has led to the creation of new sovereign economies, thus adding to the number of such economies. In its transition from a market economy, Croatia's management of economic policy, and particularly trade policy, has attracted the interest of scholars and experts. Why should a small country such as Croatia liberalise its foreign trade policies? Several arguments, which are more or less common to all transitional economies, can be put forward.

The Need to Liberalise

Former Yugoslavia[2] was an economy of quite different preferences than those of the Republic of Croatia. The foreign trade policy of former Yugoslavia was based on various factors, but the major objective of foreign trade policy during the last two decades of the republic's existence was to provide enough revenue for the federal budget, a phenomenon that is common to both developing and transitional economies. The necessity to raise fiscal revenues through customs[3] and import duties[4] operating through the price mechanism of imports was also crucial in determining the general level of protection given to domestic production, in particular to safeguarding employment. Job security was of special concern to policy makers throughout the socialist world.

An additional task of foreign trade policy was to protect the balance of payments. During balance of payments crises[5] quantitative restrictions and/or other administrative instruments were used to curb imports.[6] However trade policy was characterised by lack of coordination and inconsistency and it did little to foster healthy economic growth, in order to provide a competitive environment in the domestic market. In essence, the foreign trade policy of the time promoted inward orientation[7] with no explicit intention of doing so. Today, policy makers in Croatia are pursuing an outward orientation, which requires different levels and structures of protection and a different set of instruments of protection.

The transitional period is presenting a whole array of additional problems. Privatisation and the changing role of the state in an emerging economy requires an entirely new approach to the protection of the domestic market. Stability of employment was sacred in the earlier system of self-management, but this is no longer the case and not all domestic production is protected. Today fiscal revenues are used to benefit the state and not the common good, although quasimonopoly rents from protected sectors would be collected also by private persons, not just by the state-owned companies. The currently rapid institutional and personnel changes are making it difficult to maintain control over the system; that is, public administration is even less efficient than it is used to be. This calls for a different approach to the protection of the domestic market.

In 1989 former Yugoslavia had a population of approximately 23.7 million[8] and GDP stood at approximately US$71.76 billion.[9] According to the 1991 census the Republic of Croatia has a population of around 4.8 million and its GDP is approximately US$10 billion. Due to the dissolution of Yugoslavia, the size of the internal market has reduced drastically,[10] bringing about the changes in both the pattern and the size of regional flows of goods, services and factors of production and thereby necessitating changes in foreign trade policy towards liberalisation.

The break-up of former Yugoslavia had a significant impact on foreign trade flows. Both exports and imports were previously dependent upon bilateral state contracts and agreements between states, especially exports of capital goods to developing countries. Certain inputs are no longer available domestically and have to be imported. Former agreements ranged from barter (for example capital goods exports in exchange for imported oil) to limited free trade areas (for example between former Yugoslavia, India and Egypt). Most of these agreements have now ceased to exist.

The stabilisation programme adopted by the Croatian government in 1993 has succeeded in checking inflation. The real effective exchange rate has appreciated, which means that the costs of stabilisation are being borne by the export sector and by domestic producers of importables that have to compete with increasingly competitive imports. Today exchange rate stability exists, partly due to the invisible excess supply of foreign exchange caused by decrease in the unregistered foreign exchange balances of private sector, the privatisation of state housing and other means of production, humanitarian aid and default on a portion of international debt, and partly due to Croatia's restrictive monetary and fiscal policies. Given these conditions, the current account deficit does not pose a threat to exchange rate stability, but as soon as conditions change the deficit problem will start to threaten the stability of the foreign exchange rate and that of domestic prices, necessitating a change in foreign trade policy.

The last, but not the least important fact is that former Yugoslavia had no incentive to participate in regional integration projects such as EFTA and/ or the EU. Now, given the trends of European integration, Croatia has two possible options: to liberalise to the extent it may participate in the European Free Trade Area or to apply for membership of the European Union. Both alternatives imply immediate and at least partial liberalisation of foreign trade policy.

The Path Towards Liberalisation

Successful liberalisation of foreign trade policy demands a gradual approach. Several points need to be emphasised here, which could lead to a change in the level and the structure of protection.

Firstly, customs tariffs should, in principle, reflect the different structures of demand for protection. The overall level of protection should be lower than it was in former Yugoslavia, and sectoral preferences should fit-in with new development priorities. This means that most items should have reduced customs protection or no customs duty at all. Reform of customs tariffs should be based upon the concept of effective protection and long-term development strategy of Croatia. Of course, there can be no immediate jump into a free trade world since the possibilities of paying for the adjustment costs are limited. Hence the liberalisation should be gradual, with clearly defined goals and time schedules. What is even more important is that the position of the administration should be credible and transparent as far as the reform process is concerned.

Secondly, additional import duties should be phased out over a reasonable period, and the length of this adjustment should allow for fiscal reforms to take place so that the differential in the average tax burden between Croatia and its main trading partners does not endanger the competitiveness of domestic producers.

Thirdly, quantitative restrictions should be gradually minimised and/or replaced by customs tariffs. A temporary solution would perhaps be the organised auction of import quotas in order to make the system more transparent and reduce quasi-monopoly rents based on quantitative restrictions.

Finally, the abovementioned changes should fit into one of the two integration alternatives, thus representing a transitional path towards regional integration.

SOME LESSONS FOR ECONOMIES IN TRANSITION

What possible lessons can be drawn for other economies in transition, over and above the general need to provide freer trade and more transparent foreign trade policy? The Croatian example proves the following.

Firstly, additional sources of tax revenue should replace revenue lost because of customs tariff liberalisation and the phasing out of additional import duties.

Secondly, accession to GATT, and especially ratification of the Uruguay Round agreement, would minimise domestic political pressure on increased unilateral protection.

Thirdly, depending on the specificity of each sector during the transition, selective production subsidies should be used in accordance with GATT rules.

Finally, the role of the state must change. Besides administering the necessary instruments of foreign trade policy, the government should move towards becoming an information broker, providing information on foreign trade opportunities and investment opportunities to both foreign and domestic residents. It must also assume the role of an educator in foreign trade practices; that is, organise seminars on international business practices, introduce foreign language courses, establish an international exchange of students and so on to facilitate foreign trade.

CONCLUSIONS

Small economies in transition, as experience shows, have little or no choice but to change their foreign trade policies in order to provide for both freer and larger international trade. The greater the share of GDP affected by international trade (directly or indirectly), the greater the possible benefits for their economies. However liberalisation should be associated with numerous additional economic policy measures, and should be gradual. Where possible, integration with free trade areas and/or customs unions will ensure further growth incentives.

Notes

1. See, for example, Helpman and Krugman (1986, 1989).
2. 'Former Yugoslavia' will be used throughout when referring to the Socialist Federal Republic of Yugoslavia in order to avoid confusion with the so-called 'Yugoslavia' under Milošević.
3. On average, nominal protection supplied by the 1978 customs tariff amounted to some 10 per cent during the 1980s and the beginning of the 1990s.
4. Three measures were used: customs registration duty (1 per cent of C.I.F. imported value), a special duty on imported goods (7.5 per cent during the 1990s) and duty for tax equalisation of importables (7.5 per cent during the 1990s). A further special duty was levied on some imported agricultural products.
5. In Croatia such a crisis took place between 1980 and 1987.
6. During the crisis 90 per cent of imports were subject to quantitative restriction.
7. See *World Development Report* (1987).
8. *World Development Report* (1991), p. 205.
9. *World Development Report* (1991), p. 209.
10. A further reduction in the size of the internal market was caused by the 1991 war.

References

Bhagwati, Jagdish (1988) *Protectionism* (Cambridge, Mass.: MIT Press).
Cheasty, Adrienne (1990) 'The Fiscal Implications of Reducing Trade Taxes', *Finance & Development*, vol. xxvii, no. 1, pp. 37–9.
Dornbusch, Rudiger (ed.) (1993) *Policymaking in the Open Economy* (Oxford: Oxford University Press).
Grossman, Gene M. (1992) *Imperfect Competition and International Trade* (Cambridge, Mass.: MIT Press).
Helpman, Elhanan and Krugman, Paul (1986) *Market Structure and Foreign Trade* (Cambridge, Mass.: MIT Press).
Helpman, Elhanan and Krugman, Paul (1989) *Trade Policy and Market Structure* (Cambridge, Mass.: MIT Press).
Pritchett, Lant and Sethi, Geeta (1994) 'Tariff Rates, Tariff Revenue, and Tariff Reform: Some New Facts', *The World Bank Economic Review*, vol. viii, no. 1, pp. 1–16.
World Development Report (1987, 1991) (Washington: World Bank).

12 Constraints on Monetary Policy for Transitional Economies

Pero Jurković

THE FISCAL CONSTRAINTS

The interdependence of fiscal and monetary policy is well known.[1] While fiscal policy determines the magnitude of the total balance of public revenue and expenditure, monetary policy determines the way financing is to be carried out. Thus, public revenue and expenditure balance; that is, public sector deficit or surplus becomes the deciding factor of interdependence between fiscal and monetary policy.

Generally speaking, this is the case in economies where these two economic policy components have a clearly defined function. Experience shows that it is not true for economies in transition from central planning to open market. In the latter case the public sector still includes state-owned that is, not yet privatised companies. Such companies have retained many characteristics of their socialist heritage, such as the so-called soft budget constraint; that is they operate outside the fundamental rules of financial discipline. The soft budget constraint may manifest itself as operational losses, as insolvency, or both. In the majority of cases state-owned companies were able to fund at least a part of their operations through government subsidies, by deferring payments, or by taking out various kinds of soft loans.[2]

Obviously, under such conditions no policy based on liquidity, including monetary policy, can be efficient. It goes without saying that any arbitrary increase of debt in terms of its effect is almost equal to the effects of monetary-base creation. Control over channels of monetary issue is lost because of the spreading chain of claims among businesses, which increases interenterprise arrears,[3] leading ultimately to inflation and the collapse of the economy.

Over and above these constraints standing in the way of an efficient monetary policy in economies in transition, the Central Bank (the monetary authority) too is encumbered by a number of parafiscal functions, such as:[4]

- open lines of credit to the budget;
- indirect monetisation of fiscal deficits;
- subsidy elements in the system of refinancing loans;
- uncontrolled use of secondary liquidity sources;
- the way of public debt creation.

During the period of structural adjustment most countries in transition experience a considerable decline in economic activity,[5] which reduces their already relatively low fiscal capacity. The imperfect tax system and a high degree of tax evasion (due to inadequate control over the discharge of tax liabilities, among other reasons), also limit the possible growth of public revenue in these countries.

Downward inelasticity of public expenditure, or the impossibility of its short-term reduction, is also present in countries undergoing transition. The inflexibility of public expenditure is even more pronounced in these countries because of the additional demand created through the financing of public needs that are characteristic of the restructuring phase of the economy. This is invariably true in the case of financing welfare programmes that focus on off-setting (at least partially) the consequences of an increase in unemployment.

Because of all this most countries in transition fail to avoid deficit financing of public expenditure. In these countries, the chance to avoid the use of deficit financing lies in the augmentation of domestic savings, since foreign borrowing might not be possible. However as domestic savings in these countries are low, the only way out is to resort to financing budget expenditure (and other public expenditure items) by direct government borrowing from the central monetary authority. This is certainly the least acceptable and perhaps the most inflatory way of financing such expenditure.[6] Such an approach gears monetary policy directly towards government revenue. Its original functions are either influenced or pushed into the background. In most cases, government borrowing from the Central Bank is seen as its vested right to use short-term loans to bridge the gap between an uneven flow of revenue and expenditure. However, more often than not such short-term loans turn out to be long-term ones because they cannot be repaid on time.

In addition to this direct line of credit, in transitional economies there is strong commercial bank and business pressure to monetise deficits in the economy. Such pressure could be due to commercial bank illiquidity arising from potential losses (bad assets) inherited from operations formerly managed by debtors and not by creditors; to the sustaining of loss-making companies (public and private) by covering their losses (including wage) through loans; to the insolvency of banks and other businesses; or because of sloppy public debt servicing and deferred settlement of other claims to other businesses. In such cases banks (often including the Central Bank) fail to resist the demands for such loans. Since they *de facto* belong to the public sector, the effects of indirect monetisation does not differ in any respect from direct lines of credit to the budget, apart from the fact that the entire financing process becomes less transparent.

In economies in transition the refinancing of loans granted by the Central Banks involves a subsidy element (such as lower than market interest rates and/or negative real interest rates), whereby this institution again assumes a para-fiscal role. In most cases the situation involves so-called selective credits to specific sectors (for example agriculture) or activities (such as exports). As a rule, selective credit is granted at below-market interest rates, either directly or by subsidising part of the interest payment from the budget. It is often granted under every favourable conditions, such as longer terms of repayment, preferential interest rates and so on. The allocational inefficiency of such an approach hardly requires detailed explanation. The existence of such loans is mostly explained by various social interests (usually political), but it is actually an excellent example of lobbying, of the activity of vested interests and of rent-seeking activities[7] in these economies. In addition to allocational inefficiency, monetary policy that relies to a large extent on selective programmes of refinancing hardly needs to be flexible and efficient.

Variation in the liquidity of commercial banks and other financial institutions is a phenomenon common to all economies. Hence by granting liquidity loans – discount windows – the Central Bank helps commercial banks to overcome such conditions. However in some economies in transition there is widespread use of so-called secondary liquidity sources, meaning a variety of automatic windows outside the control of the Central Bank. Such a blatant violation of financial discipline is made possible by inadequate regulations governing the national payments clearing system and improperly defined final settlement clauses.

This exaggerated use of secondary liquidity sources hardly differs from other forms of monetary-base creation, except for the fact that it escapes the control of the monetary authority. Under such conditions, of course, there is little left to form a solid base for an efficient monetary policy.

The manner of public debt creation in a country is of extreme importance for its monetary policy. Due to a limited fiscal capacity, substantial inherited liabilities and the additional expenditure required to restructure the economy, economies in transition generally experience a shortfall between revenue and expenditure and turn to public debt as a way of financing public expenditure. The size of public debt compared with GNP often reaches a high level in both absolute and relative terms.

Another related problem is the way of public debt creation. In the first place, public debt often arises as a result of direct borrowing to finance the budget, and not through the issue of government bonds and their sale in the financial market. Furthermore a large part of public debt in such countries is used to cover expenditure that has already been incurred. Obviously, the burden of such expenditure is shifted to future generations. Such a monetary-base creation disqualifies public debt financing as one of the most important monetary policy instruments in open market operations. This in fact means that government bonds will not be traded in the secondary market. It also is an underlying reason for the retention of a greater scope of discretionary measures used in the monetary policy of such countries than would otherwise be desirable. It is precisely such decisions that sustain all the other parafiscal monetary policy functions.

While considering the constraints on an efficient monetary policy originating in the fiscal domain, one can not neglect the relationship between these policies. Bearing in mind the above considerations, it must be pointed out that the more restrictive the fiscal policy, the more limited the scope of public sector deficit financing. In view of the prevailing state of affairs in economies in transition, it is practically impossible to achieve such an objective. In the context of stabilisation efforts, this automatically clears the way for the Central Bank to adopt as restrictive a monetary policy as possible. In economies in transition, because of its limited scope monetary policy is often so restrictive that it becomes counterproductive. A greater degree of fiscal restriction would allow for a more flexible monetary policy stance.

THE CROATIAN CASE

Since achieving monetary independence in late 1991, to a certain extent Croatia has succeeded in separating monetary policy from fiscal policy. Croatia had already introduced a two-tier banking system in the mid-1960s, considerably earlier than many other transitional economies.[8] At the present time there are about fifty commercial banks, but most are relatively small.

Table 12.1 NBC balance sheet (net, per cent)

	1991 (Dec.)	*1992 (Dec.)*	*1993 (Dec.)*	*1994 (April)*
Assets:				
NBC foreign assets	0.0	47.5	85.0	85.8
Claims on government	37.6	14.0	11.1	11.5
Claims on banks	62.4	38.5	3.9	2.7
Total	100.0	100.0	100.0	100.0
Liabilities:				
Monetary base	82.8	73.8	47.4	55.7
Foreign liabilities	0.0	0.0	3.2	2.0
Other liabilities (net)	17.2	26.2	49.4	42.3
Total	100.0	100.0	100.0	100.0

Until recently the status of the monetary authority and monetary policy instruments were not sufficient to ensure efficient monetary management. Therefore an independent monetary authority – the National Bank of Croatia (NBC) – was set up. Responsible only to parliament, its primary goal is to stabilise the national currency. Other economic policy goals may be pursued as long as they do not hamper attainment of the primary goal. Accordingly the legal status of the monetary authority in Croatia is defined along similar lines as those in Germany, Switzerland and Austria.

Monetary policy instruments have also been gradually changed in terms of strengthening their allocational neutrality. In 1993 the inherited selective credit instruments were abandoned because of their pronounced discriminatory character in terms of allocation. The function of the Central Bank has shifted from lending (refinancing facilities) to the creation of a monetary base through foreign exchange transactions between the Central Bank and commercial banks in the foreign exchange market. A part of the monetary base is now being created by extending loans to the government, but strict limits have been set on this. In compliance with the National Bank of Croatia Act, the government may only borrow from the Central Bank on a short-term basis in order to bridge the gap between revenue and expenditure, and the amount of such borrowing must not exceed 5 per cent of the planned volume of current budget revenues.

Changes in monetary policy can best be seen from changes in the balance sheet of the NBC (see Table 12.1). Foreign assets increased their share in the balance sheet from zero in December 1991 to 86 per

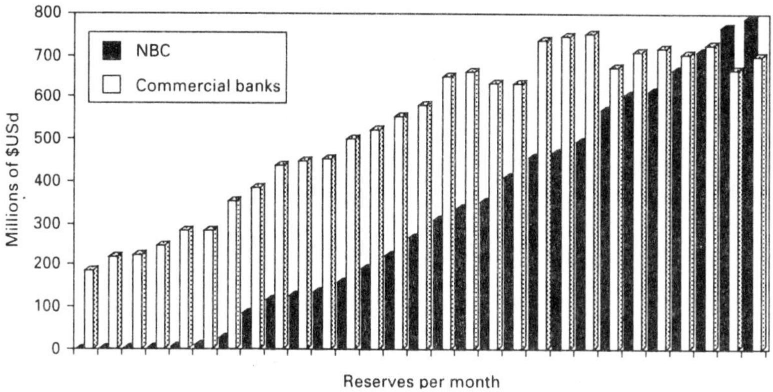

Figure 12.1 Foreign exchange reserves, January 1992 to May 1994

cent in April 1994. Credit to commercial banks decreased from 63 per cent in December 1991 to less than 3 per cent in April 1994. At the end of May 1994, international reserves, which were virtually zero at the time of monetary independence, amounted to about US$800 million (see Figure 12.1).

In spite of all these changes the para-fiscal character of the Croatian monetary authority has not changed completely. Thus subsidised loans to government, the collection of seigniorage and implicit deposit insurance remain among the Central Bank's activities.

Due to the regional war, Croatia inherited high inflation and many transitional problems. Inflation became a real threat to the reforms that were set in motion in 1993. Thus curbing inflation became the top priority and a necessary precondition for further transformation of the economy. Until such time, seigniorage implied a substantial redistribution of capital to current expenditure; that is, *de facto* disinvestment. Part of the investment fund was shifted to the current budget through high (but real negative) interest rates, which also meant that customers were being indirectly subsidised. The problem was solved only after the establishment of price stability and real positive rates of interest (see Figures 12.2 and 12.3).

One of the main problems to persist in the Croatian banking system is the uncontrolled (automatic) use of secondary liquidity resources by illiquid banks. This phenomenon thwarts the efficient management of monetary policy and the efficient supervision of the money supply by

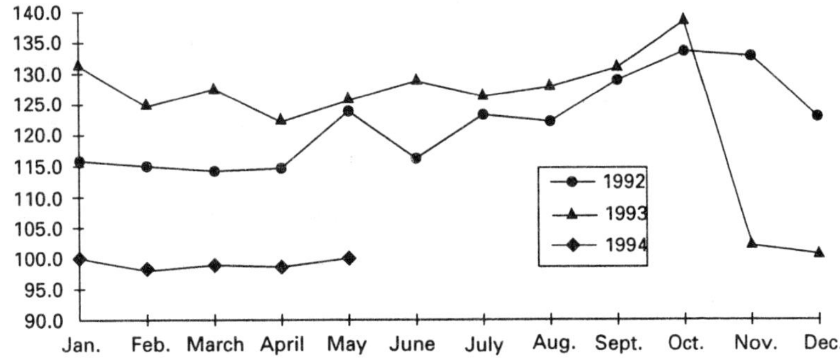

Figure 12.2 Consumer price index, 1992–4

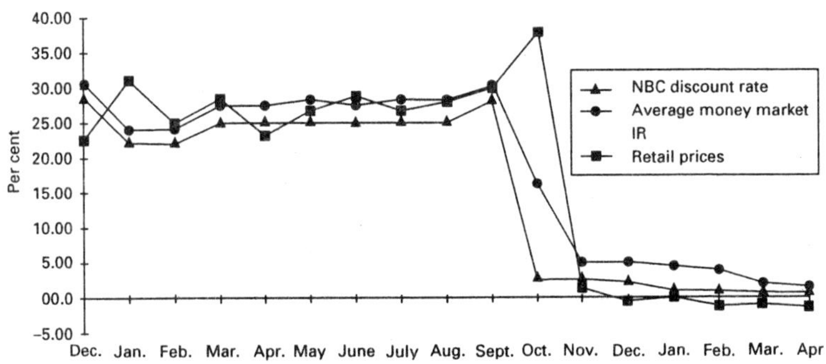

Figure 12.3 Monthly prices and interest rates, December 1992 to April 1994

the Central Bank. The problem is closely linked to the inherited insolvent-client structure and to the high war damages suffered by these clients. It is a classic example of violation of financial discipline and disregard of the hard budget constraint principle.

A way out of the situation is perhaps to be found in the rehabilitation of illiquid banks or the liquidation of insolvent banks. The Rehabilitation Act has been enacted, and ways for its most efficient implementation are being sought. Essentially this involves:

- sorting out the portfolios of banks through replacing (via the State Bank Rehabilitation Agency) insolvent banks' non-performing loans

with own investments, partly in cash and partly in government bonds, and
- preventing any recurrence of insolvency among the rehabilitated banks through the simultaneous restructuring of loss-making clients.

An important reason for the lack of financial discipline in Croatia's banking system is to be found in the present payments clearing system. In spite of some changes, the system has remained basically unchanged. It is fairly well equipped with advanced technology, but only one institution (ZAP – the domestic payments clearing agency) is allowed to operate. The system has some inherent drawbacks that are hampering effiicient monetary policy enforcement. Specifically, this means that even today Croatia is failing to implement the so-called double-cover principle. In practical terms this means that the bank can not always avoid slipping into a negative balance on its given account. The problem is further complicated by the fact that all payments are still settled exclusively by the ZAP. Thus commercial banks can not gain daily access to the assets and liabilities of their customers, nor to their own account. The payment system involves an imbalance between settlement and clearing functions, the former dominating the latter.

Another major constraint on the efficient functioning of the monetary and overall financial system in Croatia is the extensive chain of arrears among companies and other businesses – a phenomenon that is characteristic of countries undergoing transition. As in many other countries, the origins of this problem in Croatia can be traced to the inefficient inherited economic structure, a lack of firm determination to penalise those customers who fail to comply with the elementary rules of financial discipline, and the absence of a mandatory bankruptcy procedure. According to available data (to the end of March 1994), the volume of such arrears in Croatia was roughly equal to the total amount of currency in circulation. The negative implications of this situation hardly need to be discussed. This is, *de facto*, a forced redistribution of income with all para-fiscal features sustaining the inefficient inherited economic structure; that is, the required economic restructuring is being thwarted. The elimination of this phenomenon is also a precondition for the establishment and maintenance of an efficient lending policy. But the lack of financial discipline is something that can not be resolved overnight.

Finally, as far as relations between monetary and fiscal policy are concerned, most of the monetary base in the country is being created through the monetary effects of foreign exchange transactions between the Central Bank and the commercial banks. A few points should be made in this regard.

First, the foreign exchange market in Croatia is marked by an excess supply of foreign exchange. This excess can be attributed to a variety of causes, such as substantial foreign exchange earnings from the tourist trade, foreign remittances, humanitarian aid, extra-institutional foreign exchange and so on. In 1992 and 1993 Croatia had a current account surplus, a capital account surplus and increased international reserves. The low uptake of foreign exchange can be attributed to a lack of demand for small investments and the generally low level of economic activity in the country.

Second, in the management of monetary policy and implementation of the government's stabilisation programme, the policy makers have opted to control monetary aggregates (monetary base targeting) rather than resort to an exchange rate anchor (floating exchange rate).

Third, because of the largely undeveloped financial market (as is the case in other economies in transition) and more specifically the underdeveloped government bond market (and other securities as well), the possibility of indirect monetary control is very limited. Therefore it is difficult to sterilise the monetary effects of foreign exchange transactions. To offset this problem the National Bank introduced new securities, the so-called NBC bills, which are sold primarily to commercial banks. At present these bills are the most important, but very expensive, instruments of money sterilisation. However because of the high cost of such sterilisation (high real interest rates to attract commercial banks), their ultimate effect is limited.[9] In order to maintain a reasonable balance in the foreign exchange market, prevent further appreciation of the national currency (which would be detrimental to the export-orientated Croatian economy) and sustain an adequate level of internal liquidity, the monetary authority must support monetary policy with an appropriate fiscal policy. The importance of fiscal policy always increases with time.[10]

CONCLUSIONS

The Croatian economy, in spite of some specific features of its own, has much in common with other transitional economies. It has transformed its monetary policy instruments and has successfully reduced inflation from hyperinflationary levels to the deflation of the first half of 1994. Monetary policy has played a very important role in the heterodox anti-inflationary plan. But to maintain the credibility of the programme (and low inflation) fiscal policy must be closely coordinated with monetary policy. In order to restructure the economy, the speeding up of economic growth is necessary; but this cannot be achieved through fiscal expansion and following the traditional Keynesian approach.

To obtain a sufficient degree of freedom in monetary policy there must be a reduction in the level of government borrowing from the Central Bank. Of course such a monetary policy orientation would also permit the allocation of financial resources to those sectors of the economy where resources would attain the highest effect. Therefore such a combination of monetary and fiscal policy would be desirable not only in terms of maintaining the success of the 1993 stabilisation programme in keeping inflation very low,[11] but fiscal restraint is also very important in terms of reconstruction of the country and speedy economic development. Bearing in mind the downward rigidities in fiscal expenditure and the pressure to increase them for various reasons (from social safety net to subsidising loss making-enterprises), this task will be very difficult indeed. It is of utmost importance to liberalise domestic resources for private investment in emerging firms[12] and prevent crowding out. The government's role is, and will remain, very important in the country's economy (as it is in every other country in the world), but the key to success is private sector initiative. Restructuring is always very painful and risky.[13] Governments can not do the job alone and fiscal restriction must enable emerging enterprises and the private sector to grow. If not, two things might happen: either the government will remain the main entrepreneur in the economy and will carry on misallocating resources, or recession will continue and no substantial change will take place. In both scenarios transitional economies will not attain their final goal: the complete restructuring of their economies and an improved standard of living.

Notes

1. See Pero Jurković, *Fiskalna politika u teoriji i praksi* (Zagreb: Informator, 1989).
2. Janos Kornai, 'Transformational Recession: A General Phenomenon Examined through the Example of Hungary's Development', *Economie Appliqué*, vol. XLVI, no. 2 (1993), pp. 181–227.
3. Eric V. Clifton and Mohsin S. Khan, 'Inter-enterprise Arrears in Transforming Economies: The Case of Romania', *IMF Staff Papers*, vol. 40, no. 3 (1993), pp. 680–96.

4. Maxwell J. Fry, 'The Fiscal Abuse of Central Banks', *IMF Working Paper*, July 1993, WP/93/58.
5. J. Kornai, op. cit.
6. Carlo Cotarelli, *Limiting Central Bank Credit to the Government – Theory and Practice* (Washington: IMF, 1993).
7. Vito Tanzi, 'Fiscal Policy, Growth and the Design of Stabilization Programs', in Mario I. Blejer and Ke-young Chu (eds), *Fiscal Policy, Stabilization and Growth in Developing Countries* (Washington: IMF, 1989), pp. 13–32.
8. See proceedings of the symposium on Central Banking Issues in Emerging Market Economies, 1990.
9. Susan Schadler, Maria Carkovic, Adam Bennett and Robert Kahn, 'Recent Experiences with Surges in Capital Inflows', *IMF Occasional Paper*, no. 108 (Washington: IMF, 1993).
10. Pablo E. Guidotti and Carlos A. Vegh, 'Losing Credibility: The Stabilization Blues', *IMF Working Paper*, WP/92/73 (Washington: IMF, 1992).
11. Mario I. Blejer and Adrienne Cheasty, 'High Inflation, Heterodox Stabilization and Fiscal Policy', in M. I. Blejer and Ke-young Chu (eds), *Fiscal Policy, Stabilization and Growth in Developing Countries* (Washington: IMF, 1989).
12. Mario I. Blejer and Adrienne Cheasty, 'Fiscal Policy and Mobilization of Savings for Growth', in Blejer and Ke-young Chu (1989), op. cit.
13. V. Tanzi, op. cit.

Additional References

Blejer, Mario I. and Ke-young Chu (eds) (1989) *Fiscal Policy, Stabilization and Growth in Developing Countries* (Washington: IMF).

Caprio, Gerard, Jr. and Ross Levine (1994) 'Reforming Finance in Transitional Socialist Economies', *The World Bank Research Observer*, vol. 9 (January), pp. 1–24.

Central Banking Issues in Emerging Market-Oriented Economies: A Symposium Sponsored by the Federal Reserve Bank of Kansas City, Jackson Hole, Wyoming, 23–25 August 1990.

The National Bank of Croatia Act, Official Gazette, 74/1992.

NBC Main Statistical Indicators, vol. II, no. 5 (15 June 1994).

Sarcinelli, Mario (1992) 'Eastern Europe and the Financial Sector: Where Are They Going?', *Banca Nazionale del Lavoro Quarterly Review*, no. 183 (December), pp. 463–92.

13 Macroeconomic Issues in Eastern Europe

Ivo Družić

Macroeconomic management problems in Eastern Europe are not a new phenomenon. With the fall of the Austrian and Ottoman Empires some 80 years ago, some 13 countries emerged in Eastern Europe that today have become key factors in the (in)stability not only of Europe but of the entire world. After all, the First and Second World Wars were triggered in the region. Now, with the end of Soviet rule, former states are again falling apart and wars are starting all over again.

In 1993, in response to these threatening events, the US and the European Union (EU) jointly started a Partnership for Peace programme for Eastern Europe. This programme has sound political reasoning in viewing Eastern Europe as a buffer zone between Russia and Western Europe. However, except for the desire to prevent the large-scale migration of Eastern Europeans to the Western countries, there is no clear economic reasoning behind the programme. This might lead to a failure on the part of Eastern European economies to adapt themselves to modern market conditions in a relatively short period of time.

In 1943 a quite opposite approach was proposed by Rosenstein-Rodan – the creation of an Eastern Europe Investment Trust (EEIT).[1] Today, in more than one way this programme seems to be more appropriate than the celebrated Partnership for Peace.

There are two basic reasons why the EEIT proposal deserves a closer look. Firstly, this approach not only attempted to solve Eastern Europe's economic problems but also took into account the world's scarcity of resources. Secondly, it correctly predicted what would happen if Eastern Europe were to adopt a specific form of industrialisation; that is, industrialisation based on the Russian model would lead to very heavy and unnecessary sacrifices because capital would have to be raised internally at the expense of lowered living standards and reduced consumption. Furthermore, the building of heavy industry in Eastern Europe would only add to the world's excess capacity.

For a number of reasons, there is no analogy between the industrialisation that took place in the nineteenth century in most Western countries and the current transition process in Eastern Europe. Firstly, instruments such as shares and loans were inappropriate in the nineteenth century because units were smaller and did not take advantage of external economies. Secondly, technical progress was the main driving force in developed countries from the beginning of the nineteenth century onwards, while in international depressed areas, as they were called then, there was hardly any technical progress but the application of given technical knowledge only. Thirdly, an increase in overhead costs and fixed capital raised the risk of loss of capital and reduced factor mobility. State supervision and guarantees substantially reduced these risks and for that reason constituted an unavoidable part of the international investment scheme.[2]

CONCEPTUAL MACROECONOMIC ISSUES

The conceptual confusion and empirical inconsistency over many macroeconomic issues in developed market economies at times causes an unbridgeable obstacle for policy makers in transition economies. Some scholars consider macroeconomics to be in such a sorry state, confused by recent experiences and driven by methodological dissention, that practically no agreement between the various schools of macroeconomic thought can be reached. At least seven schools exist: Keynesian, monetarist, new classical, new Keynesian, supply-side, neo-neoclassical and structuralist.

The first dimension by which we can classify schools of thought pertains to the treatment of wages and prices. Some of the more recent models contain, explicitly or implicitly, either real-wage rigidity in one or other sense, or real-wage stickiness. The contrasting models possess one or other kind of impediment to the adjustment of nominal wages and prices, which gives rise to stickiness in average wage or price levels. While on any given day some wages may change, most wages or prices – because of scheduling effects – remain unchanged. Furthermore, prices and wages may be simultaneously flexible all of the time or in a given time period. The local market clearing concept is one example of this framework.

The second dimension of classification refers to the concept of expectations. In a more general framework the expectations of people are treated to a certain degree as exogenous – as not entirely a function of the current state of the economy and its structure. This approach emphasises inadequate communication between the members of an economy and a consequent lack of coordination. Another approach deals with rational expectations.

Encamped under the banner of non-rational expectations and wage-price stability are those following in the footsteps of Keynes – the true Keynesians. In the same camp, but quite different in their outlook, are Milton Friedman and the traditional monetarists. While the new classical school differs in that it has adopted rational-expectations theory, the new Keynesian school departs by using models pertaining to stickiness in the money-wage and money-price levels. Supply-side macroeconomics fits the new classical mould, differing only in the roles it assigns to monetary and fiscal policy. The neo-neoclassical real theory of fluctuations also exhibits price-wage flexibility and rational expectations, though it is non-monetary in character. Finally, a group of recently arrived models from the structuralist school invoke real-wage rigidity or stickiness, with or without rational expectations.[3]

MACROECONOMIC POLICY ISSUES

When applied to a transition economy, the abovementioned macroeconomic approaches tend to influence different institutions within the same transition economy. For example Keynesian concepts may influence the Ministry of Finance, the monetarist approach may influence the Central Bank and neo-neoclassical theory may influence the Ministry of Labour. This not only causes hot theoretical debate but could seriously hinder the transition process.

The key question here is, what should transition-friendly macroeconomic management really consist of? To seek the answer to this is to court confusion. According to neo-Keynesian economists such as James Meade, Franco Modigliani and James Tobin, it is the government's role to remedy economic ills. Monetarists Milton Friedman and Karl Brunner, on the other hand, while acknowledging the effectiveness of governmental economic policies in the short run, deny any such role in the long run. In fact they attribute most economic ills to governmental meddling in economic affairs. New classical or rational-expectations economists have extended these *laissez-faire* conclusions. Robert Lucas and Thomas Sargent, the major protagonists of this group, have stunned economists with their arguments supporting the view that stabilisation policies are impotent even in the short run. At the non-conventional end of the spectrum, post-Keynesian and Marxian economists have little sympathy for the pronouncements of conventional economists. Many believe that the malady has progressed too far for the government to doctor the economy in any significant way.[4]

Regardless of these controversies, macroeconomic management in transitional economies is dutifully following the international financial institutions' usual demand-management approach through monetary and fiscal management in terms of soft or hard budget constraints. From these activities the following observation can be made: a restrictive monetary policy, or a policy of hard budget constraints, as a condition for a stable macroeconomic environment is, especially in the long run, more appropriate for transition than is a soft budget policy. Transition is bound to fail in a destabilised economy. For instance inflation mops up savings and increases uncertainty about the future value of assets for both investors and shareholders. In such a rigorous environment, privatisation might, admittedly, bring about income redistribution, but it must be recalled that no market economy has ever been built on equal incomes and wealth. Increasing inequalities are a precondition for success rather than a constraint on transition, insofar as they favour a concentration of wealth as a driving force for the growth of GDP within a new market-oriented business structure.

The question of political and ideological constraints on transition can, however, be raised. At any given moment governments need to decide whether to prioritise political or economic stability. This, however, is a delicate problem in an ongoing process of transformation and gives rise to different approaches, depending on the political circumstances in each country. If political stability is the priority at any given moment, then monetary policy will be softened, in spite of negative long-run consequences on the transition process. The climax is reached at the intersection point of the limits of the political and social endurance of the population and the marginal earnings through the activation of new resources in a transformed market-oriented economy. In other words, if the political and social endurance of the population cannot be maintained until such new resources are activated, the need for political stability could gain the upper hand, which will naturally result in the introduction of an increasing number of soft budget constraints.

Consequently a suitable and carefully balanced combination of elements of hard and soft budget constraint policies seems to be the main but difficult to achieve target of transition monetary policy, with a desirable impact on the privatisation process. The softening of monetary policy can initially have a positive impact on transition, but if these elements are pursued for too long the macroeconomic environment will gradually become distorted and distant from the criteria and value standards of the world market.[5]

According to the IMF recipe, fiscal policy complements monetary policy because of its role in alleviating the budget deficit or keeping it below 5 per cent of GDP. In spite of decreasing state outlays, budget deficits in the transition economies are not likely to remain within this IMF-set margin because of falling profits and revenues. New tax structures, including personal income tax and VAT, are not yet in place to replace the old tax structure that was so heavily dependent on the revenues of state-owned firms. The need for a social safety-net requires further development and refinement of the tax system.

While, on the one hand, reform should concentrate on finding ways of financing the budget deficit in non-inflationary ways, on the other hand it should provide, as much as possible, a liberal taxation environment as a prerequisite for encouraging entrepreneurship. It is very well known that a centrally planned economy is usually burdened with so-called physical planning, or targeting physical allocation of both human and capital resources. In such an environment the fiscal or tax policy is just a lever for filling or draining budget positions. A tax system appropriate to a market economy should not have profit as its primary revenue source. There should be very few moderate taxes so as not to interfere with incentives.[6] At the same time, as capital gains in transition periods tend to be very high there should also be significantly higher taxes, but not so high as to discourage incentives for profit-seeking activities.

When trying to meet these two objectives (that is, low business taxation and low inflation), governments are confronted with the fact that designing and introducing a new fiscal system takes time. In the meantime they are faced with the problem of inflation, since the introduction of VAT and personal income tax produces redistributive and inflatory short-term effects. Some stress the role of national governments as key creators (and therefore potential key terminators) of inflation, although inflation is the responsibility of the many players taking part in determining prices and wages.[7]

In practice this means that, in the early stages of transition, there is a strong need for temporary assistance from abroad if the main objectives of the fiscal reform are to be realised. Should foreign financial assistance fail to materialise, the progress of the transition process will, to a very great extent, depend upon the government's ability to avoid this squeeze between inflation, taxation and budget deficit.

MACROECONOMIC RESTRUCTURING ISSUES

One of the extremely sensitive tasks of transition is to restructure property rights in order to bring them into line with the framework of a market economy. However difficult the process of establishing private ownership and private enterprise may be, and how long it may take, the institutional prerequisites for initiating these processes should be created quickly. This should be the starting point for solving the immediate problems of any transitional economy.

Privatisation is the only way of ensuring competitiveness, which forms the basis of market and overall economic efficiency. The part of the state sector that should be privatised in the countries of Central and Eastern Europe accounts for about 90 per cent of the economy, so the prime objective is to reduce this sector considerably and transfer the property to private owners.

The complexity and significance of the process of privatisation can only be fully appreciated if the impact of this process is considered at all levels of the economy. At the national level, macroeconomic measures and instruments (from the allocation of resources and determination of prices, to foreign trade, exchange rate and interest rate policies) to establish private ownership rights over enterprises brings about a radical change in the conditions under which economic agents behave, and in the efficiency of the national economy as a whole.

At the industry level, privatisation brings about fundamental changes to the structure of enterprises, banks and so on. It affects production, the conducting of business, organisational activities and the legal system. It encourages the development of market institutions and makes possible the functioning of capital goods and labour markets, without which enterprises cannot operate in market terms (stock exchanges, brokers, banks, trade associations, international codes of conduct, standards and so on).

At the company level, privatisation has a fundamental impact on the allocation, control and management mechanisms of the company. It defines clearly the competence, rights and obligations (as well as apportioning risk and responsibility) of the owner, managers and workers, encouraging thereby an efficient and rational operation.

At the lowest level, along with state and parastate institutions, the individual is the single most important holder of ownership rights.

The positive impact of privatisation is evident in corporations, where it leads to motivation and involvement and is thus an irreplaceable factor of the market economic process.

The transition from a command economy to a market economy requires a radical change in the price system; that is, the transition from a sellers' to a buyers' market means reducing the level of demand to a level below the level of supply and allowing competition, not only domestic but also foreign. However this might lead to unused capacities and growth in unemployment. Under such conditions, privatisation becomes an unavoidable precondition of overcoming recession and crisis.

Various suggestions about privatisation have been made both in theory and in everyday life.[8] For theory one can choose between Friedman's *People Capitalism* and Meade's *Partnership Economy*. Four theoretically possible models of privatisation were suggested at the beginning of the transition. The first is the transition model of joint stock companies with mixed capital. The key participants in this model are the Treasury (that is, the Ministry of Finance) and foreign capital. The legal basis here is a law enabling the Treasury to separate the enterprise from the inventory of state ownership to enable further ownership transformations. This is of the greatest importance, for without further ownership changes the company may be little more than a self-managed state enterprise.

The second is the transition model of joint stock companies with shareholders. This model could be subdivided into three sub-models:

1. Dividend ownership rights are granted to the employees of a given enterprise. The consequences of this option would be dispersed or nontransferable ownership, with new employee–owners being tempted to choose immediate consumption, which would result in rapid decapitalisation. Because of the dividend this submodel has no anti-inflationary effect.
2. Shares are sold first to employees and ex-employees, and then to others. The main advantage of this submodel is its anti-inflationary effect; the main disadvantage is the lack of financial resources among the population.
3. Debentures are distributed among the population. These debentures would be equal to the value of their share in national wealth. Alternatively a voucher system would allow holders the right either to obtain shares for the equivalent value in a state enterprise or to purchase shares through representatives and brokers. If this submodel were to be applied, it should be accompanied by antimonopoly laws.

The third privatisation model is the transition model of group ownership, where some kind of representative body would be the owner and no individual shares would be issued. Owners could be workers' self-management bodies, cooperatives, municipal bodies, trade unions, foundations or public funds. The main disadvantage of this model is that those in charge are often in a position to exploit the group's property to their personal profit.

The fourth is the transition model of holding companies, either newly created by the state or those already in existance (such as banks), to which are sometimes affiliated certain state enterprises. This model could be useful in the early stages of transition, although it fails to meet the purpose for which the process of privatisation is introduced in the first place.

In practice, policy makers in transition economies are faced with two fundamental dilemmas. The first pertains to the method of privatisation, that is, whether to sell the state-owned assets or distribute them freely. The main advantages of selling are increased budget revenues and increased efficiency. It is said that the purpose of privatisation is not simply to hand out property, but to place it into the hands of more capable owners. It is further added that a precondition to this is that genuine private entrepreneurial motivation should arise from the purchase of property.[9] The main disadvantage of selling is that it is extremely slow and demands very skilful administration. A serious difficulty encountered in such sales is evaluating company assets.

The best example of the free distribution of state assets (also known as voucher privatisation) was developed in the Czech Republic, where state assets were distributed to every adult citizen in form of vouchers, with which they could buy company shares. The main advantage of such a system is that it quickly accomplishes widespread private ownership. The basic disadvantages are that it sacrifices potential budget revenues and enterprise efficiency is reduced because of the excessive dispersion of ownership. The Czech approach also shows that orientation to a certain technique and model need not be exclusive. A combination of options is more feasible, and probably the best way of coping with the variety of sectors and types of business that are in the process of privatisation. For instance some shares may be distributed, some may be sold by auction to domestic and foreign investors, others may be sold to employees, and so on. There is increasing interest in this model in the Baltic States, Romania, Russia and Slovenia.

The second practical dilemma for transition policy makers is gradualism versus jumping into a free market. Those in favour of a quick leap are more interested in denouncing gradualism than in extolling the benefits of their proposals. They stress that gradualism opens the door to an unstructured, free-for-all economy: consumers will turn to the black market and firms will produce for the black market. Households will turn to German marks and US dollars and thus provoke hyperinflation, and workers will privatise firms spontaneously. Those who are left out or fall behind will become radical. The common experience is that economic disintegration takes much longer than one thinks, but when it does come it happens much faster than one would have thought.

Gradualism may seem a low-risk strategy when events appear to be under control, but a more realistic answer is immediate radical reform, not a phased-in move towards a market economy. Temporary collapse may be inevitable one way or the other, but in the context of radical reform it may at least sow the seeds of reconstruction.[10] Furthermore, to quote a now famous sentence by a 'jump fan', 'gradualism promised incoherence, not less pain. It would be as if the British decided to shift from driving on the left to driving on the right but decided to shift it gradually – first by having just the trucks shift over to the other side'.[11]

Those in favour of gradualism are equally interested in finding faults and weakness in the jump approach rather than espousing their own cause. Sometimes they claim that there is not the slightest chance of switching on the engine of self-development without private property in all forms, but warn that the case of Poland is quite different from the case of multiethnic states because these states are not united by the authority of a single church and the colossal authority of the Pope.[12] A more specific approach in favour of gradualism argues that the experiences of transition, especially the experiences of restructuring (that is, privatisation) from NEP onwards, demonstrate that the results of dealing with mass unemployment as a consequence of jumping into restructuring activity can be as damaging as the previous difficulties that brought about the transition.[13]

It is more than evident that the potential danger coming from these processes is not the objective (privatisation) but the timing and speed of the transition process itself. This very slippery crossing from one environment to another has to be done with the main parts of the economic machine at constant work until, as with a heart transplant, the very heart (ownership) is exposed. The critical moment comes when the original heart is removed, the body is maintained to hi-tech machines, the new heart is put in and all body functions are returned to normal. One could liken the ailing Eastern European economies to the body, the centrally planned economy to the old heart, the market economy to the new heart and Western markets to the hi-tech equipment that keeps the body functioning while the transplantation is being done.

DEVELOPMENT ISSUES

Development theories, growth theories, theories of economic development, theories of industrialisation and so on have lost much of their appeal over the last two decades. First of all none have performed successfully in underdeveloped countries. Quite the contrary – many of the African, Asian and Latin American countries to which numerous world and UN experts (some of them very distinguished scholars from respected Western universities) and their growth models have been attached, have experienced very low or zero growth rates of per capita income over a very long period.

Secondly, the overall growth of less developed countries has been very poor and disappointing.[14] At the same time newly industrialised countries, with no known growth theory or model attached to them, have experienced amazingly high growth rates.

The third reason for the diminished interest in development theories, as far as economists are concerned, is that it has become clear that in the long run the distinction between economic and noneconomic factors has no significance, and it is necessary to acknowledge that economic growth must be seen as a specific aspect of general social evolution rather than as a process that can be separated from the social system and studied in isolation.[15]

For all the truth contained in these arguments, it would be highly unwise to fail to see that for years transition economies have been obsessed by growth rates as the main indicators of overall progress and improved living conditions. The Eastern Europe population has very high expectations from transition and, as in the less developed countries in the industrialisation phase, having at last obtained representative governments they assumed that the economic benefits of freedom would follow.[16]

Although the industrialisation era is long over in most of Eastern Europe, the basic problem of catching up with developed market economies remains the same. However this time it is not a matter of catching up with Western countries in iron, steel and chemical production, but catching up with information-intensive production such as advanced materials, in the research and development of new technologies and so on. For some, catching up means that industrialisation or technical progress can not be the agent of the transition process, because long before transition is possible a well-trained workforce must occupy positions of key importance to the transition economy, as in case of

Japan, South Korea and even modern Turkey. At that point the government and its development policy steps into the scene.

What the actual role of government should be in the development strategy of a transition economy is the real question. As far as ways and means are concerned little has changed. Modernisation of a transition economy can occur under the law of free-market trade and international investment, as recommended by Rosenstein-Rodan more than fifty years ago. But there is a notion that modernisation will succeed only if the various countries engaged in the process are at the same level of progress. If this is not the case (and the Eastern European countries are at a much lower level of progress than Western countries), the modernisation can be achieved only by protecting the transition economy, as suggested by Fredrich List some two and a half centuries ago.[17]

Nevertheless, it seems that for the small markets of the Eastern European countries, Rosenstein-Rodan's arguments for an open-economy strategy would be more appropriate.[18] It would be so especially because of his EEIT idea discussed above; that is, the equal partnership of Eastern European and Western European countries. Rosenstein-Rodan proposed that about 50 per cent of EEIT investment should consist of labour costs – training, housing for labour and so on. The main role of the EEIT would be to take advantage of external economies and reduce risks. The basic investment incentive for entrepreneurs would be the expectation of profits based on past experience. However, in the case of today's Eastern Europe, experience of the past could be irrelevant as the whole economic structure of the region has changed. Individual entrepreneurs' information is bound to be insufficient in this case because they cannot obtain all the data that would be available to an organisation such as the EEIT. The other reason why the idea of an EEIT has its appeal even today is that it could enter international financial markets much more easily than could individual ventures and entrepreneurs. It could easily happen that enterprises or even nationwide ventures would not be profitable enough to guarantee dividend payments out of their profits. But if a sufficiently large investment unit could be created by including all the new projects of the region, external economies would become internal profits out of which dividends may be paid.[19]

Considering all the arguments and experiences, one feels that whatever the transition development strategy chosen two basic problems remain to be solved. One relates to human resources, particularly qualifications and skills, education and employment, and declining birth rates. The other relates to technological change; that is, catching up with new technologies, including incentives, innovations and so on.

Unemployment

As far as the unemployment problem of Eastern Europe is concerned the situation has changed considerably. Birth rates have fallen to less than 0.5 per cent per annum in most of Eastern Europe, except for Albania and some parts of southern Eastern Europe that are populated by Muslims. There is still a significant excess agrarian population, with a distorted aging pattern prevailing in the countryside. It is estimated that the problem of 8–10 million surplus rural workers can not be solved in the usual manner, that is, through migration and urbanisation. In our opinion the alternatives are few. One appropriate alternative would perhaps be an expansion of small and medium-sized businesses into the countryside, attracted by lower labour costs. For this to happen appropriate tax policies and improved communications facilities are equally important. A second alternative could be the creation of temporary jobs (lasting three to four months) in public work projects such as the construction of dams, embankments, canals and so on. In Eastern Europe there is a real need for such projects as only 2–3 per cent of arable land is irrigated and the rest is subject to repeated flooding.

A far more pressing problem manifested in the first steps of transition is so-called invisible unemployment in industrial sectors. Estimates show that in the present Eastern European setting, excess industrial labour amounts to some 9–10 million people, primarily because of obsolete technology and poor industrial organisation. In solving this gigantic problem we can expect that expanded and modernised industry will reabsorb some of the excess labour, with 2–3.5 million new jobs being created over the next ten years. The best prospect for job seekers is of course a rapidly expanding service sector.

The excess industrial labour supply could be at least temporarily resolved through the creation of two million jobs (to last three to six months) in public works such as road and rail construction. For example establishing a proper highway network in Eastern Europe would involve roughly 15 thousand kilometres of roads, which are vital to the transformation process in Eastern Europe. This would naturally require an outward-looking attitude on the part of Eastern European governments towards potential Western investors in the granting of concessions, long-term land leasing facilities, unrestricted joint ventures and so on. The cost of road construction is estimated at around US$80 billion and initial feasibility studies show an average 10 per cent annual rate of return for half the mileage.

Similar attitudes and policies would be required for the construction of 8–10 thousand kilometers of double-track railway lines. The rate of return would be even higher than in the case of highways because of the immensity of the East–West merchandise trade and the likely reduction of heavy-goods traffic for ecological reasons. Investment markets could be in the range of $30 billion. Public works could also be used as requalification centres for basic training in computer and information services.

It must be clearly recognised that the overall competitiveness of Eastern European countries in international markets will depend greatly upon the stability of their labour markets, meaning that average hourly gross wages (taxes and social security included) must fall within the US$5–7 range in the immediate future.

Technological Change

As far as technological change is concerned, there is not the slightest doubt that technology and industrial organisation have very important roles to play in economic development. At the same time it would not be plausible to adopt a purely deterministic view of technological factors for they are strongly related to market resource allocation and consequently to savings and propensity to save. What markets cannot do is to deliver information about future events resulting from the present decisions of economic agents. Therefore the relationship between market signals, growth and technological change is considered a central economic issue. In essence, market economies are more or less dualistic as far as technological change and the economy is concerned.

The main problem of modern economics is, as far as distinguished scholars are concerned, establishing a stable and orderly market-clearing general equilibrium economy of the Walrasian type, which can be at odds with technological change. Dynamism and change often lead to disequilibrium in the economy, while the supply and demand of old and new products are adjusting themselves to the changed environment.

The problem of combining technological change with economic reasoning is of particular interest in a transition economy. Eastern Europe has been slow to join the technological revolution and lacks even a proper feedback and evaluation mechanism. Therefore the way that technological change is dealt with in mature market economies is of great significance to transition economies. Learning usually starts at the point at which market-oriented macroeconomics tries to comprehend the dynamics of technological change.

The major question here is whether such change is to be treated as an internality or an externality. Of course this question does not apply in the short run, when technological change is clearly the result of externalities (such as scientific advances). But the question inevitably arises in the long run, when former externalities become economic internalities; that is, when industrial organisation and labour have to adjust to new technological patterns.[20]

In this respect technological change corresponds to a concept of natural trajectories, and once established as the dominant influence on engineers, designers and managers it becomes a long-term technological regime associated with a characteristic institutional framework.[21]

In an environment of technological change the basic problem for transition economies in Eastern Europe is to avoid the so-called locked-in dependent development that characterised a fair number of LDCs. The paradox that appears here is that prior capital accumulation is needed to produce new capital, prior knowledge is needed to absorb new knowledge, skills must be available to acquire new skills, and a certain level of development is required to create the infrastructure and economic agglomeration to make that development possible.[22] Numerous debates revolve around the possibility of breaking away from this vicious circle, but if it is possible, what are the entry costs and what should be the point of entry to a new technological framework for a transition economy?

The cost of entry usually consists of four elements: the fixed investment cost, representing the absolute minimum entry cost for a producer; the cost of closing the knowledge gap, embracing the cost of obtaining knowledge and information to serve as a platform for the generation of new or innovative knowledge; the cost of closing the experience and skill gap, which concerns the gaining of management and marketing experience and learning new skills; and the cost of compensating for a lack of externalities such as suitable financial services, transport facilities, basic utilities (water, electricity, telecommunications), a legal and institutional framework, and so on.

The point of entry is viewed as the second essential element of the catching-up strategy, implying that entrepreneurship is at its core. Optimum entrepreneurship could be defined as the solution of a dynamic programming problem and the successful implementation of this solution; or to make it simple, entrepreneurship could be defined as the carrying out of new combinations.[23]

CONCLUSIONS

It follows from the above that transformation from a centrally planned to free market economy requires a coordinated performance of structural change, short-run economic policy and long-term strategic decision making, including an R&D policy. This simultaneous multi-level activity could be called macroeconomic management of the transition economy. Instead of carefully evaluating this extremely difficult, interrelated set of agendas, most literature on the transition process deals either with restructuring or with policy model issues, often treating them inadequately as separate issues. At the same time conceptual and especially development issues are left almost completely out of the picture. Our conclusion is that until a consistent and complex synthesis of these multilevel transition ingredients is carried out, there can be no lasting success in transition.

Notes

1. Rosenstein-Rodan's analysis and his proposal could come as a surprise to many, but its enduring quality is a result of sound reasoning. The proposal was for an Eastern European Investment Trust to cover the whole area – from Russia to Eastern and Central Europe, and extending to Germany and Italy. He envisaged a single market, to be encouraged and sponsored by Western countries. See Rosenstein-Rodan (1943), pp. 245–55.
2. See Rosenstein-Rodan (1943), p. 248.
3. Edmund Phelps has delved into the confusing world of macroeconomic theory. He constructed a consistent scheme that resulted in seven precisely defined and formalised macroeconomic models. See Phelps (1990), pp. x–xii.
4. In a highly provocative manner Arjo Klamer has confronted different macroeconomic policy models. Interviews with prominent representatives of various schools of thought enabled him not only to delve to the very roots of the dissent between macroeconomic policy models, but to rethink them within a new theoretical framework. See Klamer (1992), p. vii.
5. See IRMO (1992), pp. 10–11. IRMO (the Institute for International Relations, Zagreb, Croatia) carries out internationally sponsored research on the transition process in Eastern Europe.
6. See Dornbusch, 1993, p. 116.
7. Janos Kornai is very specific in his claim that externalities and internalities

deflect government activity and that a huge budget deficit is a prime cause of inflation. Therefore neither an external lending nor an internal stabilisation policy will have any effect if public spending – that is, the deficit – is not significantly reduced (Kornai, 1990, p. 106).

8. Jadwiga Staniszkis has developed a model of privatisation that borrows heavily from the Polish experience. The Polish experience is relevant to the rest of Eastern Europe for two reasons. Firstly, Poland was the first Eastern European country to face the full impact of transition following Jeffrey Sachs' once celebrated do-it-all do-it-now policy model. Secondly, all possible transition models have been discussed in Poland. For details see Staniszkis (1991), pp. 52–6.
9. See Kornai (1990), pp. 82–4.
10. See Dornbusch (1993), p. 111.
11. Sachs and Dornbusch are vigorous opponents of gradualism. In condemning the careful step-by-step approach to transition Sachs has denounced his opponents with witty but sometimes caustic remarks (for details see Sachs, 1992, p. 342).
12. In fact, R. W. Davies has paraphrased a comment of the famous Russian economist Shatalin, once in charge of *Perestroika*, which shows that Sachs' opponents could be resourceful too. Unfortunately neither have done much to ease the burden of transition. For details see Davies (1991), p. 127.
13. Judith Shapiro has produced a sober assessment of the costs of transition. In her comparative analysis of early reforms to contemporary transition models she has succeeded in identifying the types of costs that are seriously endangering transition. Presenting the case of so-called *sovznak* and *chervontsy*, which were money surrogates that showed enormous inflation during the first market-oriented reform in the 1920s in the USSR, Shapiro has exposed the dimensions of a crisis that could annihilate the transition endeavour before it really starts. For details see Shapiro (1991), p. 158.
14. For an elaborate analysis see Singer (1991), pp. xvii–xxiv.
15. See Bruton, 1967, p. 298.
16. D. E. Apter undertook a study of LDCs some thirty years ago, when foreign aid was dependent on the willingness of LDCs to conduct overall political and economic adjustment to conform with Western standards. As far as popular expectations in Eastern Europe are concerned, his statements still apply. See Apter (1965), p. 152.
17. See Hoselitz (1967), p. 200.
18. Rosenstein-Rodan (1943), p. 250.
19. Ibid, p. 251.
20. For details see Boyer (1988), p. 67.
21. The link between technological change and economic growth during the process of transition appears to be of utmost importance. Nevertheless research on this problem is scant. This lack could cause serious delay in or even failure of the transition. Although Dossi *et al.* do not deal with transition in particular, their work has relevance to a transition economy for it discusses in detail the relationship between economic growth and technological change. The success of transition could to a great extent be judged by its ability to catch up with developed market economies in

terms of growth and standard of living. Without a wise and complex policy that adopts and augment technological changes in developed Western countries, transition has little chance of succeeding. For details see Freeman and Perez (1988), pp. 45–7.

22. See Perez and Soete (1988), p. 459.
23. This subject is rarely studied, although it could account for the major malfunctioning of the command economy. In addition lack of research on this topic could be the main cause of scholars' surprise at the velocity of the changes in Eastern Europe as well as their inability to approach the situation in a proper manner (see Granick, 1983, p. 224).

References

Apter, D. E. (1965) *The Politics of Modernisation* (Chicago: Chicago University Press).

Boyer, R. (1988) 'Technical Change and the Theory of Regulation', in Dosi *et al.* (1988), pp. 67–94.

Bruton, H. J. (1967) 'Contemporary Theorising on Economic Growth', in B. F. Hoselitz, *Theories of Economic Growth* (London: Collier-Macmillan), pp. 239–58.

Davies, R. W. (1991) 'Soviet Economic Reform in Historical Perspective', in C. Merridale and C. Ward (eds), *Perestroika: The Historical Perspective* (London: Edward Arnold), pp. 117–37.

Dornbusch, R. (1993) *Stabilisation, Debt, and Reforms* (New Jersey: Prentice Hall).

Dosi, G. *et al.* (eds) (1988) *Technical Change and Economic Theory* (London and New York: Pinter).

Freeman, C. and C. Perez (1988) 'Structural Crises of Adjustment: Business Cycles and Investment Behaviour', in G. Dosi *et al.* (1988), pp. 38–66.

Friedman, M. (1990) 'An Interview', *Privredni vjesnik*, Zagrels, vol. xxv, no. 9, pp. 237–40.

Granick, J. (1983) 'Institutional Innovation and Economic Management: The Soviet Incentive System, 1921 to Present', in F. V. Carstensen and G. Guroff (eds), *Entrepreneurship in Imperial Russia and the Soviet Union* (New Jersey: Princeton University Press), pp. 224–30.

Hoselitz, B. F. (1967) 'Theories of Stages of Economic Growth', in B. F. Hoselitz (ed.), *Theories of Economic Growth* (London: Collier-Macmillan), pp. 193–238.

Klamer, A. (1992) *New Classical Macroeconomics* (Brighton: Wheatsheaf), p. vii.

Kornai, J. (1990) *The Road To A Free Economy* (New York: W. W. Norton).

IRMO (1992) *Macroeconomic Policy Reform and Private Enterprise in Central and Eastern Europe* (Zagreb: Institute for the Development of International Economic Relations).

Meade, J. (1989) *The Economics of Partnership* (Aberdeen University Press).

Perez, C. and L. Soete (1988) 'Catching up in Technology: Entry Barriers and Windows of Opportunity', in G. Dosi *et al.* (1988), pp. 458–79.

Phelps, E. (1990) *Seven Schools of Macroeconomic Thought* (Oxford: Oxford University Press).

Rosenstein-Rodan, P. N. (1943) 'Problems of Industrialisation of Countries of Central and South-Eastern Europe', *The Economic Journal*, June – September, reprinted in A. N. Agrawala and P. N. Singh (eds) (1956), *The Economics of Underdevelopment* (Oxford: Oxford University Press), pp. 246–56.

Sachs, J. (1992) 'The Plunge to Capitalism', in L. H. Leyman (ed.), *Eastern Europe: Transformation and Revolution 1945–1991* (Lexington: D.C. Heath, pp. 340–4.

Shapiro, J. (1991) 'The Costs of Economic Reform', in C. Merridale and C. Ward (eds), *Perestroika: The Historical Perspective* (London: Edward Arnold), pp. 138–58.

Singer, H. W. (ed.) (1991) *Development Perspective for the 1990s* (New York: St. Martin's Press).

Staniszkis, J. (1991) *The Dynamics of Breakthrough in Eastern Europe* (Berkeley, CA: University of California Press), pp. 52–6.

14 Financial Sector Reform: Scope and Sequencing

Tomás J. T. Baliño*

Over the last twenty years or so financial liberalisation has become a key component of the reform process. Countries in Latin America, Asia and Europe have endeavoured to liberalise their financial systems, generally moving from financially-repressed regimes[1] to systems in which interest rates have become free or liberalised and credit is allocated according to market criteria. This liberalisation marks a dramatic change from postwar thinking, which was characterised by controlled interest rates and strong government intervention in the allocation of financial savings.

The main reason for the change in views was the realisation that interest-rate controls had led to financial disintermediation, which forced both surplus– and deficit-producing units to find noncontrolled intermediaries to deal directly with one another, or to abandon their intention to save and invest. This repression caused lower aggregate savings and investment and lower investment efficiency, which in turn hindered economic growth. Also, controlled interest rates aggravated inflation, as economic agents avoided holding financial assets (such as money) in favour of durable assets or foreign exchange.

In the mid-1980s another type of reform was undertaken in economies moving away from central planning towards a market orientation. This reform was not limited to countries that were abandoning socialism: for example Hungary in 1985 and China in 1984 began to reform their financial systems while continuing as socialist countries. However the pace of reform accelerated with the political changes in Central and Eastern Europe, the former Soviet Union and the Baltic states. A key transformation in these cases was the replacement of the monobank with a two-tier banking system, comprising both a Central Bank and a network of commercial banks.

CHALLENGES OF FORMER CENTRALLY PLANNED ECONOMIES

Liberalisation of the financial sector in centrally planned economies poses major challenges. In such economies financial flows were of secondary importance. Consumers had some freedom of choice, but their influence on production decisions was indirect. The overall plan determined enterprise decisions as to what and how much was produced, when, by whom, and to whom it was sold. Enterprises with approved production plans did not have to worry about obtaining finance as the monobank would include the necessary loans in its credit plan. Conversely a firm that accumulated financial assets was not free to invest them as it wished and had to conform with the plan. Moreover the state was free to confiscate any financial assets of an enterprise that exceeded what was deemed adequate. Thus, in practice enterprises were viewed as part of the state rather than separate legal entities.

The role of the financial system was mainly to ensure that the expenditure of enterprises as in line with the plan. Banks (usually a monobank) were not concerned about risk analysis as they were lending to state concerns.

Thus the financial sector is probably the area most in need of reform when a country moves away from central planning and towards the market allocation of resources. In this situation practically everything has to be created, including a legal framework to underpin the market economy. That framework should include laws on bankruptcy, collateral, securities, and notably a Central Bank act and a general banking law. In addition financial institutions have to be created anew or drastically transformed. Often this task is made more difficult by the scarcity of appropriately trained staff. Although the people in most of the former centrally planned economies were well educated, their training in economic and legal disciplines was from the perspective of central planning and socialism. Thus typical graduates were unfamiliar with basic market disciplines such as financial analysis, credit evaluation and accounting in a market environment.[2]

RESULTS OF THE REFORMS

Financial reforms have succeeded in increasing the size of the financial system, measured by the amount of assets held by the public relative to GDP. Other positive effects of the reforms – such as their contribution to raising the volume and efficiency of investment and increasing growth, or improving a country's balance of payments position – cannot easily be measured, since financial reform has typically formed only a part of the broader reform effort.

However some financial reforms have ended in crisis, as was the case in Argentina, Chile and Uruguay in the 1970s. The experiences of these countries ended in the early 1980s with deep financial crises, characterised by sharp increases in the debt/equity ratios of enterprises, bank failures, an overvaluation of the exchange rate corrected by large devaluations, and a large foreign debt. For instance in Argentina more than 70 banks had to be liquidated in the two-year period immediately following the start of the crisis in 1980. In the Philippines, the financial liberalisation that was carried out from 1980 to 1984 was accompanied by a severe financial crisis in the years 1981–6, during which a large number of financial institutions failed, and real credit to the private sector contracted sharply (by about 53 per cent between 1983 and 1986).

SEQUENCING ISSUES

Economists and policy makers have been analysing how to implement financial liberalisation and the steps that need to be taken in order to minimise the possibility of failure. What sequencing must be followed in order to achieve the desired results? There are several aspects to this questions: how should the macroeconomic sequencing be organised; how should the liberalisation of the financial system be implemented; and what specific issues should be addressed in economies in transition from central planning to market systems?

Macroeconomic Sequencing

Various economists, such as McKinnon (1973, 1982, 1991) and Edwards (1984), have discussed the optimum order of financial liberalisation, and there is a general consensus that fiscal balance must have the highest priority. In many countries, that requires the elimination not only of central governments recorded deficit but also of the deficits created by the social security systems, public enterprises, provincial and local governments, and the quasi-fiscal deficits such as those often hidden in the balance sheets of the Central Bank and the commercial banks. The latter can be particularly important in developing countries and in planned economies, which have often directed commercial banks to extend credit at preferential rates, sometimes to borrowers of doubtful creditworthiness. In those circumstances, liberalising interest rates without taking other measures can lead to a serious financial crisis, as interest payments rapidly increase the weight of government and private-sector debt. The hazards of adverse selection and moral problems can lead to poor loan portfolios and expectations of a government bailout.

McKinnon suggests that liberalisation of the domestic capital market should come after the price level has been stabilised and the fiscal deficit eliminated. Otherwise real interest rates and the real exchange rate will be too volatile, and this will create too much risk in the system. Moreover high inflation has been associated with changes in relative prices (Blejer and Leiderman, 1979), which can lead to distress borrowing.[3] Trade liberalisation should come simultaneously with the liberalisation of domestic prices. Full capital liberalisation, according to McKinnon, should come at the end of the process of liberalisation.

> Only when domestic borrowing and lending take place freely at equilibrium (unrestricted) rates of interest and the domestic rate of inflation is curbed so that ongoing depreciation in the exchange rate is unnecessary, are the arbitrage conditions right for allowing free international capital mobility. Otherwise the premature elimination of exchange controls on foreign capital flows could lead to unwarranted capital flight or an unwarranted buildup of foreign indebtedness or both.[4]

In principle, the above suggestions make sense, provided they are not interpreted to suggest that reform should be a protracted exercise spread over several years. Delaying reforms creates problems of its own. First, experience suggests that certain controls, such as those on capital movements, are easily evaded. In fact countries with extensive capital controls have been unable to prevent capital flight, which suggests that such controls are hard to implement or are ineffective.[5] Second, it is difficult to make general statements about what to liberalise at each stage; often a country's particular circumstances make it easier to liberalise a certain sector rather than another, and this may not coincide with the optimal sequencing mentioned above. Third, there are the costs of delaying reforms in any area, which vary across countries.

Perhaps the best way to implement the sequencing recommendations for macroeconomic reform is not to delay certain reforms until others are in place, but rather to accelerate the completion of the whole reform process, so that only short lags obtain between one reform and the next. That would not only achieve the purposes of the reform faster but would also minimise the problems that any wrong sequencing might create. Rather than analysing whether all the ideal conditions are in place to eliminate a particular regulation or distortion, policy makers should analyse whether keeping that regulation or distortion in place any longer has a net positive social benefit. More broadly, neither policy makers nor the public should have any illusions that economic liberalisation will be a painless process, free of set-backs. It will not. The task of the policy maker is to try to ensure that over time the benefits of the liberalisation package outweigh its costs.

Components and Sequencing of Financial Sector Reforms

The discussion in the previous section focused on the broad macro-economic setting in which financial liberalisation takes place. This section concentrates on the components and the sequencing of financial reform itself, with particular emphasis on centrally planned economies in transition.

McKinnon (1991) analyses the main issues in macroeconomic sequencing that need to be addressed to attain financial equilibrium and price-level stability during liberalisation. He suggests that central government controls can be fully dismantled only after

> The monetary – financial – fiscal system has [been] converted from the passive mode that had simply accommodated the planning mechanism into an active constraining influence on the ability of decentralised enterprises, households, and even local governments to bid for scarce resources.[6]

A first step in the transformation of the banking system of a formerly centrally planned economy has to be the establishment of an independent Central Bank, focusing on macroeconomic issues, and of a network of commercial banks that can be entrusted with the micro-economic allocation of credit. That step is essential in order to avoid perpetuation of the situation where the Central Bank decides who gets credit and for what purpose, while neglecting its overriding responsibility: to maintain the value of the currency.

The Central Bank needs quickly to acquire a minimum of expertise in several key areas, including monetary management, payment systems, banking supervision and regulation, and foreign exchange transactions.

The bank also has to build up its capability to gather, process and analyse economic data.

Monetary management is virtually a new activity for the Central Bank of a former centrally planned economy. Moreover it is a difficult activity, even for well-established Central Banks. They will need to set out a monetary programme that determines permissible growth in credit and takes into account the country's demand for money and balance of payments objectives, the extent of economic growth and inflation. Quite often this exercise initially has to be done on the basis of crude information about the economy's behaviour and with the use of deficient data. However this is better than continuing to carry out monetary policy in a piecemeal fashion, in which aggregate credit and money is not programmed but simply the aggregate result of many decisions made about individual credits. As better data become available and Central Bank staff become more familiar with modern analytical tools, more reliable estimates of the demand for money and credit can be obtained. This would also make the Central Bank better able to analyse and forecast the main sources of monetary growth, such as government spending and revenue flows.

The reformed Central Bank also needs to acquire new instruments to control aggregate credit expansion. It no longer grants credit directly, a power that after reform is given to commercial banks. Therefore instruments are required to control the aggregate amount of credit without interfering with the commercial banks' powers of deciding which credits to grant. Various instruments can provide that control: credit ceilings, reserve requirements, Central Bank credit to commercial banks and open market operations. However some of these instruments are better than others – for example credit ceilings can be effective in keeping total credit under control when technical difficulties impede the use of other instruments. Nevertheless the instruments create significant distortions, such as curtailing competition among banks and discouraging deposit mobilisation. Thus, ideally, they should be used only temporarily until it is possible to rely solely on the other instruments listed above. In fact the monetary authorities should use the breathing space provided by the credit ceilings to improve their techniques to implement monetary policy with indirect instruments. Thus policy makers should introduce indirect instruments early in the reform process and use them to manage monetary policy within the limits set by the credit ceilings. The latter can be phased out by making them gradually less binding as indirect instruments begin to provide sufficient control.

A properly functioning payments system is a prerequisite for developing money and foreign exchange markets and is crucial for the implementation of effective monetary policy through indirect instruments. Typically the setting up of such a system is a significant challenge for previously centrally planned economies and is at the heart of the transformation from a monobank to a two-tier banking system. Rather than acquiring the most sophisticated payments technology, the monetary authorities should focus on ensuring that the payments system achieves the following targets:

1. The ability to process payments within a reasonable period.
2. The ability to minimise the risk to participants, including the Central Bank.
3. The ability to provide an adequate channel for the Central Bank to implement its monetary policy. A key requirement is for the system to provide prompt final settlement of interbank obligations by debiting and crediting the Central Bank's accounts.

Banking regulation and supervision is another key area to develop. As mentioned above, expertise in this matter is rare in formerly centrally planned economies and the supervisory authority, typically the Central Bank, faces several challenges: to establish an appropriate regulatory and supervisory structure; to assist banks in acquiring the skills needed to analyse credits and observe prudential norms; and to design strategies to deal with the large number of problem loans that banks in such economies typically hold.[7] Particular attention should be paid to licensing. While competition in the banking system requires freedom of entry to new institutions, the supervisory authority will need to ensure that only banks with a good chance of survival enter the system. Moreover, initially the bank may wish to regulate the number of new entrants, so as to keep pace with its supervisory capacity.

CONCLUSIONS

Financial liberalisation is a key part of economic reform. It stimulates financial savings and channels them to the most productive uses. Regardless of how liberalisation is implemented, it will not succeed if it is not supported by policies conducive to economic stabilisation and growth. Fiscal balance is a key component of those policies; a monetary policy that keeps inflation low and forces economic agents to face a tight budget constraint is another. Moreover price liberalisation is a prerequisite for the economy to give the right signals to the financial system regarding the allocation of resources.

Liberalisation of the financial sector requires the Central Bank to focus on monetary stability and the commercial banks to concentrate on credit allocation. The Central Bank of a former centrally planned economy has to deal with several challenges at once: divesting itself of commercial banking operations; learning to manage money and credit policy through market mechanisms; setting up a payments system that is able to process payments rapidly and safely; establishing prudential regulations in line with those existing in market economies; acquiring the capability to supervise other banks; and developing a programme to deal with the stock of bad loans that is typical of transforming economies. This is a tall order; the good news is that several Central Banks in former centrally planned economies are well on the road to meeting these challenges.

Notes

1. This terminology was made popular by Shaw (1973) and McKinnon (1973). It refers to the distortion of financial and capital markets caused by government regulation and taxation of such markets.
2. This varies between countries. Some of them, for example Hungary and Poland, have been experimenting with market reforms for some years and have begun to train people in at least some aspects of the market economy.
3. Distress borrowing is defined as borrowing to stave off the bankruptcy of a borrower with little or no possibility of repaying its debts.
4. McKinnon (1991), pp. 9–10.
5. See Mathieson and Rojas-Suárez (1993).
6. McKinnon (1991), p. 3.
7. Those strategies should include helping banks and the government to elaborate a policy to address the problem of insolvent enterprises.

References

Baliño, Tomás J. T. (1991) 'The Argentine Banking Crisis of 1980', in V. Sundarajan and Tomás J. T. Baliño (eds), *Banking Crisis: Cases and Issues* (Washington: International Monetary Fund).

Blejer, Mario, and Leonardo Leiderman (1979) *On the Effects of Inflation and Relative Price Variability on Output and Unemployment: Some Empirical Evidence*, Discussion Paper No. 28 (Boston: Boston University, Department of Economics).

Edwards, Sebastian (1984) 'The Order of Liberalization of the External Sector in Developing Countries', *Princeton Essays on International Finance*, no. 156.

Mathieson, D. J. and Liliana Rojas-Suárez (1993) 'Liberalisation of the Capital Account: Experiences and Issues', *IMF Occasional Paper*, No. 103 (Washington: International Monetary Fund).

McKinnon, Ronald I. (1973) *Money and Capital in Economic Development* (Washington: The Brookings Institution).

McKinnon, Ronald I. (1982) 'The Order of Economic Liberalisation: Lessons from Chile and Argentina', *Carnegie-Rochester Conference Series on Public Policy*, vol. 17, pp. 159–86.

McKinnon, Ronald I. (1991) *The Order of Economic Liberalisation: Financial Control in the Transition to a Market Economy* (Baltimore: The Johns Hopkins University Press.

Shaw, Edward S. (1973) *Financing Deepening in Economic Development* (New York: Oxford University Press).

Sundararajan, V. and Tomás J. T. Baliño (1991) 'Issues in Recent Banking Crisis', in V. Sundararajan and Tomás J. T. Baliño (eds), *Banking Crisis: Cases and Issues* (Washington: International Monetary Fund).

15 Japanese FDI and Economic Policy

Kiyoshi Abe

Direct investment abroad by Japan is a relatively new phenomenon but it is attracting much attention from the rest of the world. Foreign direct investment (FDI), which is influenced by strategic decisions made by companies, is sensitive to macroeconomic circumstances abroad and is subject to greater risk than is domestic investment. FDI can exert a considerable influence on both the investor and the recipient, and its policy implications are significant.

This chapter will review Japanese FDI, compare its current stage with that of other advanced countries, and analyse its economic effects and the implications for macroeconomic policy.

A REVIEW OF FDI

In the 1950s and 1960s Japanese FDI was relatively small and mostly oriented towards the development of natural resources. Japanese companies in Asia, the Middle East and Latin America invested in natural resources such as oil, natural gas, iron and copper ores, which were then shipped to Japan for processing.

In the 1970s, thanks to an improving balance of payments, the country's foreign investment in manufacturing grew rapidly. Labour-intensive Japanese industries moved from Japan to Asia's low-wage, resource-rich economies. Japanese investment abroad expanded especially during the period 1978–84.

The first half of the 1980s witnessed the increase of Japanese investment in industrial countries due to mounting trade friction. In order to circumvent this friction, Japanese companies established factories in Europe and the US in order to retain and expand their local-market share. Due to the sharp rise of the yen during the latter half of the 1980s, foreign investment accelerated and peaked about 1990. This period was characterised by an increasing number of industrial countries receiving Japanese investment and by the growing importance of

Table 15.1 Contrasts in investment

Investment in the US and EU countries		*Investment in Asian countries*
Keep local market share	The motive	Export to Japan and other countries
Large	Local market	Small
Few	Imports to Japan	Many
Yes	Trade friction	None (or little)
Yes	Protectionism	None (or little)
Equal partners	Local suppliers	Unequal partners
High	Local wages	Low
Large	Effects of higher Yen	Large
Supportive	Government attitude	Supportive

Source: SANWA Research Institute, 1993.

assembling industries and of nonmanufacturing sectors such as finance, insurance and real estate. This trend has continued into the 1990s.

TWO TYPES OF FDI

A review of Japanese FDI suggests that there are two types: investment in industrial countries (mainly in the US and the countries of the EU), and investment in developing Asian economies. Caution is needed, however, because the difference between the two kinds of FDI is not always clear, as shown in Table 15.1.

THE FDI STAGES

There are three stages in the relationship between foreign investment and trade, although the distinction between the stages is often ambiguous. Exports and imports are affected by FDI, and the relationship between these two factors changes from stage to stage, as explained below.

- Stage 1: exports of components and capital goods from the investing country to the host country increase with FDI because they are not initially available in the host country. Local production of components and capital starts.

- Stage 2: with the increase in contact with local industries, the exportation of parts, components and capital goods from the investing country tends to peak and then decrease. Local production increases and replaces items previously imported from the investing country.
- Stage 3: local products become more sophisticated and local customer needs are satisfied before excess production is exported to third countries and the investing country. If the local market is large, it will take time for exportation to commence. If the local market is small, exportation commences soon after local production has begun, thereby benefiting the host country directly. With the resulting decrease in the investing country of domestic production, imports increase correspondingly.

Most Japanese direct investment in the US and the EU countries seems to be at Stage 2, although there are some exceptions. Japanese car exports to the US, for instance, are declining and being replaced by cars made by Japanese companies in the US. The same trend applies to the manufacture of televisions and other electrical products in the US and Europe. It is expected that the number of Japanese companies at Stage 3 will increase in the near future. Many Japanese companies in Asia, however, have already reached Stage 3 due to the small size of the local markets, although the companies are still dependent on essential supplies from Japan. Thus elements of Stages 1 and 2 remain.

THE EFFECTS ON THEN DOMESTIC ECONOMY

FDI exerts a considerable influence on trade, employment and other aspects of a country's domestic economy, although the negative effects tend to be exaggerated. There are three main effects on the trade balance: export-inducing, export-substituting and import-reducing. Consideration of these effects makes it possible to estimate the overall effect of FDI on the country's trade balance. A SANWA report, *Effects of Overseas Production on the Domestic Economy*, compares the US with Japan and shows the effects of FDI on the trade balance (Table 15.2).

The total negative effect of FDI (accumulated stock) on the US trade balance during the period 1982–7 amounted to US$8.3 billion per year on average, or about 0.2 per cent of GDP. The overall US trade deficit exceeded US$100 billion during the same period, while the trade deficit on industrial goods exceeded US$27.1 billion per year on average. The negative effect of FDI was relatively small. The main reasons for

Table 15.2 Negative effects of foreign investment on trade balance

	1987–91	*1994–2000*
US	$10.0 billion per year (0.2 per cent of GDP)	Data not available for the period
Japan	$4.3 billion per year (0.2 per cent of GDP)	$17.2 billion per year (0.4 per cent of GDP)

Source: SANWA Research Institute, 1993.

the deterioration of the US trade balance, therefore, were not so much US direct investment abroad as a buoyant domestic demand and the high dollar.

During the next period, 1987–91, the negative effect increased to US$10 billion per year, or about 0.2 per cent of GDP. The overall US trade deficit exceeded US$115 billion on an annual average during the same period. The negative effect of FDI was also relatively small.

The negative impact of FDI in the US tends to be exaggerated and the SANWA study shows that it is not as large as generally thought. Macroeconomic factors have played a part in the worsening of the US trade deficit, and these should be taken into account.

When considering Japan, the SANWA report points out the similar negative effects that FDI has had on the Japanese trade account. During the period 1987–91 the reduction of the trade surplus due to FDI amounted to US$4.3 billion per year, or about 0.2 per cent of GDP. The corresponding figure for the US is also about 0.2 per cent, as shown above. In this respect, Japan seems to have caught up with the US.

In forecasting the future from 1994–2000, the decrease in Japan's trade surplus due to FDI will amount to US$17.2 billion per year, or about 0.4 per cent of GDP. This percentage is double the corresponding ratio for the period 1987–1991 (0.2 per cent). The forecast is based on the hypothesis that Japanese foreign investment as a whole will increase at an annual rate of 10 per cent (20 per cent for Asia, 0 per cent for other areas) from 1994 to 2000.

Investment abroad entails a decrease in domestic employment. About 0.14 million jobs were lost in Japan from 1987 to 1991, according to the SANWA input–output calculation on FDI. It is noteworthy, however, that domestic jobs as a whole increased during the period by 1.46 million due to the effect of large macroeconomic measures that boosted domestic demand. The negative effect of FDI was thus relatively small.

According to this hypothesis, between 1994 and 2000, 0.95 million jobs will be lost in Japan as a result of production being transferred abroad. Although this figure is not large, it is considerable compared with the impact of other macroeconomic elements on employment (higher yen, increasing imports and so on).

AN INTERNATIONAL COMPARISON

Japan, as a relative newcomer to foreign investment, is in the process of catching up with other advanced countries. In terms of direct investment flow, Japan ranked number one in the world for the years 1989, 1990 and 1991. When comparing Japanese foreign investment with the FDI of other advanced countries the following facts emerged.

First, in terms of capital accumulation Japan still lags behind. The cumulative sum of annual FDIs from 1970–90 was US$421.5 billion in the US, followed by US$233.6 billion in the UK and only US$201.4 billion in Japan. The cumulative sum at the end of 1991 was US$231.8 billion in Japan but US$450.2 billion in the US.

Second, Japan's overseas production is at a relatively early stage. The ratio of overseas production to domestic production in manufacturing industries increased from 3 per cent in 1980 to 6 per cent in 1990. The 1990 ratio for Germany and the US was, however, 10 per cent and 25 per cent respectively, far higher than for Japan. The ratio of overseas production to exports is only 70 per cent in Japan, but exceeds 300 per cent in the US.

Third, many Japanese companies abroad still rely on imports from Japan rather than on local supplies, a tendency not conspicuous among US and EU companies abroad. The fact is that Japan has only just begun to invest abroad, unlike the UK, which has been doing so since the nineteenth century.

Fourth, cross-investment or mutual investment (investment within the same industry) occurs less often among Japanese companies than in the US and Europe. The same is also true of mutual trade, for instance there are many mutual investments among car manufacturers on either side of the Atlantic, but not across the Pacific.

Fifth, Japanese foreign direct investment is often a form of export substitution. For example, Japanese companies are operating in the US to replace exports from Japan, thus maintaining its market share in the US.

Sixth, in terms of Kindleberger's famous six stages of the balance of payments, the UK and the US are ahead of Japan and Germany. According to JETRO's 1984 White Paper on International Trade, the former two have entered the adult-creditor-country stage, while the latter two are at the young-creditor-country stage.

Seventh, compared with those of industrial countries, the profit rates of Japanese FDIs are low. According to one survey the profit rate of US subsidiaries during the 1980s was on average about 15 per cent of total sales; whereas according to Bank of Japan statistics, that of Japanese subsidiaries during the 1980s averaged about 4 per cent. Similar contrasts exist between German and Japanese subsidiaries. The reasons for the low Japanese profit rates are:

- competitive parallel movements of Japanese companies;
- large initial investment costs;
- small-scale production;
- unfamiliarity with local conditions;
- green-field type investment, rather than merger and acquisition.

Exceptions are those Japanese companies with a long history of overseas production, who tend to report net profits. They are familiar with local conditions and are able to utilise local advantages. They are internationally oriented and can spread currency risks abroad. Some set their prices rather high, as do their local competitors.

THE INCREASING IMPORTANCE OF OVERSEAS PRODUCTION

International companies with strong competitive advantages have been engaged in foreign investment for many years. The increasing disadvantage of producing in Japan has forced these companies to move their factories abroad. A major problem for Japanese subsidiaries is how to keep existing production facilities running while avoiding major financial losses in the host country.

During the high-yen period of the late 1980s, Japanese foreign investment grew side by side with investment in domestic plant and equipment, thereby preventing an industrial hollowing-out of the Japanese economy. This stock-adjustment process came about because Japanese business perceived there to be a shortage of capital stock in domestic industry.

Since the rise of the yen in 1991, in contrast, it has been felt that there is an excess of capital stock in the economy and therefore domestic investment has fallen out of favour, to the advantage of existing overseas facilities. The $1=Y100 exchange rate since June 1994 has necessitated still further reliance on overseas production and the current situation in Japan looks similar to the US situation in the past.

The inflated dollar in the 1970s and early 1980s pushed US business abroad. US multinational companies were said to be floating in a network of global production. Dependence on overseas production became the norm and of utmost importance. Japan today is in a similar position. Here are just some examples of major Japanese multinational companies that are becoming increasingly reliant on overseas production (*Nihon Keizai Shimbun*, 5 October 1993):

- Hitachi has shifted the production of compressors for small refrigerators to its plant in Thailand. VTRs will continue to be produced in Japan, but only those at the top of the range.
- SONY plans to expand its overseas production from the current 35 per cent to 50 per cent in three years.
- Matsushita Electric has shifted the production of some simple VTRs and radio cassette players to its Malaysian plant.

There are many other similar examples. It is considered normal for domestic products with declining competitiveness to be produced outside Japan. In October 1993 JETRO conducted a survey of Japanese multinational companies that revealed the increased emphasis on overseas production. Ninety per cent of the companies questioned said that they intended to increase overseas production, and 8.5 per cent stated that overseas production already exceeded domestic production, compared with 6.7 per cent five years earlier. Sixty-eight per cent intended to increase the volume of imports from their subsidiaries abroad, compared with 35 per cent in 1988. A further 7 per cent envisaged increased imports by 1998. When asked about industrial hollowing-out, 65 per cent said that this was possible, but could be avoided by an appropriate policy mix, 25 per cent thought it very likely and 9 per cent considered it unlikely.

JAPAN'S EXTERNAL ECONOMY IN TRANSITION

The increasing importance of overseas production reflects some fundamental changes. Traditionally, Japanese investment has been aimed at long-term, rather than short-term returns. High priority has been placed on securing local markets and retaining market share, even at the cost of short-term profits. This aggressive attitude is well known, even notorious. Thanks to financial back-up, Japanese companies have been able to endure initial losses for future high returns. Whether this approach will continue is an important question for the following three reasons.

In the first place, many large-scale production systems have already been established abroad, especially in industrial countries, and global networks of Japanese multinational companies are more or less in place. The time has now come for these companies to recover their initial costs and generate income.

Second, in order to reap large profits Japanese companies must resort to mass production as small-scale production does not pay. However, Japanese companies are finding it difficult to maintain good relations with their partners in the host countries. For this reason they have to maintain a low profit profile and thus prices can only be gradually raised.

Finally, the collapse of the 'bubble economy' in Japan has made it difficult to maintain its traditional market-share-oriented strategy and profitability is considered increasingly important. A low-profit investment strategy cannot be maintained any longer as low-cost funds are hard to find.

Japan's foreign investments from 1985–91 were at the top of the list but dropped to fourth place in 1992, recovering somewhat in 1993. The 1992 value was 43 per cent lower than in 1991. This sudden drop in 1992 resulted from the burst of the bubble and was a reaction against the rapid increase during the late 1980s.

The future growth of Japanese foreign investment will undoubtedly depend upon conditions in the host countries. There is a cautious attitude towards further investment, and this is especially true of Japanese investment in industrial countries. A survey carried out by the Export–Import Bank of Japan in December 1993 suggested that some Japanese companies intended to resume direct investment during 1994, targeting China, Indonesia, Vietnam and Thailand.

It turns out that four years were required for recovery from the collapse of the bubble economy. The Wako Economic Research Institute suggests that Japanese corporate profits will start recovering in early 1995. The post-bubble restructuring efforts may thus soon start to bear fruit.

POLICY IMPLICATIONS

There are leading new industries and declining old industries. There is a need for a selective foreign investment policy, whereby policy makers choose which products are produced at home and which abroad. Calls for such selective policies are common among industrial leaders in Japan, who claim that such policies, coupled with an appropriate domestic policy, will prevent industrial hollowing-out from becoming serious in Japan. The author shares their view.

Foreign direct investment is playing a positive role in the regional revitalisation of host countries, which could later reflect positively on the Japanese economy. Japan needs to learn to live with others in a kinder, gentler way and thus Japanese-affiliated companies must harmonise with the local interests of host countries.

A low price strategy can no longer be considered fruitful and Japanese companies need to shift to a high-price, high-quality product strategy. In this context Japan could learn from the experiences of German companies. German products are popular everywhere in the world, even at high prices. Germany has a relatively open market. Its exports are sizable, but it also imports large quantities. It does not pursue foreign markets as aggressively as Japan does, and thus the Germans are not resented as strongly.

The era of Y100=US$1 has just begun and it has become essential to internationalise Japanese companies. The resulting increase of overseas production presupposes a kinder and gentler symbiosis.

Domestic macroeconomic policy should attempt to minimise the deflationary effects of Japanese FDI on domestic employment and production, maintaining a stable expansion of domestic demand. Since social capital in Japan is still deficient, the 1994 MITI (Ministry for Trade and Industry) White Paper called for sustained growth in domestic investment.

On the microeconomic level Japanese policy makers should pay heed to those industries with comparative advantage that can produce higher value added goods. Their research and development needs to be supported by new investment and the freer interindustry migration of labour-selective governmental measures. The government should also pay proper attention to industries with comparative disadvantages, so that FDI-related deflationary effects can be reduced.

CONCLUSION

The internationalisation of Japanese businesses could continue, provided macroeconomic policy is properly geared to this end. Corresponding selective policies are increasingly required. MITI's policy should shift towards localisation on a global scale, although some Western critics point out that there exists only global nationalisation from Japan.

References

Abe, Kiyoshi (1993) 'Japanese Direct Investment in the USA: Direct Investment, Hollowing-Out and Deindustrialization', in K. Abe, W. Gunther and H. See (eds), *Economic, Industrial and Managerial Coordination Between Japan and the USA* (London: Macmillan).

Dunning, John (1982) 'Explaining the International Direct Investment Position of Countries', in J. Black and J. Dunning (eds), *International Capital Movements* (London: Macmillan).

JETRO (1984) White Paper on International Trade.

JETRO (1994) White Paper on Direct Investment.

Kindleberger, C. P. (1963) *International Economics* (Homewood, Ill.: Irwin).

Ostrum, Douglas (1992) 'Japan's Multinational Corporations at a Turning Point' (Washington: Japan Economic Institute).

SANWA Research Institute (1993) 'Effects of Overseas Production on Domestic Economy', Monthly Report, no. 11.

Yamada, Hasashi (1993) 'Balance of Payments Disequilibrium and the Reduction of Surplus', *Japan Research Review*, vol. 3, no. 9.

Index